THE ORVIS® — GUIDE TO —

FLY FISHING

THE

ORVIS®

— GUIDE TO —

FLY FISHING

More Than
300
TIPS for
**Anglers of
All Levels**

Tom Rosenbauer, David Klausmeyer, and Conway X. Bowman

SKYHORSE PUBLISHING

Skyhorse Publishing books may be purchased in bulk at special discounts for sales promotion, corporate gifts, fund-raising, or educational purposes. Special editions can also be created to specifications. For details, contact the Special Sales Department, Skyhorse Publishing, 307 West 36th Street, 11th Floor, New York, NY 10018 or info@skyhorsepublishing.com.

Skyhorse® and Skyhorse Publishing® are registered trademarks of Skyhorse Publishing, Inc.®, a Delaware corporation.

Visit our website at www.skyhorsepublishing.com.

10 9 8 7 6 5 4 3 2

Library of Congress Cataloging-in-Publication Data is available on file.

Print ISBN: 978-1-62914-532-7
Ebook ISBN: 978-1-63220-081-5

Printed in China

Table of Contents

Introduction to *The Orvis Guide to Fly Fishing*

I'M REALLY PLEASED TO BE A PART OF THIS BOOK OF FLY-FISHING TIPS. I'M HAPPY TO collaborate with two of the greatest names in fly fishing—Conway Bowman and Dave Klausmeyer. I've been fortunate enough to call both of them friends for many years, and typically we get to hang out together at industry-related events, which is fine, but we've also been able to fish together, which is always better. What I've long been impressed with over the years has been the tremendous knowledge both Dave and Conway have—but without a micron of ego. In any sport you find a lot of people with talent and many others who are humble and open-minded, but it can be rare to find rich lodes of both in one individual.

You hear old-timers saying, "I never had videos or YouTube or even any good instructional books when I was learning. I was self-taught and learned the hard way, by experience." But what they usually fail to mention is that they learned a generation ago, when everyone had more free time, when people took vacations for two weeks at a time. Besides, when these people learned they were probably teenagers who had all the time in the world and many opportunities within bicycle range, whose lives weren't as regimented as kids today, and who had twelve hours a day to spend outdoors without their parents even knowing what county they were in.

In today's world, we don't have the same amount of free time. With all the supposed productivity gains we've obtained through computers and smart phones, people today have less freedom for leisure activities and take shorter vacations than ever. So we take classes designed to shortcut a couple years of learning on your own into a day or two. And they really work. I know that people who have just left a good fly-fishing class are about where I was after five years of hacking away on my own.

And then these freshly minted students take fishing trips for the first time and realize a couple things—first, that no matter how much instruction you had in a classroom, there are always these little tips that make a daunting task easy. And second, that no matter how much time you spend fly fishing you always want more.

You're not alone—we *all* anticipate and cherish every trip. Conway only has to travel a few miles to sight-fish for carp and bass. He can smell the ocean from his house, and it's a short run offshore to sharks and tuna and yellowtail. I have a trout stream in my backyard. Dave ties flies and writes about them and photographs them eight hours a day. People send him boxes of cool fly-tying materials every day. Yeah, we get to do it more than most, but we still treasure our times on the water or at the vise, and we understand that nothing is more annoying than when a task that looks simple turns into a disappointment, and you know that just one little tip would make the annoyance go away so you can get back to having fun. If only someone would whisper that tip in your ear.

There is nothing more frustrating than to look forward to a trip, finally arriving, only to be thwarted by casting into a crosswind or trying to attach a wire leader but forgetting which knot to use. Or perhaps you've set aside a Saturday afternoon in the winter to tie some Parachute Adams for next season, only to discover you don't really know how to tie parachute hackles. This book is designed to head off those questions before they spoil your precious day, or at least make it less fun and successful than you had hoped.

But how do the three of us know what questions will be important to you? How do we know what tips to pass on? As the editor, sometimes-writer, and godfather of the Orvis fly-fishing books, I've picked my co-authors carefully. Conway Bowman grew up trout fishing with his dad, but as he married and had a family, he knew he had to fish closer to home, so he became intimate with carp and bass fishing in the lakes near his hometown of San Diego and also was a pioneer in developing techniques to catch the small (if you can call 100-pounders small) mako sharks that are abundant a few miles off the coast of his home town. But what really turns Conway on is teaching. Watch him on one of his TV shows. There is nothing of the "Hey, look at me" bravado you see on most shows, but you get the impression that all this guy wants to do is to share what he's learned with you.

And Dave Klausmeyer, as the longtime editor of *Fly Tier* magazine, spends his day reading emails or listening to phone calls from people who want to be better fly tiers, and then he spends his time agonizing over exactly how he will fill his pages with stories and pictures that will help all his readers get just a little bit better at something every time they pick up an issue.

And me? As I write this I am coming up on the four millionth download of my podcast, where I answer questions from listeners every week. Through emails and phone calls for requested podcasts, I sense the frustration in words or hear the panic in phone calls when some aspect of fly fishing just seems to be impossible to master or annoying to perfect. Conway, Dave, and I have learned to anticipate these questions, because we hear them every week but also because we've been there. We may not always have the answers, because we're learning every time we pick up a rod or sit down at a vise. We have fishless days and we've had evenings when we sat down at the fly-tying vise and, after two hours of struggle, ended up with a bunch of flies whose best use would be to slice all the materials off with a sharp razor blade and use the hooks for something else.

So let the three of us share tips from frequent questions that we *have* found solutions for. Come fish with us, come learn with us, as we all discover how to squeak the best out of those too-short hours and days when we're out of cell service and forgetting everything except the sound of the rushing water of a trout stream; or tuna crashing bait on a tranquil offshore day; or sitting in a quiet study at the fly-tying vise after the family is asleep, creating what is sure to be the next Woolly Bugger or Copper John. It's only fishing, but it sure is addicting.

—Tom Rosenbauer

THE ORVIS®
— GUIDE TO —
BEGINNING FLY FISHING

101 TIPS for the Absolute Beginner

Illustrations by
BOB WHITE

Preface by
NICK LYONS

Tom Rosenbauer

SKYHORSE PUBLISHING

Contents

Preface

IT LOOKS IMPOSSIBLE. AND CERTAINLY TOO COMPLICATED. BUT THERE IS A MOMENT in the life of the beginning fly fisher when he suddenly turns a corner. What seemed unintelligible now makes good sense. What seemed disconnected is marvelously all part of a coherent process. What was impossible—casting a fly beyond one's shoelaces, choosing a fly with even a faint chance of gulling a fish, "reading" the water, catching a trout or a bass or a pike or a bluefish—now is something one has done and something one can expect to do again many times.

Ah, it's not only possible, but great fun. There is a kind of electric shock when a fish strikes your fly, and a quiet satisfaction.

Fly fishing can indeed seem impossible. There seem to be a thousand occasions for error. Mostly, the people I've met who have tried and then not pursued fly fishing fall into a variety of different camps. Some find it too fussy; some are frustrated trying to learn the few basic casts. Some lose their first couple of fish because their knots didn't hold. Some like spinning or bait casting or trolling or catfish grabbing and don't know why they should change. Some are afraid to fail. Some try fly fishing and don't master it enough to find pleasure there. I felt many of these issues myself when, after a childhood fishing in other ways—quite successfully—I began to *not* catch fish with a fly rod.

I had no mentor, but I persisted. And when I finally got to doing it fairly well, and with decent success, I found that the further I practiced and the more time I spent on the water, the more proficient I became at it, the more inexhaustible its pleasures were. I have now fished far and near with immense pleasure. And I have become fascinated by how people learn and how they develop.

This nifty little book by Tom Rosenbauer will save the novice much of the discomfort I felt and will bring him—or her—to a position of some confidence. I have read previous books by Tom, and all reveal his special clarity and helpfulness. He is a superb fly fisher and an excellent, patient teacher.

What makes *The Orvis Guide to Beginning Fly Fishing* particularly valuable is that it is the distillation of many years of teaching novices and more advanced fly fishers what they need to know to fish better. Tom knows all of the questions most frequently asked, and he knows the most practical and helpful answers he has given.

The questions: answering these is the heart of this book.

Here are the central problems beginners have, the questions that have kept them from progressing at a decent rate. Clear, practical, genuinely helpful advice—that's what this book provides.

How I wish I'd had Tom's book when I had so many of the basic questions, when I knew so little I once threaded a fly line through the little keeper ring (used to hold the fly on the end of your line) and wondered why I couldn't cast.

This little book is chock-full of valuable answers and hints and tips—and it will quickly get you on the water, catching a variety of fish, enjoying yourself greatly.

Bravo, Tom!

—**Nick Lyons**
February 2009

Introduction

YOU WALK INTO A FLY SHOP, REVOLVE AROUND THE FLY BINS FOR A FEW MINUTES, wander back to the wall full of gadgets, then finger the endless file of fly rods that all look the same. You've been told you need something called a tippet to go fly fishing, but don't have a clue what a tippet looks like, whether it attaches to the rod or the reel, or how much one costs. Meanwhile, the shop manager is deep in quiet discussion with a couple of weathered young guys who are probably guides, and although she looks friendly, you're afraid to ask such a basic question, so you leave unfulfilled and frustrated.

This is your book. In close to forty years of teaching fly fishing—in print, on the Web, in schools, and through podcasts—I've heard it all. I've also heard the same questions over and over through the years, and they really don't change much with each generation of new fly fishers. Fly fishing is easy in concept (you cast a tiny lure out there on a weighted line with a skinny leader, and a fish bites it) but we often get caught in the nuances. How quickly do I strike? How long should my fly stay on the water? How quickly do I gather line?

I've tried to pre-empt these common questions by setting them down in manageable bites that will answer your questions and get you jump-started quickly. There are many comprehensive books on fly fishing, but often you just need a quick answer and don't have time to read through a chapter or two to get it. I think you'll find many of your questions are answered here. I hope I've provided quick enough answers to get you going, and to encourage you to study the topic in more depth with other resources, including the list of essential books I've provided in the last chapter.

Fly fishing is popular and visible today. It's elegant, intellectual, and it takes you to the most beautiful places in the world. Looking at general-interest magazines and television commercials, you'd think every third person in North America is a fly fisher. Yet as far as we can determine, out of forty million anglers in the United States, only about five million are serious fly anglers. The attrition rate of this consuming sport is high because in order to do it well you have to do it often, and most people today don't think they have the time to fly fish often and thus never become proficient enough to feel comfortable. Part of the problem is that adults and children just don't have enough free time in their lives, but more specifically, people think they have to get on an airplane and fly to Montana or the Bahamas to have fun fly fishing.

In fact, most of us have a place to fish with a fly within five miles of our homes. Steelhead run rivers in the middle of Rochester and Chicago and Cleveland. Largemouth bass, tarpon, and exotic peacock bass lie ready to grab a bass bug in the canals around Miami. World-class carp fishing with a fly is found almost everywhere, even in downtown Denver and Los Angeles. I learn something new every time I go fly fishing, even though I've been doing this for so many years and live on the banks of a trout stream. You will, too, and the skills you develop while having fun catching eight-inch sunfish in Central Park will serve you well when you *do* find time to take that exotic trip.

—**Tom Rosenbauer**
February 2009

PART

I

Getting Started

1

How do you get started if you don't have a mentor?

IN THE FIRST PART OF THE TWENTIETH CENTURY, FLY-FISHING SKILLS WERE PASSED from parents, patient relatives, or friends to novice fly fishers. A lucky find at a local library might turn up a ragged copy of Ray Bergman's *Trout*. But without the advantage of helpful videos, modern photographs, and clear illustrations, learning fly fishing without a mentor was an exercise in frustration. Today, you have rich sources of information, from hundreds of books and DVDs to free resources on the Internet. But when you need to ask, "What went wrong with my cast?" or "How should I present that dry fly?" these sources fall mute.

The best place to begin is at a fishing school. The emphasis in schools and clinics is on fly casting, which is the most difficult aspect of fly fishing to master, and whether you learn to cast from a school or on your own, make sure you're comfortable with the basics of casting before you go fishing. Most schools are run by people with proven skills at teaching fly fishing and you'll benefit from their experience at identifying quick ways to improve your fly casting. You can choose from independent schools, classes run by tackle companies, or free clinics held by local fly shops. But not everyone has the time or the inclination to learn in a classroom setting. To some they are a painful reminder of high-school algebra. Others are too anxious to get right on the water and enjoy the calming sunshine of a June morning in the middle of a river.

The next best option is a reliable and understanding fishing guide. Some guides are comfortable with novices and others have neither the temperament nor the patience to spend the day removing a client's flies from streamside brush. If you want to learn on a guide trip, explain to the guide that you are a rank beginner—do not overestimate your skills, as a guide can see through your deception after a few casts—and that you are interested as much in learning technique as you are in catching fish. If the guide seems reluctant on an initial phone call, make a polite exit and try a different guide. And pick your location carefully. Saltwater fishing for bonefish or tarpon, fishing for trout on rivers that are termed "technical," or steelhead fishing in the middle of winter are not places to learn. Fishing for trout in stocked or wilderness waters where the fish strike eagerly, chasing small striped bass or redfish in saltwater estuaries, or fishing for bass and panfish in lakes are experiences that will teach you important skills and still allow an expectation of a fish on the end of your line.

You may not want to pay for a guide or a fishing school because of economics or principle. Finding a mentor is difficult but not impossible these days. First, in any social situation, try to identify yourself as a beginning fly fisher. It's amazing how many fishing buddies have come together this way, and the bonding that can happen when two fly fishers realize a common passion in an otherwise boring or uncomfortable event is almost instantaneous.

Join a local Trout Unlimited, Coastal Conservation Association, or Federation of Fly Fishers chapter. These organizations often have a circle of members who take great pleasure in introducing new people to fly fishing, and if you show interest in volunteering for local stream improvement or cleanup projects you'll get acquainted quicker than you would by sitting in the back corner at monthly meetings.

The most unreliable but sometimes the most satisfying way to learn more about fly fishing is by finding an impromptu mentor on the banks of a trout stream or on a lonely beach at dawn. But you have to be careful about whom you ask for advice. Avoid groups of three or four people fishing close together—they are probably fishing pals taking a trip together and you may feel like the new kid in school trying to sit down at the lunch table with the football team. I would also avoid the lone angler with a tense, crouched posture staring intently at the water. This guy has just traveled for hours to do battle with a trout and does not want to be distracted with small talk.

Along the banks of a river, you can sometimes find friendly anglers willing to answer your questions, no matter how basic.

Look for the lone angler standing on the bank with relaxed posture who seems to be in no hurry to get into the water. He's already been on the river for a week, or is retired and fishes there every day, and may be very generous with advice and helpful hints. Approach him slowly and away from the water so you don't spook any fish that may be close to the bank, offer a pleasant greeting, and read his tone of voice and body language. If he offers some advice, listen, and once he starts fishing, ask if you can watch what he does. Just stay on the bank and don't wade into his pool, as there is nothing that betrays your lack of knowledge more than crowding a fellow fly fisher.

2

The best way to practice your casting

THERE IS NO FLY-FISHING CIRCUMSTANCE WHERE CASTING POORLY WILL OFFER AN advantage. I recently hosted a week-long bonefishing trip to the Bahamas where one angler went fishless until the very last day. Despite being a good sport about it, I could sense his frustration welling up and I knew he was not having a good time. Although the weather was cooperative and not windy, he was still not able

You can practice casting wherever you have enough room. No water required.

to place a fly with any accuracy because he had not taken the time to practice his casting before the trip. On his last morning on the islands, I woke him up at dawn and made him practice, without the distraction of feeding fish or the pressure of a guide watching over his shoulder, on the lawn in front of his hotel room. After an hour of practice he was placing his fly wherever he wanted at forty feet. That day he caught and released three bonefish, and when I caught up with him at the dock after fishing I was worried his smile would pop his jaw out of its socket.

You must feel comfortable with that fly rod in your hand before you spend time, money, and emotional capital on a fishing trip. And there is no substitute for practice. Find a place where you have fifty feet behind and in front of you, with perhaps twenty feet of clearance on each side. This can be your lawn, a park, a rooftop, parking lot, alley, or a deserted gym. Water is essential for practicing casts like the roll cast or spey cast, but for the overhead cast, which you'll use 90 percent of the time, dry-land casting is fine. Try to practice when no one is around so you won't be distracted and won't have to answer platitudes about how many you've caught.

Use the same line you'll be fishing with. Most of the time this will be a floating line, but if you plan to use a sinking line, practice with one because you'll need to adjust your timing for the denser character of the line. Never cast without a leader. Fly lines are designed to be cast with a leader on the end, which slows the casting loop at the end and offers air resistance that adds the finishing touch to your cast. Finally, tie to the end a piece of brightly colored yarn that mimics the size and air resistance of the flies you'll be using. If you have old flies, cut the point off one and use that instead. Place an object thirty or forty feet away. Now work on your accuracy. The ability to hit a six-inch target at forty feet about 20 percent of the time means you're ready to go fishing, as long as the other 80 percent of your casts are not far off.

Avoid the temptation to cast the entire fly line. Few fish are caught at seventy feet, even in the ocean, and casting the whole line is like eating before you learn to chew. If you will be fishing in the ocean or a on very wide river, back up and stretch out your casts to fifty or sixty feet, but remember that accuracy still counts at that distance. If you can't hit the target, you are better off wading closer to the fish or asking your guide to move the boat closer.

Try to practice casting in the wind. The chances of fishing on a totally windless day are slim, so be prepared. Practice with the wind in your face, when you'll ease up on your back cast and put more speed into your forward cast. Then turn around and cast with the wind, which is not as easy as it sounds. Wind behind you pushes your back cast down, which can spoil your casting loops or fire a fly into your ear on the way forward. Then play with crosswinds. For a right-hander, a left-to-right wind is safe and easy because the wind pushes the fly away from you, and all you have to do is aim upwind to make your fly land on target. A right-to-left wind is another story for a right-hander. You should avoid this dangerous wind, which pushes line into your body, if possible. If you can't avoid a crosswind, practice casting across the front of your body or actually turn around and cast behind yourself, dumping your "back cast," then turn around to face your target after the line hits the water.

Don't kill yourself with practice. You are much better off casting thirty minutes a day for three days than spending an hour and a half in a single session, because once your arm gets tired the practice ends up being a workout instead of a tune-up. Fly casting at this distance requires very little strength—it's almost all timing—so if your arm gets tired, you've been doing it too long or you are gripping the rod too hard.

(In fact, a loose grip on the rod actually improves your casting because it dampens vibrations and smoothes out your cast.)

Casting practice is a chore, but you should resist the plan that you'll straighten out the kinks once you hit the water. Even world-champion casters practice regularly, and if you're not totally confident in your ability, a few hours of practice will exponentially increase the success of your next fishing trip.

3

The two knots you must be able to tie on the water

THERE ARE SCORES OF FLY-FISHING KNOTS, AND AT FIRST THE NUMBER OF KNOTS you'll see can be confusing. Most of these can be done at home, with lots of light and plenty of time to practice; for instance, tying a nail knot to a fly line to attach a leader or tying an Albright knot to attach your backing can be done before a fishing trip. But once you're on the water, you will change flies or lose them, so you'll need to be practiced at tying a fly to the tippet. You'll also need to tie two pieces of tippet material together when lengthening your leader or adding a lighter piece of material if you choose to step down to a much smaller fly. For nearly every situation except fishing for big-game species like sailfish or tarpon, the only knots you'll need are a clinch knot and a surgeon's knot.

The clinch knot is used to tie two pieces of monofila-ment leader or tippet material together. It works with nylon or fluorocarbon equally well. If you've done any spin fishing or bait casting, you probably already know this knot. There is a variation of this knot called the improved clinch knot, but it's neither improved nor necessary—the basic one works just as well and is easier to tie and to tighten.

The surgeon's knot connects two pieces of monofilament. Like the clinch knot, it is equally strong with nylon or fluo-rocarbon, and it also works perfectly to connect these two unlike materials together. In contrast to the hard-to-tie bar-rel or blood knot, it works with materials of widely differ-ent diameters. For instance, whereas a barrel knot connecting 5X to 2X material (a difference of 0.003 inch) will break easily, a surgeon's knot connecting the same two materials will retain nearly 95 percent of the strength of the lighter material.

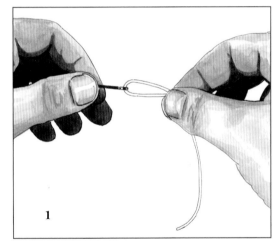

1

Clinch Knot

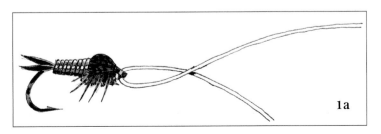

1a

Clinch Knot

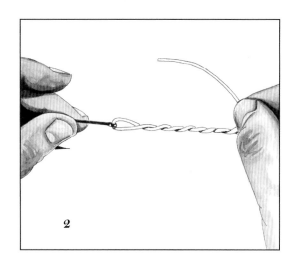

2

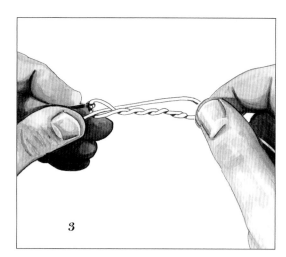

3

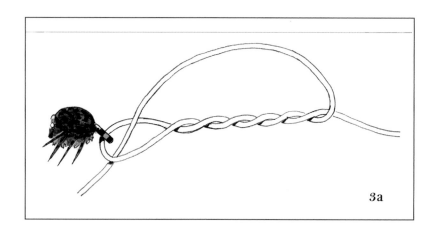

3a

4

Surgeon's Knot

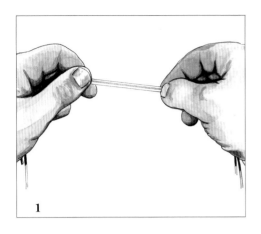

1

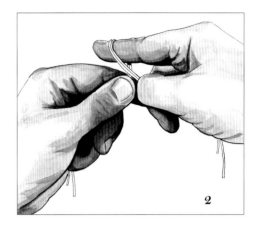

2

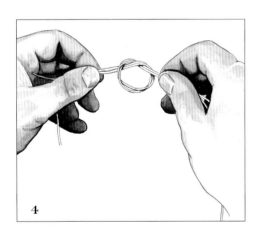

3

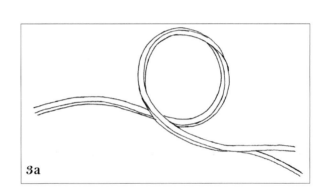

3a

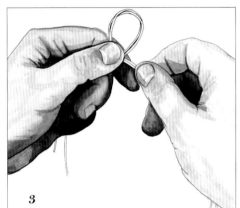

4

5

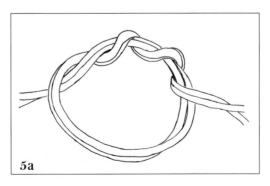

5a

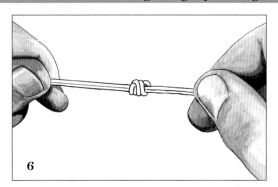

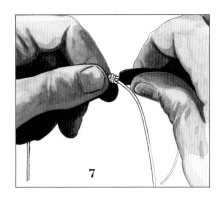

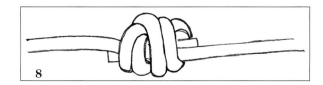

There are scores of knots that perform the same tasks as these two, but these are the ones I use on the water, and the only time they've failed me is when I forgot to wet my knots (a bit of saliva as lubricant helps them tighten firmly) or when I neglected to test a knot before presenting a fly to a fish.

4

Exactly how much fly-fishing gear do you need to get started in trout fishing?

A VERY COMMON AND NATURAL REACTION FROM PEOPLE WHO WANT TO BEGIN FLY fishing is, "There is so much stuff! What do I need to just get started?" One of the allures of fly fishing is that it can be so complex and many people enjoy the accumulation of new gear. But it does not need to be that way. My advice is to start small and then just add to your tackle collection when you really find a need for something new.

Here's an example of how simple it can be. I live on a small trout stream. The other day when I got home from work, I realized my wife Robin had locked me out and I didn't have a house key. Now, I always keep a rod and reel rigged and ready to go, hanging on a couple of nails behind the house. Still in my street shoes and office clothing (granted, the Orvis dress code is pretty casual, but it's still not what I would consider fishing attire), I grabbed my rod and reel, with a small streamer fly already attached to the leader, and walked down to the river.

I have one pool on my property where I can cast without getting into the river. I made about three casts, hooked and released a ten-inch brown trout, and walked back to the house. It was pure luck. If I had lost that fly in the trees I would have been dead in the water (excuse the pun). If I needed to get into the water to get a better angle on a cast, I would have ruined my shoes—plus, the water was cold.

So here is bare minimum:

- A fly rod
- A floating fly line to cast the fly (you'll want a floating line 95 percent of the time for trout fishing)
- A fly reel to hold the line
- A leader to present the fly, to smooth out the cast, and to keep the heavy fly line away from the fish
- A fly

Whether you fish a pond or a stream, eventually you'll want to get into the water. The fish might be farther than you can cast, or you might not get enough back cast room by standing on shore. In a lake the answer is a canoe, kayak, rowboat, or float tube. In a stream, the answer is a pair of waders, or at least a pair of wading shoes and shorts if the weather is warm enough.

You don't need a lot to go fly fishing—a rod, reel, line, leader, a box of flies, and maybe a pair of waders and a waist pack to carry a few things.

What happens when you lose a fly, or the fish won't eat the one fly you have? You can carry a bunch of flies in a pocket, but I don't recommend it. You can be like the famous fishing writer Nick Lyons and carry extra flies in an old Sucrets tin. Or you can buy a fly box or two and keep your flies neat and secure.

Leaders break and get too short after a lot of fly changes, so you'll eventually want to replace the terminal end of your leader, known as the tippet. Smart anglers carry at least three different sizes of tippet material on spools because flies much larger or smaller than the one you're using now might require a different size tippet.

Some of us use our teeth to cut leader material, but as you get older the enamel wears away and you just can't get a nice clean, close cut with those old choppers. Plus, your dentist will wag his finger at you. So a pair of fisherman's snips will make your knots neater and save your teeth for corn on the cob after you retire.

If you fish with dry flies, unless you only use flies made from closed-cell foam, you'll need a silicone-based fly floatant to keep them floating. For releasing fish and for crimping the barbs down on flies, a pair of forceps helps. You can fish nymphs without a strike indicator and split shot, but you'll eventually want to get them.

About the only truly dangerous aspects of fly fishing are falling in a fast current and getting a hook stuck in your eye. Polarized glasses can ease your fears with both—they'll cut glare from the water and let you see submerged holes and rocks, and they'll keep an errant hook from sticking in the most vulnerable part of your anatomy (any other place is painful, but more embarrassing than anything else). A hat also protects your head from hooks and keeps glare out of your eyes. Your standard baseball cap works as well as anything.

You can keep all this stuff in a pocket, but eventually you'll either need to buy a shirt with lots of pockets or wear something else to carry your gear. The traditional garb is a fishing vest with pockets, but the popularity of fishing vests is being challenged by new lightweight chest packs.

So to the very basic list mentioned earlier you'll probably want to add:

- Waders
- Wading shoes
- A fly box or two full of basic trout flies
- A few spools of tippet material
- Fly fisherman's snips
- Fly floatant
- Split shot
- Strike indicators
- Forceps
- Polarized sunglasses and a hat
- Vest

Of course, as you progress in fly fishing you'll discover lots of other neat gadgets for making your time on the water more fun, but with the gear listed above I could happily fish all year. At least in my backyard.

5

What to get after the essentials

ALTHOUGH YOU CAN FISH WITH JUST THE BASIC STUFF FOR THE REST OF YOUR LIFE, eventually you'll discover some gadgets and gear to make your time on the water easier and more fun. Some anglers decry the proliferation of gadgets that can hang from a fishing vest, but others enjoy trying new widgets and feel they're part of the allure of fly fishing. Just don't rush into the acquisition of gear too quickly. Wait until you've got a few trips under your belt. Keep a mental or written list of problems you have, and then look for solutions in your local fly shop, tackle catalog, or hardware store.

Here are some suggestions of things that aren't essential, but that I find to be truly useful on the water:

- A rain jacket. If you primarily fish in waders, get one of the "shorty" styles that won't hang in the water when you are wading. If you fish from a boat or from shore, you can get away with a longer style.
- Fingerless or thin neoprene gloves for cold-weather fishing, and thin sun gloves for tropical and high-mountain fishing in warm weather. Skin cancer is a real threat to fly fishers, and gloves are as essential as a hat if you're sensitive to ultraviolet rays.
- Knot tying tools. If you have trouble with knots, many clever tools have been invented to make knot tying easier.
- A diamond file for sharpening hooks. It's a lot more convenient and economical to sharpen a hook than to throw away a three-dollar fly.
- A net. Fish are easier to land, photograph, and release with a net. You can land many fish with your hands, but you'll lose more at the final moment. The amount of time spent battling with a fish will be cut in half when you carry a net.

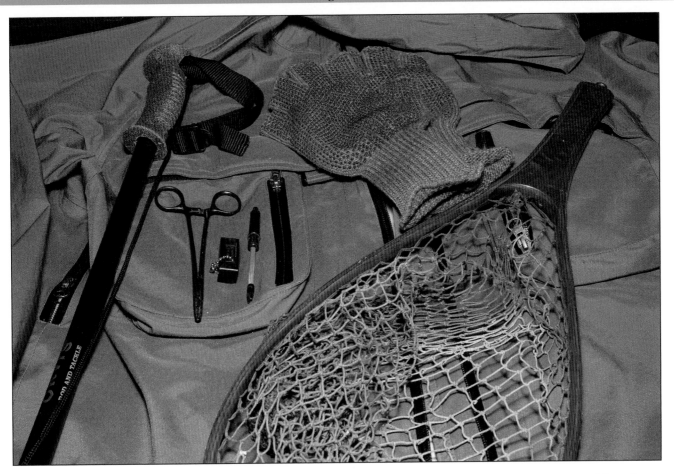

After you acquire the essential gadgets, think about a rain jacket, wading staff, a few tools, a net, and a pair of fingerless gloves if you plan to fish in cold weather.

- A net retainer with a quick-release mechanism to keep the net out of the way until you need it.
- A wading staff if you fish big rivers. Having a third leg makes a big difference. Many wading staffs collapse and stay out of the way until you need them.
- Sunscreen and insect repellent. Why be miserable?

6

Planning your first fishing trip

I WOULD NOT SPEND A LOT OF TIME OR MONEY ON YOUR VERY FIRST FLY-FISHING trip. You'll make mistakes, you'll realize your casting limitations, and you'll have plenty of questions that you may have to research after your trip. It doesn't make sense to waste a week of your valuable time and thousands of dollars for a trip to New Zealand, or even a day of time and a hundred miles on your car, when you can find a place for your first trip much closer to home.

My first suggestion would be to find the closest pond or lake. There are few ponds in the lower forty-eight states that don't have a population of sunfish or other panfish. These feisty little guys strike

A patient guide will help you enjoy your first big fly-fishing trip.

eagerly, they aren't spooky, and fly selection is not critical as long as you fish a fly that's small enough to fit into their diminutive mouths. They also tend to hang close to shore so you won't have to worry about long casts or dealing with waders or a boat. You'll fine-tune your casting and will learn how to strike fish, how to strip in line to bring them to hand, and how to release them. Don't forget to bring a pair of forceps, as these fish often swallow a fly with such abandon that it gets lodged beyond where you can reach with your fingers. If the pond has small largemouth or smallmouth bass, so much the better. They are slightly harder to catch, but bass under ten inches are more eager than their adult relatives.

You can also find panfish or large minnows like fallfish and creek chubs in streams close to home. These streams may be ignored by most anglers because they don't have any trout or other gamefish, but you're just out there to practice—and besides, it helps if you don't have to worry about who is watching your technique. In addition, the current in these streams will teach you about manipulating your fly in moving water, something that most of us forget about when practicing in the backyard or on casting ponds.

7

What to do when you first get to the water

A LITTLE OBSERVATION BEFORE YOU ENTER THE WATER AND BEGIN CASTING WILL make your fishing day more productive and fun. Whether you're launching a boat or wading a river, take a few minutes to observe the water before disturbing it with your presence. The best fish in a body of water are not necessarily a half mile upstream or on the other side of the lake—fish take the best habitat for feeding, regardless of how close it is to an access point, and you might frighten some nice fish by making premature waves.

Try to observe the water from a high vantage point if possible, which gives you a better look into the water than you would have at the water level. I often climb a hill above the water before fishing, even if it means getting out of breath for a few minutes, because it helps to slow me down and also alerts me to deep pockets or submerged objects in the middle of the river that might harbor nice fish, stuff I would never see if I just waded into the water. Once you've scoped the water for inanimate objects, look for fish.

Look for subtle dimples of trout taking tiny insects, wakes in the shallows from cruising redfish, or smallmouth bass crashing minnows in the shallows. Next, look for prey. Are there baitfish in the water? What size and shape are they? Are there insects on the surface or in spiderwebs along the bank? A few minutes of careful study may help you pick the best fly of the day.

For the sake of others and for your own fishing success, look for other anglers. Disturbing another angler might spoil someone else's day and even evoke harsh words, and following another person in a river or on a lake forces you to fish water another angler has already fished, water that is probably already disturbed and devoid of feeding fish.

Although few anglers carry them, a small pair of binoculars can greatly enhance your initial surveillance. Is that a big log out in the middle of the river or a twenty-inch brown trout? Are those insects mayflies or caddisflies? Is that shape along the bank that's just out of sight a dead tree or another fly fisher waiting for the hatch?

Usually, the best way to start a day on the water is to sit and quietly observe the water, looking for feeding fish or likely fish-holding spots.

8

Fly fishing in urban areas

YOU MAY FEEL SELF-CONSCIOUS FISHING CLOSE TO A SIDEWALK OR ALONG A BUSY highway, subject to long stares and smarmy comments from pedestrians, but some of the best fishing you have might be right under your nose. I've caught steelhead in downtown Rochester, New York, and Grand Rapids, Michigan. I've stalked carp in sight of the Denver skyline and on a golf course in Houston. You can catch striped bass within the city limits of San Francisco and New York, peacock and largemouth bass (plus tarpon and bonefish!) in Miami, and trout in the suburbs of Atlanta.

Because boat traffic and swimmers disturb cautious gamefish, the best time to fish urban areas is from dawn until the first rays of sunlight hit the water, which probably fits in best with your work schedule, anyway. Multiple-piece rods and a minimum of tackle also allow you to commute by car or bicycle or train with your tackle right after fishing, and if you wear waders, a pair of wrinkle-free pants lets you arrive in the office with no one the wiser.

I don't know of a single urban area in North America that does not have fly-fishing opportunities within the city limits. It might not be as peaceful and prestigious as the Florida Keys or wilderness trout, but that doesn't mean the fishing is any less appealing or challenging. The more you fish with a fly the better you'll get, and fishing close to home a few days a week, even if it's bluegills in Central Park, will sharpen your skills for that summer trip to Alaska. There is not a better way to start your day, and I guarantee you'll forget about the noise and bustle around you in short order.

You don't have to travel to the wilderness to catch fish on a fly. This hefty lake trout was caught on a fly in the middle of Grand Rapids, Michigan.

Equipment

9

Pick a rod by line size

THE FIRST DECISION ABOUT PICKING A FLY ROD HAS NOTHING TO DO WITH YOUR height, weight, strength, location, or casting skill. The physical weight of a fly rod is also insignificant. The first thing to decide is what line size you need. Every fly rod made is designed for a specific line size (although some may handle several with some adjustment in casting style). These sizes are based on the weight in grains of the first thirty feet of the line, regardless of whether the line floats or sinks, because it's the weight of the line bending the rod that lets you cast. Luckily, you and I don't need to memorize these grain weights because all fly-fishing manufacturers use a number system that ranges from 1 through 15, where each line size correlates to a grain weight. It's used by every maker of fly rods throughout the world.

The smaller the number, the lighter the line. Lighter lines, in sizes 1 through 4, deliver a fly with more delicacy. They cast small flies and light leaders best, but don't cast as far as heavier lines and don't handle the wind as well. As lines get heavier, in the 5 through 7 range, they lose some delicacy but gain in their ability to deliver larger flies and longer casts, and you won't have to fight the wind as much. These middle sizes are most often used for trout and smallmouth bass. Sizes 8 through 10 are considered the basic rods for long casts, big flies, and lots of wind, and are the sizes most often used by saltwater, bass, and salmon anglers. But they splash down heavier and won't protect a light tippet as well as the lighter rods. When you get into line sizes 11 and heavier, you're really looking at a rod designed to fight big fish, because once you get to a 10-weight rod, you've probably maximized the distance you'll get and going heavier only gives you more power to turn the head of a big tarpon or shark.

Fortunately, the flexibility of the rod needed to throw each line size corresponds perfectly with its purpose. Rods designed for lighter fly lines are very flexible, so it's easier to play a trout on a two-pound tippet with a flexible 4-weight rod. If you fish a leader with a two-pound tippet on a 9-weight rod, you'll most likely break most fish off on the strike because the stiffer rod is not as good a shock absorber, and besides, fishing a heavy 9-weight line on top of spooky trout will send most fish running for cover before they even see your fly.

Just by looking at this small stream with clear water you can expect that a 4-weight line would be about perfect.

Playing a small trout on a 9-weight rod is not much fun, anyway, because the rod will hardly bend against the wiggles of a ten-inch fish. And playing a ten-pound redfish on a 4-weight might be fun for a few moments, but the lighter rod just does not have the strength to land a big fish sounding under a boat, something a stiffer rod will do with ease.

10
How long should your fly rod be?

I ONCE ASKED A TOURNAMENT CASTER IF THERE WAS AN OPTIMUM ROD LENGTH for casting, ignoring all the other tasks we ask of a fly rod. Without hesitating, he answered "eight and a half feet." The physics of fly fishing are not easily understood, and air resistance, line weight, loop shape, and line speed all come into play, so I won't begin to theorize as to why eight and a half feet is the optimum length. But if all you ever wanted to do was cast out in the open with no wind, and had no conflicting currents to worry about, you'd want an eight-and-a-half-foot rod.

But fishing is much more than casting. In small, brushy places, an eight-and-a-half-foot rod gets tangled in the brush as you walk from one spot to another, and the wider casting arc of a longer rod offers overhanging trees more chances to snatch your fly and leader. A rod that is between six and seven and a half feet long is better for brushy streams, with the really short ones best for almost impenetrable woodland brooks, while rocky mountain streams with wider banks, where if you can get midstream you have plenty of room in front of and behind you, allow rods up to eight feet long before they get clumsy.

Rods longer than eight and a half feet are best for bigger waters. It's easier to keep your back cast off the ground behind you with a longer rod, they are better at making casts over fifty feet, and when you need to mend line or hold line off the water to prevent drag, that extra six inches make a surprising difference. Nine-foot rods seem to be the perfect length for saltwater fly fishing and give a great balance between making longer casts and the ability to play a large fish. It's actually easier to play large fish on a shorter rod as opposed to a longer rod, though, and that is why 14- and 15-weight rods for huge sailfish, marlin, and tuna are usually made in eight-and-a-half-foot lengths. They don't cast as well as nine-footers, but

To manipulate a fly line over these tricky currents, a fly rod nine feet long or longer would be the most efficient tool.

these species are typically teased close to the boat with a hook-less plug or bait so casts longer than fifty feet aren't needed.

Really long rods, ten feet and over, are best when tricky currents require the angler to manipulate the fly line once it hits the water. Because the swing of a fly is so important in salmon and steelhead fishing, and these fish are often caught in very wide rivers, two-handed rods up to fifteen feet long are sometimes used with special casts called spey casts that can pick up sixty or seventy feet of line and deliver it back on target without false casting and without the line ever going behind the angler.

11
How to pick a reel

FOR FISH LIKE SMALL TROUT, PANFISH, AND BASS, A FLY REEL IS SIMPLY A LINE STORAGE device. It keeps your line neat and orderly when you walk to and from fishing, and also keeps excess line from tangling at your feet and around the clutter that fishing boats seem to attract. Nearly all of the reels you see are single action, which means that one revolution of the handle moves the spool around once. Unlike spin fishing or bait casting, where you retrieve line after each cast and a multiplying action comes in handy, it's not needed

A narrow arbor trout reel on the left compared to the heavier, large arbor saltwater reel on the right.

in fly fishing. In the past, automatic reels with spring-loaded spools and multiplying reels with gear systems were made, but these reels proved to be heavy and clumsy, not to mention difficult to maintain in good working order.

Smaller reels don't need strong drag tension, either. All that's needed is enough tension on the reel to prevent the line from back-lashing on the spool when you pull some off, and perhaps some light tension if a bass or trout pulls a few feet of line when fighting. This tension might be provided by a simple click mechanism composed of a spring and a small metal triangle called a pawl, that engages teeth on the reel spool, or it can be from a small disc drag system. The main considerations when looking for a small reel are how nice it looks and how much it weighs, as the more expensive reels are lighter and more attractive than the less expensive entry-level reels.

Many fish run a hundred yards or more when first hooked. Big trout, salmon, steelhead, and most saltwater species will yank from five feet to a hundred yards of line during a battle, and it's difficult to put tension on a reel by grabbing the fly line with your fingers, as it is neither precise nor uniform, and grabbing a fly line when a fish is running usually leads to a broken leader. These fish require a mechanical, adjustable break system or drag to help you tire them; otherwise they'll just swim away until they steal all your line and backing. Fly reels for these species employ a disc drag system like the brakes on your car, and these drags are most often made with a cork or plastic disc against the aluminum frame of the spool. These bigger reels also require extra capacity for the one hundred to four hundred yards of backing you'll need. Thus, when looking for a reel for these species, check the capacity to make sure it will hold the line size you have plus the maximum length of backing you'll need.

In big-game fishing for tarpon, marlin, sailfish, or tuna, where the fish run as fast as a car and may keep up the pace for hundreds of yards, drag strength is critical, as is the ability of the reel's design to dissipate the heat generated by the friction of the drag surfaces. In the middle of a battle with a marlin, lesser fly reels get so hot they smoke and then seize up completely. There is no way for a consumer to tell if a fly reel is up to this challenge, and the only way to assure yourself of a reel that will hold up is to buy a large, expensive big-game reel with a first-class reputation.

12

Large-, mid-, and standard-arbor reels

ONE ADDITIONAL DECISION TO MAKE WHEN CHOOSING A FLY REEL IS THE RELATIVE size of its arbor. Standard-arbor fly reels, the most traditional, wind the line on a narrow central arbor. Reeling in fifty feet of fly line when you are done for the day takes about one hundred cranks of the reel handle. And imagine how hard you'd have to reel to get control of a bonefish that suddenly decided to run toward the boat at full speed. Fly line also has a "memory" when coiled on a spool, so the narrower the arc a line is wound on, the tighter the coils. Fly reel designers got around both of these problems by making the arbor in the center of the reel wider, which not only makes the coils less severe, it also doubles the amount of line wound with each revolution of the spool. Not surprisingly, these are called "large-arbor fly reels."

Why would anyone wish for a fly reel that kinks up the line and takes in so little line with each revolution? Large-arbor reels are wider overall than standard-arbor reels, and on a light trout rod a large-arbor reel looks overpowering. Thus, for small-stream fishing with light fly rods, where casts are less than twenty feet

All three of these reels have the same line and backing capacity. The large-arbor reel on the left is bigger but will retrieve line twice as fast as the standard-arbor reel on the right. The mid-arbor reel in the middle is a compromise between size and retrieve ratio.

all day long, a large-arbor reel just isn't needed. For those in-between situations (or for people that just can't make up their minds) mid-arbor reels are also made in some styles.

Spools aren't interchangeable between standard-, mid-, and large-arbor reels, but don't lose any sleep over which one you pick. I've fished for small-stream trout with large-arbor reels and for years I fished for bonefish with standard-arbor reels and never felt handicapped in either circumstance.

13
Picking the right waders

WHEN PICKING A PAIR OF WADERS, REGARDLESS OF WHAT OTHER DECISIONS YOU make, the most important point is the correct fit. Waders should be loose enough to let you do deep-knee bends without constricting your movement so you'll be able to step over logs or climb a steep bank once you get to the river, but they also should not be excessively loose, as baggy waders present more resistance to the current and will also wear more quickly because the fabric chafes and eventually wears through. Buy waders at a store where you can try them on, or carefully study the size chart on a Web site and buy from a retailer that offers easy return privileges if they don't fit.

Get breathable waders. Clammy waders can ruin your day, and although those thick neoprene waders may look warm, your body condensation stays inside them all day long. (Besides, you can wear layers of fleece inside breathable waders and stay just as warm.) And you only have to wear neoprene waders once on a 90-degree afternoon under the blazing Montana summer sun to realize you made a big mistake.

Waders come in two basic styles: boot foot and stocking foot. With boot foots, the boot is an integral part of the wader and you just slip them over your socks. Some have laces for extra security and some are just plain rubber boots. They are the easiest waders to put on if you aren't very nimble. Stocking foot waders, which incorporate a breathable upper with neoprene booties, require a separate wading boot. They give you a lot more flexibility, so if your foot size does not correspond to what is common for your height and weight, your chances of getting a better fit are greatly increased. You can also pick a lightweight wading boot for travel or a heavier boot for more support on long walks or rocky streams.

The boot-foot waders on the right come with boots already attached and are ready to use. The stocking-foot waders on the left will need a pair of separate wading shoes.

14

What to wear under waders

EVEN IF YOU'RE A NATURAL-FIBER NUT, I URGE YOU TO PUT ASIDE YOUR COTTON pants when wearing waders. Cotton absorbs sweat and condensation, and when you're exposed to the open air, cotton keeps you cool, but once trapped inside waders, cotton gets ugly. Synthetic fibers like polypropylene and nylon absorb little water or wick it away from your body, and when you take your waders off they dissipate moisture quickly.

Start with a pair of light wool or synthetic liner socks, adding a pair of heavier wool socks for cold water. Be careful that your socks are long enough to trap your lower pant leg, because bare skin anywhere against waders is a sure ticket to nasty skin abrasion. For warm weather, a pair of light synthetic pants of whatever style you like is perfect. For colder weather, layer a pair of thin synthetic base-layer bottoms followed by a pair of heavy fleece pants.

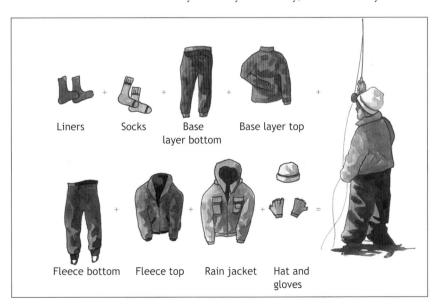

Liners + Socks + Base layer bottom + Base layer top +

Fleece bottom + Fleece top + Rain jacket + Hat and gloves =

With proper layering, you can fish all winter in comfort.

On top, for warm weather you can get away with anything you want—even a cotton shirt if you insist. For cold weather, layer like you do on the bottom—a thin synthetic base layer, a layer of fleece or merino wool over that, and for really cold weather follow with a thin jacket or vest. I find that knit fabrics under waders for both top and bottom are superior to woven fabrics because they stretch more and let you move easier, even when bundled up against the cold.

Be careful not to overdo the top layer, as the wader top breaks the wind. It's surprising how light you can go under waders. A rain jacket is essential on cold days even if the sun shines all day, because the waterproof fabric of a rain jacket cuts the wind on the parts of your body not covered by the waders.

This orange hat and vest may not be the best choice of wardrobe for sneaking up on wary trout.

15

What color clothing should you wear?

RED SHIRTS ADD A GREAT SPLASH OF COLOR and contrast to outdoor photos, but you couldn't pick a worse color for fishing. Most fish we chase with a fly rod are spooked when they see us, and blending in with the background gives you an advantage when sneaking up on the fish. For wooded streams, brown, tan, or green make you less visible, and it couldn't hurt to wear that camo shirt you typically save for opening day of dove season. In salt water, where you are silhouetted against the sky or clouds, light blue and white are the best colors. Plus, these hues keep you cooler than darker colors under the hot sun.

Mosquitoes and other biting insects are strongly attracted to the colors red and black. Blue is slightly less appealing to bugs. Light tan and light olive attract less attention from bugs than any other colors, and because these colors also help you blend into the background, they're good all-around choices for fly fishing. And you thought most of that clothing in fishing catalogs was tan and olive because fly fishers are just boring.

16
What fly line should you use for starting out?

YOUR FIRST FLY LINE SHOULD BE A TAPERED LINE OF THE SIZE CALLED FOR ON your rod. And it should float. When you look at fly line designations, you'll see something like this: "WF5F." The first two letters represent the taper, which is less important and is covered in the section below on weight forward versus double taper lines. The middle number is the line size, and it must match the designation on your rod. The last letter, F, tells you the line floats, which is what you want.

Why is a floating line so important if you won't fish many dry flies? First, it's much easier to pick up a floating line off the water when you're casting than a sinking one, because you have to lift all of the line free of the water when making a cast, and getting a submerged line moving and above the water with a single back cast is difficult. Next, you can fish nearly every kind of fly—floating or sinking—with a floating line because you can use a weighted fly or weight on your leader to sink a fly, but you can't fish a dry fly with a sinking line. Third, floating lines land much lighter on the water, and when you're starting out, you'll need all the help you can muster to keep your fly line from landing on the water too hard.

For trout fishing, I use a sinking line less than 1 percent of the time, and could probably live without ever using one. A floating line is also the basic line for Atlantic salmon, bonefish, redfish, and bass, so I'm not just suggesting this line for the novice. Unless you fish for saltwater fish in deep water or fast currents, or fish for trout in lakes in midsummer after they go deep, you may go for years without feeling the need for a sinking line.

Even in deep water, you can fish with a floating line by adding weight to your leader and adjusting your presentation.

17

When to use a sinking line

FOR MOST FLY FISHING, YOU DON'T NEED A SINKING LINE. HOWEVER, WHEN YOU need one, you *really* need one, most often when you are faced with water over six feet deep in combination with fast current or tides, and when you want your fly to swim close to the bottom for as long as possible. You *can* fish quite deep when fishing with a floating line, but at some point the amount of weight you need to add to your leader gets cumbersome, and when fishing deep with a floating line, as soon as you begin a retrieve the fly angles toward the surface, which is not always desirable.

When fishing the open ocean over deep water, it's almost essential to have a sinking line onboard.

Here is a situation when I always fish a fast-sinking line. When fishing offshore from a boat for striped bass, the fish are often suspended over the bottom at twenty to thirty feet, hovering around submerged structure, ambushing baitfish. Here you want your baitfish imitation to sink quickly and to swim close to the bottom, showing the fly to as many fish as possible before bringing the line to the surface for another cast. Here you need a Depth Charge line (a fast-sinking line combined with an intermediate running line behind it), a full-sinking class V line (the fastest-sinking standard fly line) or a fast-sinking shooting head.

Another instance where you want either a sinking line or a sink-tip line (a fast-sinking head, typically about fifteen feet long, followed by a floating running line that makes line pickup and mending easier) is when fishing streamers in fast water. Even if you want your fly to run shallow, stripping a streamer quickly with just a floating line makes the fly skim across the surface, and in order to keep the fly under water you need a sinking line to help keep it down. I also use a fast-sinking line when fishing baitfish imitations over breaking fish in open ocean, because the sinking line keeps the fly running just under the waves if you begin stripping immediately after the fly hits the water.

If you fish for trout or bass in ponds, you always hope to find them close the surface, but if their food is deep or if the water close to the surface is too warm, fish may stay deep throughout the day. The best way to fish for trout or bass in more than twenty feet of water is to use a sinking line using the countdown method. Make a long cast and count to ten or twenty (or your lucky number if you wish) before retrieving your nymph or streamer. If you catch a fish on the first cast consider yourself lucky. Now you know how long to let your fly sink. If not, increase your count until you catch fish or hang bottom. If you hang bottom on successive casts, decrease your count by a small amount until you stop hanging up, because fish can see a fly above them but won't notice a fly that is below their level.

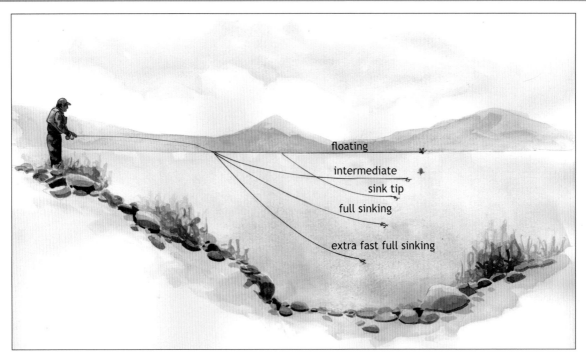

floating

intermediate

sink tip

full sinking

extra fast full sinking

18

What's the difference between a weight forward and a double taper line?

THE MOST COMMON FLY LINE TAPERS ARE WEIGHT FORWARD (WF) AND DOUBLE taper (DT). Both are the same for the first thirty feet of line, so if you never cast beyond thirty feet, the difference is irrelevant to you. Beyond thirty feet, weight forward lines taper for about six feet to a thinner portion called the running line, which is then level or un-tapered until the end of the line at ninety feet. Weight forward lines are best for distance casting because the thin running line offers less resistance to the wind and to the guides on the fly rod, so this line pulls extra line from your hand and propels it forward more easily. So a weight forward line seems to give you the best of both worlds—the same characteristics at a short distance as a double taper, plus the ability to make long casts beyond thirty feet.

A double taper line beyond thirty feet increases in diameter very gradually to a ten-foot level section right in the middle of the line, after which it begins to slowly decrease, ending in a mirror image of the first forty-five feet of the taper. Why, with all the advantages of a weight forward line, would an angler ever want a double taper line? The bigger mass in the middle of a double taper is easier to mend once on the water so it is helpful in tricky currents. When making long (over forty-foot) false casts with a dry fly, a double taper with its gradual increase is easier to hold in the air. A double taper line roll casts beyond forty feet better than a weight forward, which loses all its power if you attempt a long roll cast because the skinny

A double taper line is perfect for roll casts, longer false casts, and mending line in tight spots like this.

running line does not offer enough mass to keep the line moving. And, finally, when the end of a double taper line gets worn out and loses its floating qualities, the line can be reversed so it will last twice as long. Thus for someone who fishes either small streams or mostly dry flies, a double taper line lasts twice as long as a weight forward.

19
How to connect a leader to a fly line

CONNECTING A STIFF, CLEAR MONOFILAMENT LEADER TO A SOFT, FLEXIBLE FLY LINE requires more than your average Boy Scout knot, although when I was first learning to fly fish, one book told me to use a sheet bend knot. It was thick and clumsy and did not hold well, so once I discovered the nail knot it was a revelation. A nail knot is smooth and very strong, and when tied properly the coating will come off a fly line before the knot fails.

To make the smoothest connection of all, cut the loop off your leader (if it came with a pre-made loop, which most do these days) and nail knot the leader right to the line. However, if you want to move from a seven-and-a-half-foot leader to a twelve-footer, you have to cut off the nail knot and tie another one. This is not something you want to do a couple of times a day, and you lose a small piece of fly line every time you do. Still, if I have a fly line like a 2-weight on which I know I will always use the same leader throughout the season, I'll nail knot a leader to the line because it is the smoothest connection possible.

Many fly lines these days come with loops already attached to the end of the line. The loop might be a piece of heavy monofilament nail knotted to the line, a hollow braided loop glued to the line, or the line may

Nail Knot

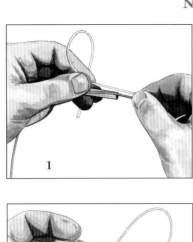

1

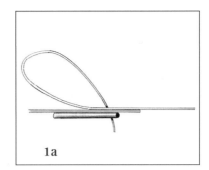

1a

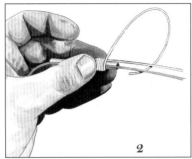

2

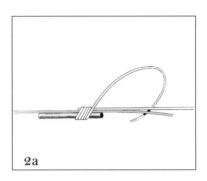

2a

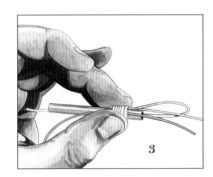

3

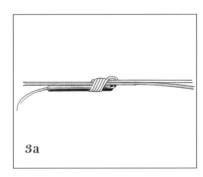

3a

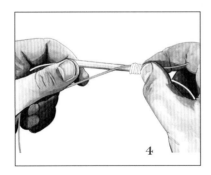

4

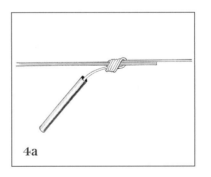

4a

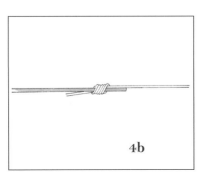

4b

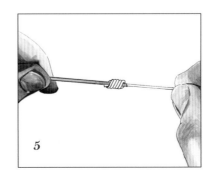

5

be made with a self-loop at the factory where the line is pulled around and fused to itself. With a permanent loop on your line, when you want to change leaders all you do is make a simple loop-to-loop connection. No knots, nothing to trim, and pretty slim once it's cinched down. If your line did not come with a pre-made loop, just tie a six-inch piece of .023-inch nylon to the end of the fly line and tie a perfection loop on the other end.

Perfection Loop

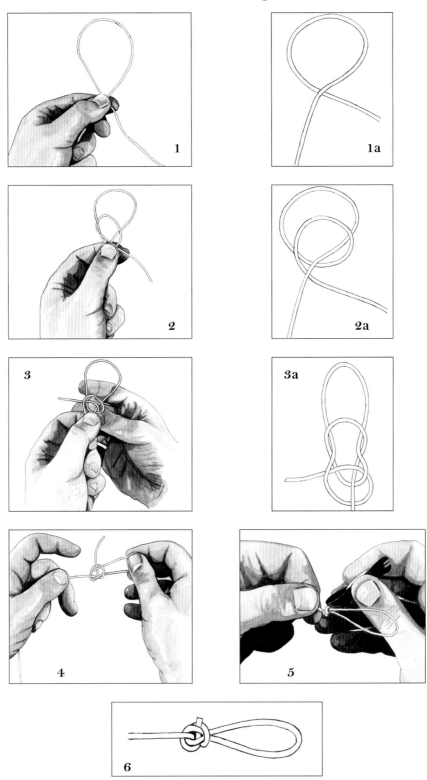

Loop to Loop

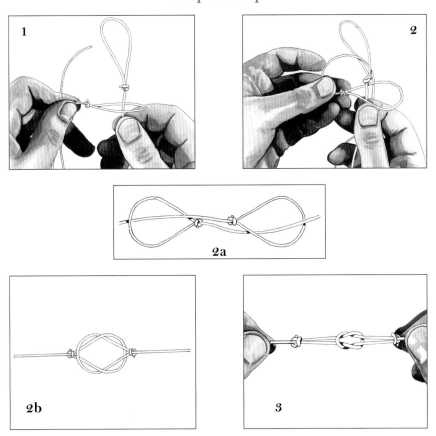

20

What is backing and how do you tie it to your reel and line?

IF YOU FISH FOR BIG TROUT OR SALTWATER FISH WITH A FLY ROD, SOONER OR LATER you'll run out of fly line when a fish makes a powerful run. Fly lines are ninety or one hundred feet long, and some fish will run more than a hundred yards before you can stop them. Backing is your insurance. It's thinner than fly line, so you can get lots of it on a spool. Backing comes in two flavors: braided Dacron and braided gel-spun polyester. Both are thin, supple, and strong, but gel-spun is half the diameter of Dacron in the same strength so you can pack more of it on the spool. It's also much more expensive, but if you need two hundred yards of backing on a spool but can only fit one hundred yards of Dacron on it with the fly line you want to use, you'll have to go with gel-spun.

Because most fly lines break at about twenty-five pounds, you only need twenty-pound Dacron or thirty-five-pound gel-spun (it doesn't come any smaller) backing for trout lines. Some big-game fly lines have a stronger core, so you may see fifty-pound gel-spun offered for these special lines.

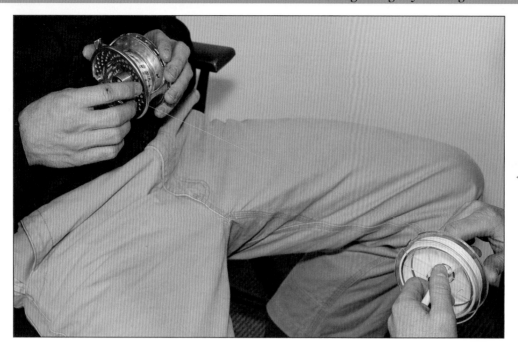

When winding on backing, it's helpful to have two people—one to crank the reel and the other to hold the spool of backing on a pencil.

If you can, try to buy your fly reels already mounted with line and backing. Most fly shops have a special line-winding machine and will do it for you for free or for a modest fee. If you have to do it yourself it's time-consuming but no big deal. First tie the backing to the spool with a couple half hitches or an arbor knot. Chances are you'll never get down to the backing and will never see this knot again. Then, get a helper to put a pencil through the center of the plastic spool that holds the backing and wind it on your reel, level-winding the backing slowly back and forth over the spool arbor so it doesn't bind or cut into itself. Your helper should keep tension on the spool to make sure your winds are tight.

Arbor Knot

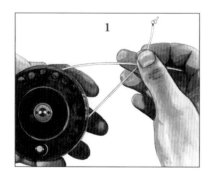

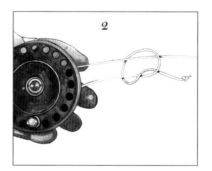

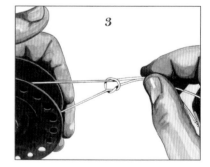

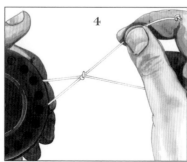

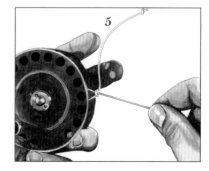

When you've wound all the backing on the spool, tie it to your fly line. The simplest way to attach backing to a fly line is with an eight-turn nail knot. It's fine for trout fishing and for smaller saltwater fish. If you're going for fish over twenty pounds, a fail-safe way to attach backing to the line is with a loop-to-loop connection. Tie a large loop in the backing with a surgeon's loop (large enough to pass the plastic fly line spool through when you make the loop-to-loop connection). Then make a self loop in the fly line by doubling the line over itself for about two inches and then securing it by tying three separate nail knots over the loop with twelve- to fifteen-pound-test monofilament. Now make a loop-to-loop connection and wind the fly line on your spool the same way you did the backing.

21
What is a tippet and what do you do with it?

THE TIPPET IS THE LAST PART OF YOUR LEADER, THE PART WHERE YOU ATTACH your fly. When you buy a new knotless leader, the tippet is an integral part of the leader, not a separate piece. Over the years, fly fishers have determined that a leader made from 25 percent heavy butt section, 50 percent quick step-down taper, and 25 percent level tippet casts best. If you run your fingers carefully down a knotless leader you can feel these transitions. The level tippet allows your fly to land softly on the water.

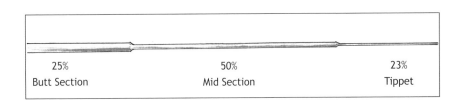

| 25% | 50% | 23% |
| Butt Section | Mid Section | Tippet |

Sooner or later, you'll tie so many flies on the tippet that it will get too short. You'll see your fly land with a big splat, which tells you it's time for either a new leader or just a new tippet. So you can either waste a few bucks and tie on a whole new leader, or, if you're smart, you'll have spools of tippet material in your pocket so you can just tie on a new tippet with a surgeon's knot. Two to three feet is standard for a tippet—any shorter and your fly might land too hard; any longer and the leader may not straighten completely because the tippet end is too air-resistant. In general, a shorter tippet is easier to cast in the wind and a longer one is better if you're fishing in moving water with lots of conflicting currents.

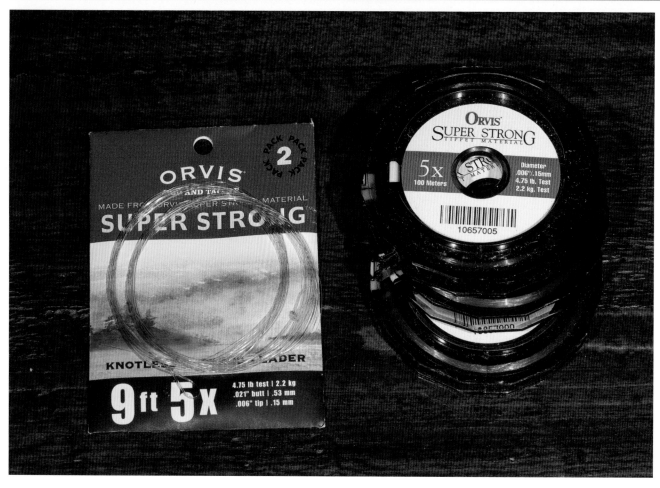

You'll need a spool of tippet in the same size as your leader, and one size smaller and larger in case you decide to fish bigger or smaller flies.

PART

III

Casting

How do you cast in the wind?

THE COMBINATION OF WIND AND FLY FISHING SCARES MANY PEOPLE AWAY, BUT with a few basic tips you can easily fish in winds up to about twenty miles per hour. Above that it does get pretty hairy. Here are some guidelines for casting on windy days:

Side-arm casting

Turning your cast to the side on a windy day will give you better control of your line.

- Keep your casts short. Spend more time getting close to fish. Fish are not as spooky on windy days so you can afford to creep right up on them.
- Cast side-armed instead of directly overhead. The wind is lighter closer to the water, and by casting at 90 degrees to the vertical you keep the fly and line farther away from your head.
- With a tailwind, put more energy into your back cast and aim it higher, and put less energy into your forward cast. With a headwind, reverse the process.
- If you have a crosswind, try to make sure the crosswind does not blow the fly across your body. Turn around and cast, or change positions.
- Shorten your leader and tippet and try to use flies that are less wind-resistant.
- On long casts with a light wind, I would rather cast into the wind that with it. I find that a wind behind me pushes my back cast below the tip of the rod and ruins my forward cast. I find it easier to let the wind help me on my back cast, and then I overpower the forward cast.

23

How do you increase the length of your casts?

MOST FISH OF ALL TYPES ARE CAUGHT AT FORTY FEET OR LESS, BUT EVENTUALLY you'll need to reach out and touch a distant spot, especially if you do any fishing in salt water. The first thing to remember is that excessive false casts, which are the normal response to a long cast, are counterproductive. The more your line is in the air, the greater the chance you'll eventually screw up. Take your time and slow down. Hold some loose line in reserve, either in big coils or in a stripping basket. Increase your false casts to about thirty-five or forty feet, which is where the rod really begins to flex and pick up energy. Make no more than three false casts. On the last one, release the excess line and aim your rod tip slightly higher than you would on a shorter cast, to help the extra line clear the guides on the rod.

Remember that as you increase the length of line you cast, your timing will be a bit slower because it takes longer for the line to straighten behind you. Also, raise your arm up above your head and increase the length of your casting stroke. On a short cast, the rod should move mostly up and down. On a long

Increasing your false casts to about forty feet and holding some line in reserve will help you make longer casts.

cast, you should add length to your stroke by moving the rod back and forth in addition to up and down. Yes, you will go beyond that sacred two o'clock position you learned from your uncle, but you need the longer casting stroke to move the longer line.

Most people can cast well up to fifty or sixty feet (depending on the rod and the caster) without adding a double haul to the mix. However, to increase your line speed (and the amount of line you can shoot on each cast) you'll eventually want to learn the double haul, especially if you're faced with wind. The double haul is simple in principle and difficult in execution. When you raise the rod into your back cast, you haul downward on the line with your other hand. The line hand then drifts back to meet with the casting hand as the back cast straightens, and as the rod hand moves forward on the forward cast, the line hand again hauls downward and then releases the shooting line.

There are as many styles and opinions on how much to haul and when to do it as there are casting styles. It often helps to haul on the back cast and let the line fall to the ground behind you. Then take a look at your hand position (hands should be together as the back cast straightens) and make the forward cast with a haul. You'll be amazed that even with the line on the ground behind you, a decent forward cast is possible because of the increased line speed you generate with the double haul. Keep practicing it until you suddenly feel the fly line try to jump from your hands—then you've got it.

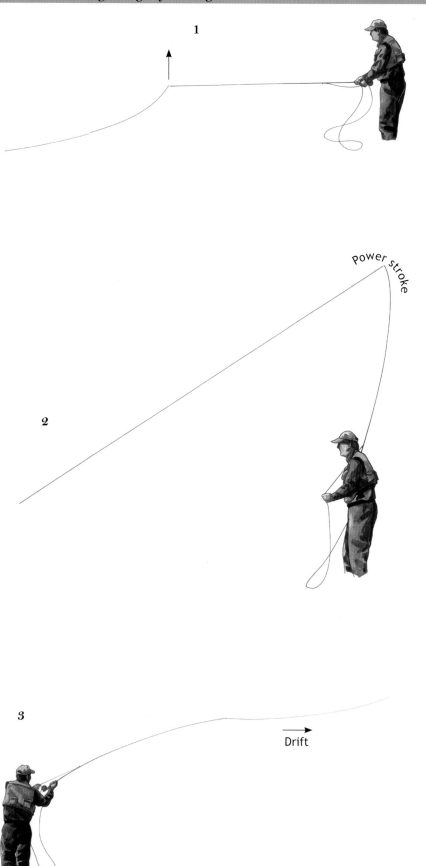

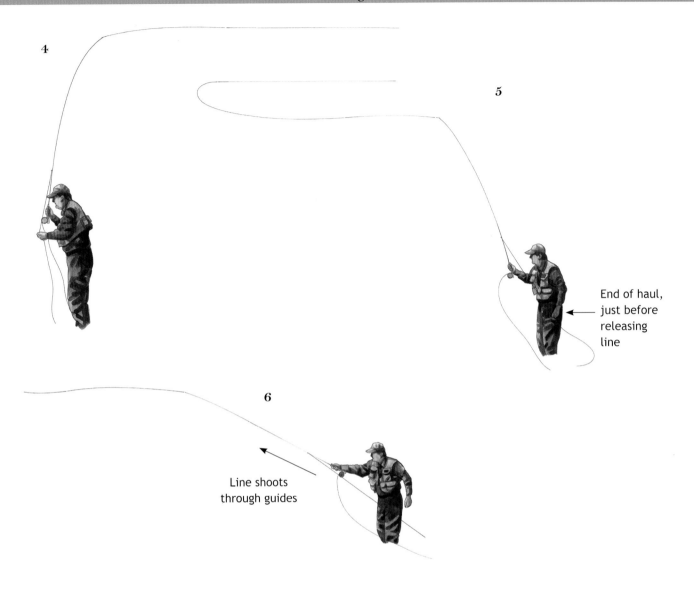

4

5

End of haul, just before releasing line

6

Line shoots through guides

24

How should your leader, line, and fly land on the water?

SOMEWHERE, SOMEHOW, A SUPPOSED EXPERT TOLD NOV- ICE ANGLERS THAT THEIR fly should land on the water before the line and leader. I know this because year after year, when teaching in the Orvis fishing schools, I'd have students ask me how to make their fly land first. You can do it, but I've never figured out why you'd want to.

With this nice loop straightening above the water, the line, leader, and fly will all land at about the same time, taking advantage of their air resistance.

In order to slow down the tremendous forward speed of your line and leader so your cast does not slam on the water, you must take advantage of their air resistance. The best way to slow down the cast and present the fly with accuracy is to be sure the line, leader, and fly all straighten above the water at the same time. Two feet above the water is about right. The key to accomplishing this is to get a nice straight back cast, a quick power stroke that drives the tip of the rod forward, and then a seamless follow-through with the rod until the tip of the rod is parallel to the water.

25

Keeping your fly line slick

SMOOTH, SLICK FLY LINES CAST BETTER, SHOOT BETTER, AND FLOAT BETTER. Lines pick up dirt and algae when used, and they simply have to be cleaned. Commercial line dressings make them feel slicker at first, but these concoctions end up attracting more junk to the line's surface and defeat the purpose. Some people clean their lines after every fishing trip, while others do it once a season. The ideal frequency depends on how much algae is in the water you fish and how much you drag your line along the ground. But cleaning a line is so simple that most of us should do it more often.

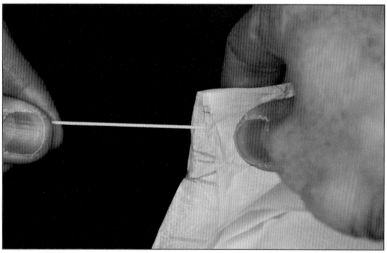

Dirt collects on the surface of the fly line and keeps it from floating and shooting well. All you have to do is wash the line in warm soapy water and run it through a paper towel to remove it.

Simply take a soft cloth or paper towel and wet it with warm water to which you've added a small amount of dish soap. Now strip the line off your reel in nice loose coils in a room free of cats, dogs, and small children, or outside on the lawn. Once all the line is off your reel, run it through the cloth, applying enough pressure to make the fly line squeak a little. Then work back the other way with a clean, dry cloth. You may find that once you strip off half your line it already looks slick and pristine (unless you cast the whole fly line when you fish), so you may be able to stop after about forty feet.

26

How to keep from hanging up in trees and brush—and what to do about it

OKAY, LET'S FIRST ESTABLISH A FACT OF LIFE. EVERYONE GETS HUNG UP IN TREES OR streamside brush. *Everyone*. Fly fishers who tell you different are either lying or never fish in those tricky places where the best fish lurk. All you want to do is minimize your hangups.

Keeping a few points in the back of your mind will help. For instance, the best place to position yourself in brushy streams if you are right-handed is from the middle of the river to the left bank (looking upstream) if you have the option, because most right-handers cast a little off to the right. Always look behind before you cast and make a few practice false casts. This is not just a rookie move—everybody does it. Don't forget that the longer your cast, the harder it is to control, especially on windy days, so if you keep getting hung in the trees shorten up a bit.

If (sorry, *when*) you get hung up in a tree, the worst thing you can do is to yank on your line with the rod. Yanking on a fly caught in a tree often puts a severe strain on a fly rod— one it was not designed for. Either carefully lay your rod on the bank and then pull on the line and leader with your hands, or point the tip of the rod directly at the fly and walk backward.

Everybody gets hung up in trees. This, however, is not the best way to retrieve a stuck fly. It's much better to back up, keeping the rod tip pointed directly toward the fly. ▶

27

What rod action do you need?

I HESITATE TO OPEN THE MESSY BOX OF JARGON THAT FLY FISHERS USE TO DESCRIBE rod actions, because few people understand what a fly rod really does. But in the convoluted world of choices in fly rods today, we all need guidelines besides just length and line size. You'll hear the words fast, medium, and slow to describe rod action. To one person, fast means a rod that bends more close to the tip than it does down into the middle of the rod. To other anglers, a fast rod is one that's stiffer than others of the same configuration. Or you'll hear rods described as "still" or "soft." Orvis uses a standard that, I believe, is less confusing because it describes exactly how a rod bends under a given load, and can be measured and duplicated from one rod to the next. This system uses the terms tip-flex, mid-flex, and full-flex. A tip-flex rod bends mostly at the tip and a lot less in the middle, mid-flex bends down into the middle of the rod, and in a full-flex action, the rod bends right down into the handle.

Obviously there are degrees of each action, but putting rods in those broad terms is enough. So what do these terms tell you about what the rod will do for you? A tip-flex rod develops higher line speed and tighter casting loops, which means it is a rocket ship that will shoot a lot of line. It also has more reserve power for long casts, and most anglers feel this action has better accuracy on long casts. A full-flex rod is great for short casts and light tippets; because the rod bends so much it acts as a superb shock absorber. It's also more fun with small fish because the rod bends so easily. A mid-flex rod, naturally, is somewhere in between and is a great compromise between close-in accuracy and power for distance.

In a small mountain stream like this, a full-flex action will load the rod better on short casts.

You might find you like one action type for all your rods. That's fine; one of the actions just might fit your personality and casting style. For instance, if you are a type-A person you might always want a tip-flex rod, and if it takes a life-threatening situation to get your pulse going, you might want a laid-back full-flex rod all the time. I prefer a tip-flex for saltwater fishing where I know I'll have a lot of wind and will be forced to make frequent long casts. For small-stream trout fishing I like a real full-flex action. For basic trout fishing I like a mid-flex. Fortunately, reliable fly shops will let you "try before you buy" so if you're not sure, you can experiment with different actions before you decide on the right one for you.

28

When you need a roll cast

WHENEVER POSSIBLE YOU SHOULD USE THE STANDARD OVERHEAD CAST. IT'S MORE accurate, you can cast farther when you need to, and it lands on the water more softly. However, you will encounter times, especially on small streams or on bigger rivers where you can't wade out very far, when streamside brush makes a back cast impossible.

Getting ready for a roll cast in a tight spot

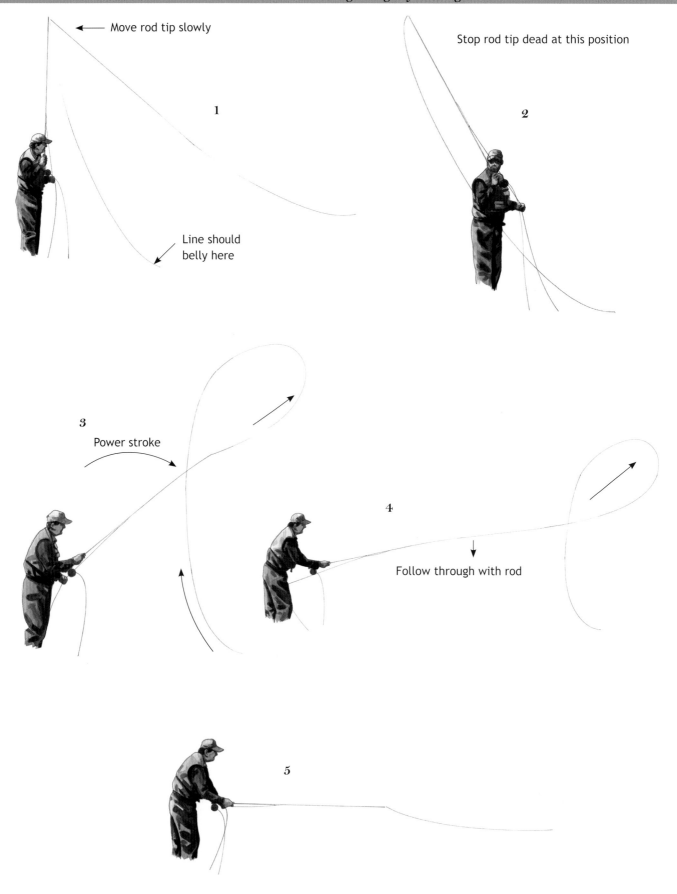

Move rod tip slowly

1

Line should
belly here

Stop rod tip dead at this position

2

3

Power stroke

4

Follow through with rod

5

Also, because the roll cast does not require an existing bend in your rod in order to propel the line forward, as an overhead cast does, it's perfect for those times when for some reason you've ended up with a pile of line at your feet. You can start with a quick roll cast to get the line out on the water in front of you. Then you'll be able to develop a bend in the rod for an overhead cast because the straight line, without slack, will begin to bend the rod immediately and will build up enough energy to flex the rod and drive the line behind you for a back cast.

The roll cast is almost intuitive and takes about five minutes to learn. Just move the rod tip back slowly until you get a semicircle of line behind the rod and slightly off to the side. A quick point with the tip of the rod will drive the line out in front of you with no back cast.

29

Why does your fly keep hitting your line?

FLY CASTERS OFTEN GET FRUSTRATED WHEN THE FLY CATCHES THE ROD, FLY, OR leader on its path, and this happens most often on the forward cast. The first thing to check is the wind—make sure you don't have a crosswind blowing the fly into your rod. With no wind to blame, the most common reason for this problem is a closed or "tailing" casting loop.

A nice loop like this one won't catch on itself.

Tailing loop fly hits
radar line

To understand what happens on a bad loop like this, you have to first see what happens on a good loop. Examining your own casting loop is tough. You're not at a good angle to see what's happening. My advice is to watch a good caster in action, either live or on a video. You see that a good casting loop on the forward cast looks like the letter J turned on its side, or a candy cane. As the forward cast unrolls, the bottom of the loop gets longer and the top gets shorter. In a good cast, the top loop always stays above the bottom loop. A tailing loop happens when the top of the loop drops below the bottom, and the fly catches on the line.

Tailing loops can be tough to correct, and the only therapy is practice. Some casters respond better to knowing what their hand and arm are doing wrong, and others find it easier to correct problems just by thinking about the rod and line. A tailing loop is usually caused by the caster using too much wrist on the forward cast, too soon. The weaker wrist muscles are better at giving the forward cast that final crisp snap, so when you make a forward cast, try to initiate the cast with your forearm and follow up with a wrist snap. If you find it easier to relate to what the rod and line are doing, remember that the tip of the rod has to get out of the way of the line quickly, and the best way to do this is to concentrate on pointing the rod straight out in front of you, at waist level, as quickly as possible.

A good tight loop

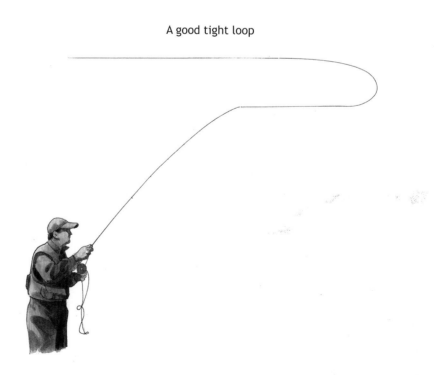

30

Why does your line pile up on the water?

THE FLIP ANSWER TO THIS QUESTION IS, "YOU ARE DOING SOMETHING WRONG ON your cast," but, truly, almost anything you do wrong will give you puddles of line instead of a nice straight cast. However, two errors are the most likely suspects. First, examine a bad cast and determine if the line is piling right in front of the rod tip, or if it's slamming on the water some distance out from your position.

Line piling right in front of you is almost always caused by a poor back cast and then not putting enough quick power into the forward cast. When you practice casting, turn around and watch your back cast *every time*. Not putting enough power into the back cast, or dropping the rod tip too far behind you, dumps the line below the tip of the rod so that it can never form a good casting loop on the forward cast. Once you are able to drive the line up and behind you so that the line at the end of the back cast is straight and parallel to the water, it's a simple matter to point the tip of the rod quickly in front of you. It's hard to make a bad forward cast with a great back cast.

Line slamming into the water, surprisingly, does not come from too much power on the forward cast. It comes from aiming the tip of the rod *at* the water rather than straight out over the water. If the tip of your rod never drops below a horizontal angle on the forward cast, you can put as much power as you want to in the cast—your line will never slam on the water.

Great casters make full use of the rod's bend to develop casting energy.

Casting from a boat

IN ONE RESPECT, CASTING FROM A BOAT IS EASIER, ESPECIALLY IF THE BOAT IS stable enough for you to stand in, because you have more elevation above the water, so it's easier to pick up line and it's easier to keep your back cast high. However, boats present their own challenges, and if you're prepared to deal with them your time on the water will be easier.

First, most boats are full of cleats and seats and other gear that can grab your fly line when you make a cast. Try to remove as many obstructions as possible around your feet, or cover them with a wet towel or a piece of mesh if they can't be moved. Whereas most of us are pretty casual about where we strip our line when wading, when casting from a boat it helps if you pay more attention to where each length of line is placed when you're stripping it in. Some anglers like to use a stripping basket in a boat, which is a device used to catch all your excess line after stripping it in. A plastic trash bucket can be used as a stripping basket in a pinch—just fill it with a little water to keep it weighted down and to keep your fly line slick.

You must also pay attention to the living obstructions in a boat. For instance, in a drift boat, where there is typically an angler in the bow and one in the stern with the guide sitting between the two, the territory over the length of the boat is a forbidden land—in other words, never cast straight in front of or straight behind a boat unless you want a very unhappy guide. And with two anglers casting at the same time, even if they are casting to different sides of the boat, it's very easy to tangle the back cast of one angler with the forward cast of the other. It's always the responsibility of the caster in the stern to watch out for trouble because the angler in the bow can't see what is going on behind him.

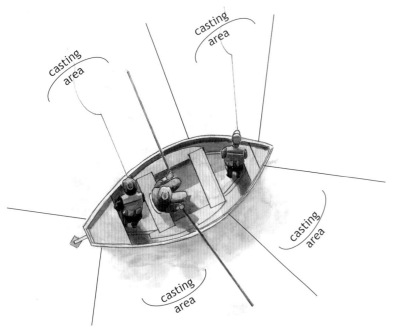

Ordinarily, the right-hander in the stern of this boat would be casting in the other direction so he could watch the other angler's back cast and not cast over the head of the guide in the middle. But all three of these guys are guides so they'll probably be OK.

Techniques

Which direction should you move when fishing a stream?

BEFORE YOU DECIDE WHICH DIRECTION TO FISH, YOU SHOULD HAVE A BASIC strategy in mind. Will you be fishing primarily with a dry fly, nymph, wet fly, or streamer? Dry flies are best fished at an upstream angle to prevent drag, and because dry-fly fishing is usually practiced in shallow water where fish can see the surface, working against the current keeps you behind the fish, in the blind spot in their rear quarters. Swing a wet fly or a streamer on a downstream angle, and by working slowly downstream, you can cover all the likely water by swinging the fly across the current, taking a few steps downstream, and repeating the process.

You can fish nymphs at almost any angle you can think of, depending on water conditions and the rig you're using. The most popular way to fish nymphs is across-stream, casting on a slight upstream angle, so when fishing them you can move either upstream or downstream. If the water is shallow it's a good idea to work upstream, as you would with a dry fly, so you can sneak up on the fish. If the water is swift and it's too much work to constantly fight the current, you may prefer to move slowly downstream.

This angler is swinging a wet fly downstream, making a few steps between each cast so he covers all the water.

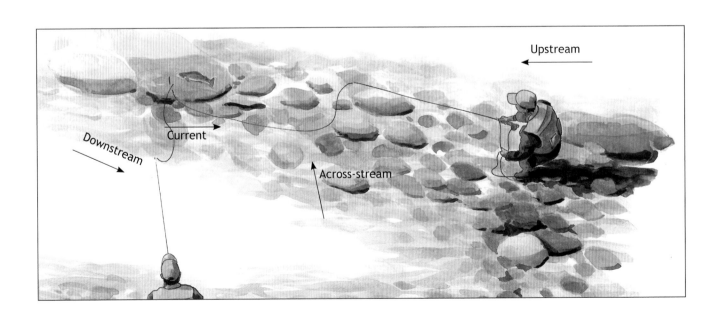

Upstream

Downstream

Current

Across-stream

33

Do you need a net or can you use your hands?

NETS CLUTCH AT BRANCHES AS YOU WALK through the woods and are just another piece of gear hanging from your fishing vest. Do you really need one? If all the fish you catch are smaller than twelve inches, it's probably just as easy to land the fish by hand, cradling each fish gently in the water while holding the leader and freeing the fly with a pair of forceps. However, this gets tougher as the fish get bigger and friskier, as once a fish gets close to you it takes about twice as long to maneuver it to hand as it does just to scoop it up in a net. You'll also lose more flies and more fish because of last-minute headshakes that wouldn't have occurred if the fish was already safely in a net.

Small trout can be easily handled without a net. ▶

34

How to land a fish without losing it

MOST FISH ARE LOST AT THE STRIKE OR DURING THE FINAL MOMENTS OF LANDING. The rest of the stuff in between might be exciting, but it's not where many fish are lost. To be sure of landing a fish, the best approach is to have a buddy with a net, preferably the long-handled variety so your assistant doesn't have to get so close to the fish or swipe the water for the fish. In a current, get your buddy downstream of your position, and once the fish gets in close, move your rod tip off to the side and downstream while the net handler holds the net under water. As soon as the fish passes above the net, a quick upward sweep captures it with a minimum of fuss. Swiping at a fish with a net is a quick path to a broken leader.

The best way to land a big fish in fast water is to have someone hold the net underwater and lead the fish over the top of the net.

Without a friend with a net, assuming you have one yourself, try to lead the fish upstream of your position with the tip of the rod, reach out and place the net under water, and then let the fish drift back in the current and lift the net under the fish. If you find yourself without a net and connected to a very large fish (or a fish that won't fit into the puny net you're carrying), the best approach is to beach the fish. Scan the shore for a shallow beach where you can lead the fish until it gets into water so shallow that is has to turn on its side. Once it does, you can back up and slide it easily into shallower water where it can't move at all.

During a close-quarters battle, whether from a boat in deep water or in a current while wading, remember that a fish can only swim in the direction its head is pointing. It is not easy merely to crank in a big fish, and it requires a lot less force to just turn the fish's head. Keeping the rod high over your head and pointed directly at the fish gives the fish only one option—to swim away from you and down, and any time the fish gains distance from you the fight will be longer. Keeping your rod to one side or another leads the fish back and forth, but it has to swim on an angle toward you if you keep its head pointed in your direction.

35
How long should your leader be?

YOUR HEIGHT AND THE LENGTH OF YOUR ROD HAVE NO BEARING ON THE PROPER leader length. It's determined entirely by fishing conditions. When using sinking lines, you should keep the fly relatively close to the fly line, because the sinking line keeps the fly swimming deep enough and a long leader may allow the fly to rise to the surface. So here, a leader of between four and six feet is about right. Don't worry about spooking the fish with your fly so close to the line—if the fish were really spooky you would not be using a clumsy sinking line anyway.

In small streams, where line speed is slower and drifts are very short, you seldom need a leader longer than seven and a half feet unless the pools are flat and calm and fish are spooky. The short leader straightens more easily on short casts. Freshwater bass are also not shy of the fly line or leader, and you can get away with the easier-casting seven-and-a-half-footer.

Basic trout fishing with dry flies and nymphs in most rivers is done with a nine-foot leader. This length keeps the fly line far enough away from spooky trout, yet is easy to straighten, even in a stiff breeze. Most saltwater fly fishing is also done with nine-foot leaders, except for bonefish, redfish, or striped bass feeding in clear, shallow water, where a twelve-foot leader may give you a slight edge in stealth. Twelve-foot leaders or longer are best when fishing for trout in lakes with a floating line, because in the smooth water of a lake's surface a trout can spot a fly line landing from a long way off. And in still pools on rivers, where conditions approach those of a lake, a twelve-foot leader may be a wise move.

Under conditions of extreme low water and very spooky fish, trout anglers may also go as long as an eighteen-foot leader by adding a few feet to the butt section and to the tippet of a leader. These ultra-long leaders are helpful in keeping the fly line well away from the fish, and in making conflicting currents less of a problem with drag because a leader is suppler than a fly line. However, an eighteen-footer requires nearly perfect casts to avoid frustration, and a mere whisper of a wind can blow one well off course, so don't try one until you've developed your casting skills.

On flat, clear water like this, a twelve-foot leader will help prevent spooking wary trout.

36

How to avoid upsetting other people on the water

I STILL CRINGE WHEN I THINK OF THE TIMES AS A TEENAGER WHEN I WADED RIGHT up the middle of a river where other people were fishing. I wasn't arrogant or confrontational, I just didn't know any better; but I must have raised the blood pressure of more than one fly fisher and I'm surprised I never got into an altercation. Somebody should have set me straight.

Your first rule of consideration starts before you even approach the water. If someone is already at a parking spot and getting suited up to fish, the right thing to do is to ask which direction he or she intends to go. If the other angler heads upstream, you have an obligation to go downstream. Never race to put on your gear to try to beat someone to the best water if he or she was there before you. It's just poor manners.

If you have to walk past other anglers to get to an un-crowded spot, stay as far away from the bank as you can. Walking close to the bank or in the shallows can spook fish and you'll spoil the fishing for people who got there before you. And if you have to cross a river, do so in shallow riffles where no one is fishing, rather than slogging through the deeper water, pushing out waves that may frighten every fish in a pool.

When a number of anglers are in a large pool, try to keep as much distance from others as possible.

Always try to find a pool or a stretch of water with no one in it. Most fly fishers enjoy their solitude, whether wading a river, paddling a kayak, or walking a lonely beach. Only enter a piece of water close to another angler if he or she invites you in—otherwise give everyone a wide berth. Fly fishers move around a lot, and just because a piece of water is empty does not mean it offers poor fishing. Besides, you may find a secret hot spot that everyone else has passed up.

37

In lakes, what do you do once the fly hits the water?

ALTHOUGH IT'S SMARTER FOR A FLY FISHER TO LEARN ON A POND BEFORE advancing to the complexities of flowing water, it's usually not what happens. Most fly fishers begin as stream trout anglers, and when faced with a huge expanse of water without current to move the fly or tighten the line, they're lost.

First, slack line is never desirable on a pond, as it sometimes is in moving water. So once the fly lands, take up any slack by stripping in some line. The best way to fish a dry fly on a pond, especially if fish are rising, is to let the fly sit there without any motion. This can get boring without any fish in the vicinity, so the key to fishing a dry in still water is to move the boat close to the fish and then try to anticipate their path and get your fly in front of them. Otherwise it's about as interesting as picking knots out of your leader. Largemouth and smallmouth bass will also attack a fly that has remained motionless for minutes, especially if the fly has rubber legs that keep wiggling long after the fly has landed.

But most flies fished on still water are manipulated by the angler. After casting, strip in line, keeping the rod tip low and pointed straight at the fly to make the fly swim through the water, until it gets about twenty feet away. Then pick up and make another cast. If no fish or obvious cover are in sight, cast at different angle until you've covered all the water within the reach of your casting skills. Experiment with retrieve speeds as well. Small nymphs imitate tiny insects or crustaceans that can't swim very fast, so strips should be short and slow; streamers imitate baitfish that swim at a faster clip, so longer, faster movements might be in order. But there are always those days when a streamer works better with a slow, steady strip and a nymph catches more fish when streaking through the water. It always pays to experiment.

In lakes, after you complete a cast the rod tip should stay close to the water's surface.

38

Is it worth fishing an area with canoe or boat traffic?

IN A WORD, NO, IF YOU CAN HELP IT. MOST GAMEFISH, ESPECIALLY TROUT AND shallow-water saltwater species like bonefish and striped bass, are wary animals, and when faced with a lot of boat traffic they either move elsewhere or stay hidden and refuse to feed. This doesn't mean you have to give up. Look for coves out of the main boat channel in lakes and saltwater shorelines, or look for side channels too shallow for boat traffic in rivers. Sometimes, fish bigger than you'd expect will live in these less-than-optimum spots in order to avoid disturbance. The other alternative is to fish at night or in early morning, when low boat traffic makes fish less nervous and more likely to feed.

◀ In a river with lots of boat traffic, you might have better luck in a small side channel that the boats have not disturbed.

Releasing fish properly

THE BEST WAY TO RELEASE ANY KIND OF FISH IS WITH A MINIMUM OF HANDLING out of the water and gentle cradling in clean water until the fish regains enough strength to swim off on its own. One of the worst things you can do is to play a fish to exhaustion. Always use a tippet strong enough to play a fish quickly, bringing it to hand while it is still "green," not half-dead and swimming on its side. A net and a pair of forceps help keep a fish immobile in the water while you remove the hook, and of course barbless hooks are much quicker to remove. If you do handle the fish, keep your fingers away from its delicate gills and wet your hands before handling it, which helps maintain the protective mucus layer on a fish's skin.

One of the biggest impediments to fish survival is the famous "hero shot," where a fish is held out of the water for many minutes while the happy angler gets ready and the cameraman gets into position. First, the person with the camera should get ready while you're still fighting the fish, and you should both plan the shot before the fish is landed, taking into account background and sun angle so you don't have to reposition while the fish is out of the water. Because fish should be removed from the water for only a few seconds or not at all to ensure survival, if you really want a nice shot, try bending down and cradling the fish in the water, close to the surface. Not only are photographs like this safer for the fish, they're more interesting than a fish held out at arm's length like a bowling trophy.

Be prepared to revive a fish for as long as you played it. Many tired fish, when just thrown back in the water, go belly-up and can't maintain their equilibrium. Apparently their gills do not work properly when they are upside-down, so they can drown if not kept upright. Find an area of clean water with slight waves or moderate current that completely covers the fish. Cradle its head and belly with your hands and gently move it back and forth to get water moving across its gills. When a fish is ready to move off on its own, it will let you know by breaking free of your gentle embrace.

The best way to release a fish is to hold it in clear water until it is able to swim away strongly under its own power. ▶

What is drag and how do you stop it?

THE EASIEST WAY TO DESCRIBE DRAG IS TO DEMONSTRATE WHEN IT IS ABSENT. Throw a twig into moving water and watch how it floats—it moves at the mercy of each little micro-current on the surface, never cutting across currents of different speed. This is how an insect drifts. Few insects have the power to swim contrary to any amount of current, and the movements they do make are tiny hops and pirouettes, not enough to throw off a wake. A fly that creates a wake telegraphs a message to a feeding fish that the object in question is not food because it does not behave like the rest of the insects.

When attached to a leader, a fly can streak across currents when the leader or line is in a different current than the fly. This will happen, eventually, on every cast you make, and avoiding drag is merely ameliorating what must happen when something is attached to a floating object. Drag can be very overt, when you can see the wake from thirty feet away, or it can be minuscule, arising from tiny current threads and invisible to an observer just a few feet from the fly. But trout can always see it.

The best way to avoid drag is to fish in uniform currents and cast straight upstream. If the line and leader float at exactly the same speed as the fly, drag won't develop until the fly is almost even with your rod tip. But fishing straight upstream is often not practical or even desirable, because on a long drift it puts your fly line right on top of the fish. So most times when fishing with a dry fly or nymph we cast at an angle that is somewhere between straight upstream and directly across the current. At this angle you'll often get a decent drag-free float for four or five feet. However, you'll often be faced with trout feeding in slow water along the far bank and fast water between you and the fish, so without some tricky moves you might get only an inch of drag-free float. Here are some of the tricks to use, either alone or in combination:

- Change positions. Often just moving a few feet will give you a longer drag-free float.
- Instead of fishing quartering upstream, fish quartering downstream. If you can, also make a quick mend upstream just before your line hits the water. This is called a reach cast, and that upstream arc in your line has to invert before the fly drags.
- Add an extra-long tippet to your leader. The tippet will land in loose coils, which will have to straighten before your fly begins to drag.
- Make a sloppy cast. By this I don't mean one that slams on the water, but an underpowered cast of controlled sloppiness that throws big piles of slack line on the water. You'll have to cast more line than you think you need because some of your line will be taken up in the loose piles on the water.

Slow current
or
Dead water

Fast current

Fly drags

41

What is the best way to wade a fast river?

PEOPLE DROWN EVERY YEAR WHILE WADING IN RIVERS. MOST OF THESE ACCIDENTS are preventable. The first rule is to always wear a wader belt. Waders with air trapped inside them are quite buoyant (no, you won't float upside down and drown; Lee Wulff proved that eighty years ago by jumping off a bridge while wearing waders) and by keeping the belt tightly cinched around your waist, you'll hold a lot of air inside. Besides, in a moderate spill you'll only get wet from the waist up.

In addition, keep these tips in mind to avoid an accident:

- When crossing fast water, always angle upstream. You will be sure you can retrace your steps to safety, whereas if you wade downstream in fast current and find yourself pushed into a deep hole, you may not be able to retreat.
- The best places to cross are in riffles and the tails of pools, where the water is shallowest.
- Keep your profile sideways to the current to present less resistance to the water.
- Use a wading staff, which adds amazing security and balance to your wading. If you don't have one and need to cross some raging currents, find a hefty stick to use as a temporary staff. It's like growing a third leg.
- Shuffle your feet along the bottom, making sure your forward foot has a secure spot before moving your other foot forward.
- Look for patches of sand and gravel, which typically show up as lighter spots on the bottom. They are much easier to negotiate than rounded boulders. (It goes without saying that you should wear polarized glasses so you can see below the surface better.)

The best way to fish a treacherous river like this is to shuffle your feet slowly, keep your profile sideways to the current, and never wade downstream when you don't know what's below you.

What to do if you hook yourself or someone else

SOONER OR LATER YOU WILL HOOK YOURSELF OR SOMEONE ELSE. HOPEFULLY YOU always wear a hat and some kind of eyeglasses so that you will not be removing a hook from a dangerous place. Barbless hooks remove as easily from human skin as they do from fish jaws, so using them is an important component of safety. But sooner or later you'll forget to de-barb a hook, or someone fishing with a barbed fly will hook you, and it's important to know how to proceed.

First, if the hook is in an eye or anywhere near it, I probably don't have to tell you get to the emergency room quickly. There is nothing you can do in this circumstance except get qualified medical care.

If the fly is lodged in an arm, cheek, or leg, the procedure for removing even a barbed hook is surprisingly easy and painless. Get a loop of strong monofilament line, about ten inches long. Place the monofilament around the bend of the hook so the open end of a loop is facing away from the eye of the fly. Wrap the open ends of the loop around your index finger. Now, while pushing straight down on the eye of the fly, give a firm, quick jerk on the monofilament. The fly will pop right out, with a minimum amount of tissue damage. Wash the wound with some type of antiseptic and make sure your tetanus shots are current.

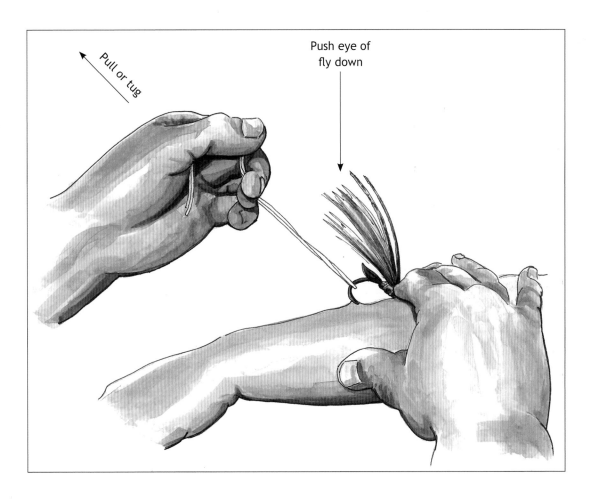

Pull or tug

Push eye of
fly down

43

Where should you hold your rod tip after casting?

A GOOD CAST REQUIRES A NICE FOLLOW-THROUGH OF THE ROD TIP, WITH IT ENDING up comfortably at waist level, parallel to the water. This is especially important when practicing, as there seems to be a natural tendency to then point the tip back up to about the ten o'clock position. I think this comes from those of us who learned to fish with a spinning rod before we learned fly casting. But this causes problems most times, as when the tip is up there swinging in the breeze it moves the line backward from where you just carefully placed it with your cast, and it leaves a big loop of line in front of you to be shoved around by the wind.

A low rod tip like this keeps your line under control, especially when fishing a streamer.

In all cases when fishing in still water, saltwater or fresh, your rod tip should move down to the surface of the water after casting. Here you have more control over your fly line, and in fact some bonefish guides recommend that you put the tip just under the surface of the water and keep it there when retrieving your fly. When fishing moving water, if you are swinging a fly downstream or making a long cast in uniform current, then again your rod tip should be held low. However, if you're fishing in places with lots of swirling currents, or if the place your fly lands is in a different current lane than where you're standing, it makes sense to hold the rod higher—high enough to keep the different current between you and your fly isolated from the fly line.

44

Why do you keep breaking off fish?

THE MOST OBVIOUS CULPRIT WHEN BREAKING OFF FISH IS THAT THE FISH WAS JUST too big for the tippet you were using. That might be the case, especially when you strike in a proper manner (raising the tip of the rod or making a long quick strip just until you feel tension), especially if the fish is moving away from you when it strikes. But most fish break off due to operator error.

Many fish break the tippet because of poor knots. When you break off a fish, carefully examine the part that returns to you: a curlicue in the end of the tippet means the knot used to tie on the fly was not tightened properly, and a missing tippet with a pigtail in the end of the leader means your tippet-to-leader knot was defective. If your tippet comes back with a clean break in the middle of it, you may have gotten a "wind knot" in the middle of it, an overhand knot that gets tied in your leader, usually due not to the wind but to poor casting technique. We call them wind knots to make ourselves feel better. Inspect your tippet often for these little overhand knots and replace your tippet if you see them, because plain overhand knots cut the strength of your tippet in half.

Sometimes the tippet material you've chosen is too light for the fly and rod you're using. Tying a 6X tippet to a size 6 streamer gives you problems because the fine tippet just won't knot well against the much bigger diameter wire used on a size 6 streamer hook. And an 8-weight rod has so much mass and backbone compared to a 4-weight trout rod that you might break a 6X tippet when striking fish no matter how careful you are.

To hook and hold large fish like this brown trout, the most important thing you can do is tie knots properly.

PART

V

Flies

45

Should you use barbless hooks? Why do they come barbed?

BARBLESS HOOKS ARE TERRIFIC FOR MANY REASONS. IF YOU HOOK YOURSELF OR another angler they slip out of your shirt or your anatomy without further damage. When you hook a fish with a barbless hook, backing it out of a fish's tough jawbone with a pair of forceps or pliers is almost effortless, which allows you to release a fish without even touching it, and will save you flies because many flies are lost at the last moment when trying to work a barbed hook free—the tippet breaks and away swims your fly. Fish caught on barbless hooks seldom work free as you expect they might, and because a barb presents some resistance to penetration, a barbless hook actually penetrates better than a barbed one.

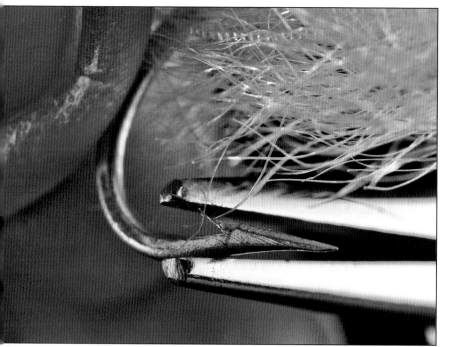

It's easy to make any fly barbless. Just crimp the barb flat with a pair of smooth-jawed forceps or small pliers.

Barbs are found on most fly hooks mainly because of tradition—not much has changed in hook design in the past fifty years, and some anglers still feel (needlessly) insecure without a barb on the hook. But don't worry; it's easy to remove the barb on any hook. With a pair of fine-nose pliers or forceps with flat jaws, crimp the barb flat. You can leave a small hump on the hook to act as a mini-barb if it makes you feel more comfortable, or you can flatten the barb all the way.

46

How do you know what size fly to use?

WHETHER YOU'RE FISHING FOR TROUT OR TUNA, FLY SIZE IS MORE IMPORTANT than color or pattern. When fish get selective about what they eat, the most obvious clue to the fraudulent nature of your fly will be that it's much bigger or much smaller than what they're eating. Shape is sometimes almost as important, but most experienced fly fishers feel that color is a distant third. Flies come in a wide range of sizes and you often have to experiment with different sizes before finding the right fly, but here are some tried-and-true guidelines.

- If you observe fish eating an insect or baitfish, try to capture a sample and place it alongside your fly. Minnows in the water and insects in the air often look far bigger than their true size.
- If you have to guess at the correct size, err on the smaller side. Fish are less suspicious of a fly that is smaller than what they are eating than one that is bigger. Common sense suggests that they'd want the bigger mouthful but empirical evidence suggests the opposite.
- If you don't see fish eating anything, look in the water. Look for baitfish and crustaceans in lakes and saltwater estuaries, or turn over a few rocks in a stream and look for aquatic nymphs. (Even if you'll be fishing dry flies, the insects will be hatching from nymphs of about the same size.) Pick a fly that is the same size as the most abundant prey you see.
- When fishing for big trout, bass, pike, or other species that ambush their food, try a small fly, something between one and two inches long, first. If that fails, try something twice as big. The same holds true when fishing for migratory species like salmon or steelhead that feed infrequently or not at all.

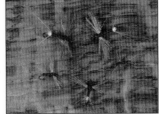

The Rusty Spinner is a great dry fly, but you'll need an assortment of sizes to match the natural insects you see.

47

How to keep a dry fly floating

IF YOU WANT TO DO THE BEST JOB OF KEEPING YOUR DRY FLY FLOATING HIGH, resign yourself to carrying two different kinds of fly dressing. Initially, you'll want to treat your flies with some kind of waterproofing—the best is the liquid kind you apply the night before, because it really penetrates the fly with silicone and the coating lasts longer. But most of us never know what fly we'll be using the next day, or just can't be bothered thinking that far ahead.

At streamside, you should first apply a standard fly floatant. It comes in a paste version that you rub into a fly or a liquid potion for dipping or spraying. All work well, but you should apply these dressings to a *dry* dry fly, in other words, one that has not touched the water yet. Otherwise they don't coat the fly very well. Once a fly gets wet, or if you catch a fish and the fly is covered with fish slime, reapplying a standard floatant doesn't work well. That's the time to introduce your second type of floatant, a dry white powder made from ground silicates and other compounds. This second type actually draws water and slime out of a fly and applies a fine coating of water-repellent powder to the fly. If you've forgotten this second type of floatant, the next best thing to rejuvenate a drowned fly is to squeeze it into a cotton shirt or handkerchief—not as high-tech and not quite as effective, but it will do in a pinch.

A couple of short, crisp false casts, of course, always help to flick moisture off your fly. And if all else fails, use a fly made from closed-cell foam. They'll float all day without a speck of fly dressing.

A bottle of white desiccant powder is your best friend when fishing dry flies.

48

How to pick flies out in a shop

ALL FLIES ARE NOT CREATED EQUAL, EVEN THE SAME PATTERN IN THE SAME BIN IN a fly shop. Flies are still made by hand, one at a time, and since you'll be paying upward of two bucks for each one it's worthwhile to be picky when selecting them. The first thing to look for is symmetry. Nearly everything fish eat has bilateral symmetry and a fly that is lumpy on one side does not look natural to the fish. And a streamer fly or saltwater fly that is not symmetrical will not swim properly in the water and may even put twists in your tippet.

When picking out flies in a shop, look for symmetry, which indicates a well-tied fly.

Next, look at the eye of the hook. It should be free of material or cement; otherwise you'll have trouble tying it on once you hit the water. Heads on flies should be neat and shiny, showing that enough head cement or epoxy has been used to seal the final wraps of fly-tying thread. On streamers, bass flies, and saltwater flies, yank on the wing and tails of the fly. If they pull out you obviously don't want that fly. Also hope that the fly shop owner does not have a "you break it, you buy it" philosophy (I've never met one that does). Hackles on dry flies should be uniform, stiff, and shiny. If the hackles on a fly are of uneven length or if they look dull, the fly will not float well.

For flies made out of deer hair or other bulky materials, or those made with dumbbell eyes like Clouser Minnows, the biggest test of a superior fly is to grab the fly by the bend of the hook and twist the fly. A perfectly tied fly will not twist around the hook shank, but one that does will fall apart easily and will also twist during casting, putting the fly off balance and almost certainly turning off the fish.

49

How to sharpen a hook

FLY-TYING HOOKS ARE MADE FROM GOOD STEEL AND ARE COATED TO RESIST RUST, but they still rust if put away wet, and delicate hook points can get out of alignment like the blade on a knife. Check your point often, especially when fishing around rocks. I can't tell you how many times I've missed several fish in a row, blaming the fish or my reflexes until I happened to check the point of my hook and found it was bent. The best way to check a hook point is to drag it across your thumbnail—if it sticks or scratches, the point is fine, but if the point just slides across the nail, you'll miss the next big fish that strikes.

A diamond file works best for bigger hooks and saltwater flies, while a fine diamond file, Arkansas whetstone, or fine ceramic will put a fine point on a small trout fly. Begin on the bottom of the hook point, stroking the fly against the sharpening surface, with the point angling just slightly into the stone. Next take a couple of licks against each side of the point. Test the hook on your nail and if it doesn't stick, repeat the process.

A good hook sharpener is cheap and fits easily in your pocket or tackle bag. It can save you hundreds of dollars a year in rescued flies, but I'd be willing to bet not one in five anglers carries a hook hone when fishing.

This rusty hook won't penetrate very well, but a few strokes with a hook hone against the point will get it back into shape.

50

How to thread a fly if you have poor eyesight

WHEN YOU HIT THE MAGIC AGE OF FORTY IT'S ALMOST PREORDAINED THAT THE EYES of flies seem to get smaller. And even young eyes have trouble threading a 7X tippet to a size 22 in failing light. Sooner or later you'll need some optical assistance, and the keys to keeping your sanity are light and magnification. Anyone who plans to fish later than 6:00 p.m. should always carry a headlamp or similar tiny flashlight that can be secured to a pocket or hat to direct light in front of you while keeping your hands free. If you somehow find yourself in fading light without a flashlight, try holding the fly up against the light of the sky.

But magnification is the real key for older eyes, and you'll probably find that those 1.5X bifocal adjustments you have on your regular glasses just don't cut it for tying on a small fly, even in bright sunlight. For fly fishing, you really need 3X or 4X magnifiers, and although these powers are not easily found in drugstore readers, fly shops sell many different styles. One is a loupe device that clips to eyeglasses, making you look like Colonel Klink in *Hogan's Heroes,* but it gets the job done. Another clips to the brim of a hat and flips

These three are all young guides and don't need close-up glasses to tie on the last fly of the day. You may not be as lucky.

down when you need it. If you choose to wear a more conventional style of reading glasses, make sure you have them attached to a lanyard around your neck or you'll donate several to the stream bottom before you wise up.

Another tip is to make sure that the end of the tippet you are trying to thread is cut straight and clean. An end that is not cut with sharp snips is duller and wider, and a curled tippet is much harder to thread than a straight one. If repeated tries to thread a fly fail, it helps to run the point of another hook inside the eye of the fly in case there is something blocking the eye. (Many fly fishers' snips also incorporate a small needle just for this purpose.)

Finally, if you're into gadgets, there are many clever products designed to help thread a fly. Most work very well and it's just a matter of finding one that you're comfortable with. Try to test drive a couple at your local fly shop before buying.

51
Should you wear a fishing vest or an alternative?

SOONER OR LATER YOU'LL NEED A PLACE TO CARRY YOUR FLY BOXES, EXTRA REEL spools, fly floatants, strike indicators, flashlight, lunch, raincoat, water bottles, and all the other paraphernalia that fly fishers accumulate. The traditional way to carry all that stuff is a fishing vest, and although when filled up they are sometimes constricting, vests work well enough if you don't plan on hiking up and down can-

Not only is a chest pack less bulky than a vest when wading, it's also easier to use on a boat.

yon walls. However, more active fly fishers favor alternatives to vests. One is a waist pack, which is fine for small streams and wading shallow salt-water flats, but not much use when wading deep. A chest pack is a stripped-down version of a vest and typically has more storage in the back, which keeps out of the way gear to which you don't need frequent access. Some chest packs incorporate full backpacks, so if you're hiking a long way and don't want to wear your waders on the trail you can stow them until you reach the water. One of the best alternatives for the minimalist is a sling pack that you can swivel in front to grab a fly box, then push back out of the way while fishing.

VI

Trout

52

Do you have to match a hatch to catch trout?

UNLIKE HUMANS, TROUT DO NOT LIKE VARIETY IN THEIR DIETS. FEEDING EXPOSES them to predators, and eating something novel that may or may not provide useful calories could be a waste of energy. So they eat what is safe, which means familiar or abundant prey. Of course they do experiment or they'd never find a new source of food, but if a recognizable morsel is available they'll invariably choose it.

So when a particular species of insect is hatching in great numbers, trout may pay attention only to something that is similar in size, shape, and color, ignoring everything else. In that case you will do best trying to

There are times when your fly has to be close to the natural as this Sparkle Dun is to the natural mayfly. But many times it's not as critical, especially when a number of different insects are on the water.

match the hatch. However, during the course of most days trout feed on a number of species of insects, crustaceans, and baitfish, and in that case they'll strike a wide variety of flies as long as the flies are within a range of what they've eaten recently. For example, several weeks after a killing frost has retired all the grasshoppers for the season, I've been able to tempt trout with a grasshopper imitation. From my experience I've found that trout keep the memory of a prey item as "safe" for about three weeks.

Sometimes there may be several insects hatching at the same time and trout may be picking off all of them. In that case, chances are if you fish a fly that looks at least close to one of the bugs you see on the water and your presentation is realistic, you'll do okay. So unless trout are feeding heavily and there appears to be only one insect present, you may not have to worry about matching the hatch.

53

Do you need to change the way you fish for different trout species?

THERE'S A COMMON MISCONCEPTION THAT BROWN TROUT ARE MORE LIKELY to feed on the surface than other species of trout, but I have never found that to be true. All the common species of trout—brook, brown, rainbow, and cutthroat—feed on the surface enthusiastically when hatching insects are abundant or when land insects like ants or grasshoppers fall into the water. However, brown trout larger than sixteen inches are far more likely to eat bigger prey like minnows and crayfish, and are more likely to become nocturnal feeders than the other species.

A very large brown trout may only feed on insect hatches once a month, lying low in tangled roots or submerged rocks, ambushing a big piece of meat only a few times each week, most likely after dark.

Rainbow trout often delight us because they are more efficient than any other species in converting food energy to body weight, and thus are more likely to feed all day long, sampling every likely tidbit that floats by. Rainbows will suspend in fast water and snack even when insect hatches are sparse, while brown trout may only respond to an insect hatch when food is truly abundant—thus the old saw that rainbow trout "like" fast water more than other species. They don't like it better; they're just able to feed efficiently in water that would exhaust other species.

Brook and cutthroat trout are often considered "dumber" than browns and rainbows because they appear to be easier to fool. Both of these species originated in ecosystems that are not as rich in food as the coastal streams that rainbows evolved in, or the rich European lakes and meadow streams where the introduced brown trout originally came from. So the flies originally used for these species were bright and gaudy. But a big cutthroat in a rich tailwater or a brook trout in a productive spring creek can be every bit as "smart" and selective as a brown trout, and will ignore gaudy flies.

The character of a river and its food supply are far more important than what species are present in determining what fishing techniques you should employ. However, over the years I have found a few maxims that seem to hold true:

- Rainbow trout will inhabit faster water than brown, brooks, or cutthroats.
- Brook trout are more sensitive than other species to high water temperatures; thus, when river temperatures get above 65 degrees Fahrenheit they will be found close to springs or in headwater streams where the water stays colder.
- Big cutthroat trout take a dry fly very slowly, and if you're used to fishing for other species you may pull the fly away from them if you don't slow down on your strike.
- Brown trout are very deliberate when taking a fly, and if you "miss" one, chances are it refused your fly at the last moment.
- Brown trout are more likely to feed heavily between dusk and dawn than other species.
- Brown trout, especially big ones, are more likely to take a streamer fly than other species.
- Rainbow trout often feed in "pods," so if you catch one chances are good that more are nearby.

Brook trout

Brown trout

Cutthroat trout

Rainbow trout

54

Where to find trout around rocks

THE NATURAL PLACE TO LOOK FOR TROUT AROUND A BIG ROCK IN THE MIDDLE of a river is behind the rock, where the fish are protected from the brunt of the current. However, the force of the current also digs a trench in front of a midstream rock and along its sides, and a cushion of low-velocity water also builds up in front of a rock. Trout will lie in all of these places, so when fishing around big rocks it's important to make accurate casts behind a rock first, then a few casts to each side, and finally in front of the rock. By starting downstream behind the rock first you'll avoid spooking trout in front of the rock with your fly line.

Getting started in nymph fishing

IN MOST TROUT STREAMS, NYMPH FISHING IS THE MOST RELIABLE WAY TO CATCH trout. Surface feeding exposes trout to predators, so unless enough insects cover the surface to make this risk worthwhile, trout stay deeper in the water column and pluck food at their level. The best way to get started in nymph fishing is with a strike indicator, because not only will it let you see when fish take your fly, it will also give you an idea of where your fly is drifting, and whether your artificial is dragging across currents in an unnatural way.

Try to keep your initial nymph rig as simple as possible. Tie a weighted nymph or a beadhead pattern to the end of your tippet and then attach a strike indicator on the upper part of your leader. The indicator should be one and a half to two times the water depth up on your leader because the fly seldom hangs straight down, and you want your fly to be suspended a few feet off the bottom. Cast at an upstream angle and watch the indicator like a heron stalking fry in the shallows. If it hesitates, wiggles, or darts upstream set the hook instantly—it's easy to miss unseen strikes to a nymph, so better safe than sorry.

Nymphs seldom drift as deep as you think, so if you don't hang up on the bottom on a dozen casts, you are probably not fishing deep enough. To get deeper, either move the strike indicator higher on your leader or add a couple split shot to the tippet about ten inches above the fly. Once you feel comfortable with a nymph rig, add a second fly by tying sixteen inches of tippet to the bend of the upper hook and adding a second fly to this piece. Two weighted flies often help you get deeper without adding shot to the tippet, and you can fish two different patterns to find out which one the trout prefer.

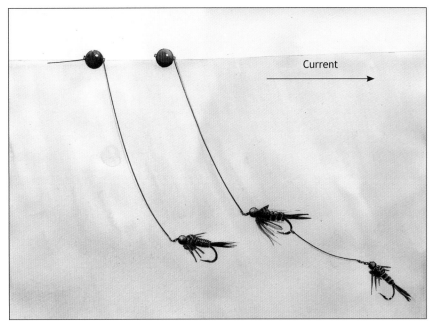

The Copper John is one of the most popular nymphs used, and features a wire body, brass head, peacock feathers for the thorax, and partridge feathers for the legs.

56

How to plan your first trout-fishing trip

IF YOU'VE NEVER FISHED FOR TROUT WITH A FLY ROD, YOUR FIRST TRIP SHOULD be with a guide. Guides do much more than row a boat and show you the best spots. Most fly-fishing guides are excellent teachers and will help you with every aspect of fishing, from rigging your leader to mak-

Fishing with a patient guide will help you learn and have a much more satisfying experience on your first trip.

ing the right presentation to landing the fish. The guide will have all the equipment you need, so you won't have to worry about having the right flies or leaders or strike indicators. A day with a guide may seem expensive at first, but consider it an investment in your education.

When planning where to go, avoid trout streams that are described as "technical" or "spring creeks." These places usually offer challenging fishing. And I'd also stay away from waters that are famous for big trout, because many places with big trout don't have as many trout, and because these places attract lots of fishing pressure and thus the fish get smart in a hurry.

57

How do you know what insect the fish are taking?

WHENEVER YOU SEE TROUT RISING, IT'S IMPORTANT TO FIGURE OUT WHAT insects are *on* the water, not what bugs you see flying. Often, one type of insect is hatching while another variety is migrating upstream, and the ones most visible to you may not be on the water at all. This is particularly common with caddisflies, because these moth-like aquatic insects, while very important to trout, live for weeks after they hatch and migrate upstream in clouds that sometimes obscure the far bank. If you see caddisflies in the air, moving purposefully upstream in a straight line, chances are they're migrating. If you see them flying in a slow, erratic pattern, or if you see them bouncing on the water's surface, they are more likely to be hatching or returning to the water to lay eggs, and thus available to the trout.

Often you'll find a large insect hatching along with smaller, more abundant ones. It's natural to pay more attention to the bigger fly (and perhaps also wishful thinking because big flies are easier to see), but if the smaller flies are more abundant the trout may be eating them and ignoring the big juicy ones. It doesn't make sense to us, but when trout zero in on one insect they may ignore all others, despite how good the big ones look.

Try to watch a fish rising to see what it takes. This is not as easy as it sounds, but if you can find a fish that is rising steadily, focus in on that spot until you can figure out what the fish are taking. Some anglers carry a pair of pocket-sized binoculars just for this purpose. If you see a fish rising to what appear to be invisible insects, there are three possibilities:

1. The fish is eating tiny, dark insects that are too small to see from your vantage point. Try a small, dark fly.
2. The fish is eating insects that ride low in the surface film. These could be spent mayfly spinners, egg-laying caddisflies, ants, or beetles. If it's evening, try a size 16 Rusty Spinner (this fly imitates a ton of mayfly spinners and is a good bet anywhere in the country). If it's during the day, try a size 18 ant or size 14 beetle.
3. The fish is eating emerging insects just under the surface. If you don't see any bubbles along with the rise form, this is often the case. Fish an emerger, or don't false cast your dry fly so it drifts just under the surface.

You can tell a lot about what a trout is eating by the way it rises. This brown trout (can you spot it just to the left of the rise?) is probably taking something very small or an emerging insect in the surface film because the rise is very subtle.

58

How does water temperature affect trout fishing?

TROUT ARE COLD-BLOODED AND MOST ACTIVE AT WATER temperatures between 55 and 65 degrees Fahrenheit. Within this temperature range, they'll feed actively, rise to the surface readily for dry flies, take nymphs aggressively, and chase streamers for six feet or more. Below 50 degrees, trout feed less often because their metabolism slows down, and as a result they won't move very far for a fly. They'll also migrate to slower, deeper pools in very cold water, so the best way to fish for trout in cold water is with a nymph fished slowly, close to the bottom.

From 65 to 74 degrees trout don't feed as readily. At these temperatures their metabolism stays high but the ability of the warmer water to hold enough dissolved oxygen to sustain them is greatly decreased, because colder water can hold more dissolved oxygen. Sustained feeding at these temperatures exhausts

In cold water, trout will not move very far for a fly, so slow and deep is the strategy.

them—in fact, catch-and-release anglers normally stop fishing at these temperatures because playing a fish when water temperatures are in the 70s can tire a fish to the point where it can't be revived. Sustained temperatures above 74 degrees will kill trout, although they can tolerate temperatures into the high 70s for short periods, as long as they aren't stressed and temperatures during the night fall back into the 60s.

If the temperature in a river approaches the high 60s in the middle of the day, the best fishing will be early in the morning, when water temperatures are at a minimum. It's often thought that evening fishing in hot weather is equally productive, but most rivers stay warm until after midnight because water cools more slowly than the surrounding land.

59

How does weather affect trout fishing?

I'M NOT A BIG BELIEVER IN THE EFFECTS OF A BAROMETER CHANGE ON TROUT FISH-ing, because a fish rising from the bottom of two feet of water to the surface experiences pressure changes far exceeding those due to atmospheric pressure, so I just can't see why a change in the barometer should affect the behavior of fish. However, I *am* a big believer in the effect of light levels and wind, and a change in barometer typically accompanies a change in cloud cover and the wind speed and direction.

Trout will feed in bright sunlight, and will feed actively if the sunny weather stimulates a hatch of insects, which often occurs in spring when water temperatures are low and sun on the water warms it enough to induce insects to hatch. However, most insects are programmed to hatch during low light levels because their greatest threats are from birds and from desiccation. Birds are less active in low light and the chances of a hatching insect drying out are much lower when it's cloudy, so often when a sudden storm darkens the sky, you'll see an abundant hatch of insects and heavy feeding by trout.

I'm really not sure why windy days inhibit trout feeding, but they seem to. In my experience, the worst weather for trout fishing is just after a cold front has passed, as the bright sunlight, lower water temperatures, and wind just seem to put the fish off. Given a choice, my favorite weather for trout fishing is a calm, cloudy, humid day. A slight drizzle doesn't hurt, either. Pack your rain jacket and enjoy the great fishing.

60

How fast should you gather line when fishing upstream?

FISHING UPSTREAM IS VERY EFFECTIVE WHEN FISHING A DRY FLY OR NYMPH, but is tiring because you must gather the line in front of your rod tip constantly. Usually when fishing upstream you're trying to make your fly drift naturally with the current, so you should gather line just as fast as the current brings it back to you—not so fast that you pull the fly, but fast enough that slack line does not gather under the tip of your rod. Slack line under the rod tip makes it difficult to set the hook, and it also makes it difficult to pick up line when you need to make a new cast.

When fishing upstream, gather the line as the current brings it back to you.

61

How much do you need to learn about insects?

THE THOUGHT OF LEARNING ENTOMOLOGY SCARES MANY WOULD-BE FLY FISHERS as it dredges up memories of high-school science class. Is it helpful to learn a little basic aquatic entomology? Absolutely, because different groups of aquatic insects have different life histories and different behavior, and knowing, for instance, that most stoneflies crawl to the shallows to hatch and don't ride the current when hatching might save you from needlessly fishing a stonefly dry fly, even if you see a lot of them in the air.

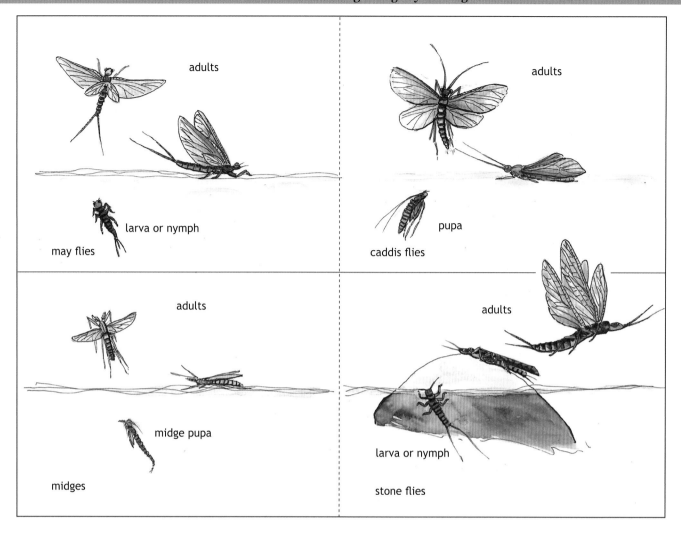

As you learn about these insects, you naturally learn more about their life history, and when you understand the behavior of trout *prey* as well as trout, you'll develop a canny instinct for predicting what the fish will do next. My advice is to learn at least to identify the four most important orders of insects and then learn a little about their life histories. These four orders are mayflies, caddisflies, stoneflies, and midges. Learning to identify the adults in the air and the larvae when you turn over rocks in a river is not hard and may even add to your enjoyment and appreciation of all aquatic life.

- Mayflies fly slowly after they hatch and look like sailboats on the water and tiny butterflies in the air. The nymphs have threadlike gills along the abdomen.
- Caddisflies skip and bounce on the water when hatching and look like moths in the air. Most caddis larvae build cases of stones and sticks, although some common species don't build cases. These "free-living" larvae usually look like green or tan grubs. All caddisflies have a brief pupa stage between the larva and adult stages that is not often seen but is very important to trout.
- Stoneflies are clumsy fliers in the air, and two pairs of wings are visible as they fly. The nymphs are flat with thick legs and tails, and crawl onto rocks along the shore to hatch.
- Midges are tiny insects with only one pair of wings and look like gnats in the air and on the water. The larvae look like tiny worms and are often bright red or green. Like caddisflies, they have a brief pupa stage and the pupae are typically dark brown or black and very appealing to trout.

62

How to decide what nymph to use

IT'S PRETTY EASY TO FIGURE OUT WHAT FLY TO USE WHEN FISH ARE RISING BECAUSE you often observe what insect the fish are eating. However, if you suspect trout are feeding underwater on nymphs, the clues aren't so obvious. One of the first things to do is to turn over some rocks to see what kind of aquatic insects are present. The best rocks to check are flat ones in riffled water because these are more hospitable for larvae. Many nymphs migrate to the shallows before hatching, so check the rocks closest to shore. Better yet, carry a small aquarium net and stir up a small bit of gravel and stones with your feet, holding the net just downstream to pick up the animals that get dislodged. The reason this is better than just turning over rocks is that some insects bury themselves in the gravel or silt and don't live on the underside of rocks, and seining in this way may turn up crustaceans like crayfish or baitfish like sculpins.

Now it's a simple matter to poke through your fly box for a fly that is about the same size and color as one of the critters you've dislodged. The most abundant one is your best bet, even if it isn't the biggest, juiciest one you see. If that doesn't work, try an imitation of the next most abundant creature.

If all else fails, just try some of the most popular artificial nymphs until you find one that works. Over the years, flies get popular because they work well in trout waters throughout the world, as the insects from a trout stream in New Zealand are not that different from the bugs in a California mountain stream. You can't go wrong with a size 14 Beadhead Hare's Ear, a size 12 Prince Nymph, or a size 18 Pheasant Tail Nymph. One of those will work most days in any trout stream in the world.

If a little olive mayfly nymph is the most common one you see when sampling the stream bed, choose your imitation accordingly.

63

How do you fish for trout in very small streams?

TROUT DON'T NEED MUCH WATER, AND IT'S AMAZING HOW MANY CAN BE IN a tiny stream that you can barely jump across. The little trickles are often overlooked by most anglers, but you can have lots of fun plucking colorful little jewels from tiny streams. Trout in small streams are usually not very picky about what they eat, but are very spooky. So the fly pattern you choose is nowhere near as critical as your approach. Work upstream so you sneak up on fish in their blind spots, and keep your profile low by kneeling or at least crouching. Short casts, obviously, are mandatory, not

Keeping a low profile and fishing straight upstream will help you approach spooky trout in small streams.

only because you may not have much back-cast room but also because most of the pools you fish will be tiny and you may only get a foot or two of drift before you have to pick up for another cast.

The most effective way to fish small streams is with a dry fly. The fish lie shallow and can see your dry fly even if they are lying on the bottom, and small streams don't produce as many aquatic insects as bigger rivers, so trout in the smaller waters rely a lot more on terrestrial insects that fall into the water—perfectly imitated by your fly coming from above. Choose a dry fly that floats high and that you can see, because trout in small streams take a fly quickly and you need to watch your fly so you don't miss any strikes. It's hard to beat a Royal Wulff, Stimulator, or Parachute Adams, all of which are highly visible and good floaters.

64
What to do when you can't see your dry fly

IT'S IMPORTANT TO BE ABLE TO TRACK YOUR DRY FLY'S FLOAT DOWN THE CURRENT, and not only so you can see when a trout takes it. Just as important is to make sure that your fly is floating alongside that midstream rock, or over a rising fish, or that your fly is not dragging unnaturally in the current. Accuracy is more important with dries than with any other type of fly, but once your fly lands on the water it might do things you wouldn't expect because of conflicting currents.

First, it's important that you see where your fly lands so you can pick it up quickly. A few false casts over your target will give you a good idea of where the fly will land. Second, try to get in good light.

The white parachute wing on this Royal PMX helps you track it on the water.

Sometimes just a slight change in position will give you a better view of your fly. I often find that removing my polarized sunglasses actually helps track a dry fly if the light is dull, because glare sometimes helps you pick out your fly better against the shiny surface. If you can, change to a fly with white upright wings like a Parachute Adams or Parachute Hare's Ear. Actually, any parachute fly will be easier to see because the wings stick up plainly.

If those tricks fail, you still have a few more. Treating the fly with silicone desiccant powder, the stuff used to re-float a drowned fly, helps it stand out better against the surface. Not only does the powder make the fly float higher, it brightens the fly a little and keeps it visible. If you are convinced you need a small, dark fly or a low-floating fly, both types that are tricky to see even under the best lighting, make your small fly a dropper. Tie on a large, high-floating dry fly you can see, and then tie about twenty inches of tippet to the bend of the big fly and add your little one behind it. Now you can watch the big fly, knowing that if the big fly drags the little fly will, too. And if you see a rise anywhere near the big fly—or if it goes under—set the hook!

65

Preparing for your first float trip

CHANCES ARE YOUR FIRST GUIDED TROUT-FISHING TRIP WILL BE IN A DRIFT BOAT with a friend or guide. With a little preparation, you'll have a lot more fun and keep the stress level for both you and your guide to a minimum.

Evening Shadows

- Be honest with your ability so the guide can plan a day on water that suits your experience level. He'll figure it out in five minutes anyway if you exaggerate.
- Most guides provide lunch, equipment, and flies—but some don't. Make sure you establish that the guide is bringing lunch and drinks before you're five miles into a ten-mile trip on a hot day.
- Don't wear wading shoes with metal cleats. They'll tear up the bottom of the guide's expensive boat. If they're the only wading boots you own, wear a pair of sandals or sneakers and only put on the wading boots if you get out and wade while on the trip.
- The guide will give you directions based on the hands of a clock. Twelve o'clock is not whatever is in front of you. It's always the front of the boat, and six o'clock is directly behind the boat.
- Pack a raincoat and try to get all your gear into one bag that can be easily stowed.
- It's best to fish and move around the boat as directed by the guide. If you want to try a cast in a different spot, ask first so you don't risk hooking the guide or falling out of the boat when you suddenly do something he didn't expect.

66

Reading currents to find trout

BEHAVIORAL STUDIES OF TROUT HAVE SHOWN THAT THEY PREFER CURRENT SPEEDS of about ten to twelve inches per second, which is about the speed of a slow walk. Try pacing it out with your foot. However, while they like to lie in water of this speed, they also like to be on the edge of a faster current, because the faster the current, the quicker food is brought to them. Thus the best place to find trout

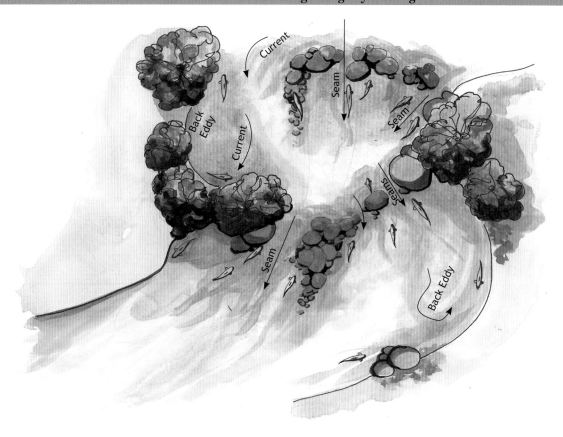

This angler is fishing to the other side of a distinct seam where fast water meets slower current.

is where fast currents meet slower water, known as a seam. You can see these obvious breaks on the edges of fast surface currents, but there are also hidden seams below the surface.

Hidden seams are found on stream bottoms with rough texture, because each rock on the bottom makes turbulence and slows the downstream progress of currents. Thus, a piece of water studded with large boulders will hold more trout than one with a smooth sand or gravel bottom. The friction of water running along a bank creates a seam as well, and here, too, a bank with a rough or uneven shoreline will hold more trout than a smooth bank where the current runs swift and unbroken.

Changes in depth also create hidden seams. Any place deep water meets shallow will be likely to hold feeding trout, as long as the shallow side is at least eight inches deep. Trout will feed in surprisingly shallow water if not disturbed, and if threatened they can quickly dart back into the depths to hide.

67

Setting the hook on trout

THE HOOKS USED IN MOST TROUT FLIES ARE SMALL AND VERY SHARP. TROUT JAWS are almost the perfect medium for sinking a hook, and if you have trouble setting the hook, the problem could be your reflexes—but it could also be the fish. Trout quickly detect the fraud in our flies, and unlike when caught with bait, they eject a fly in a flash. If you don't set the hook the moment a trout takes your fly, you'll miss the opportunity. They won't wait around gumming your fly until you get your act together. Striking to a trout is simple—just raise your rod tip enough to take all of the slack out of your line and tighten the line until you feel resistance—no more, or you can risk breaking the tippet.

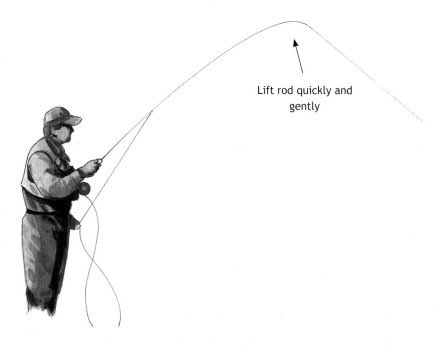

Lift rod quickly and gently

If you keep missing fish and are sure you're striking quickly enough, it may be the trout and not you. A trout that moves to a dry fly but changes its mind at the last minute because it doesn't like the fly or sees it suddenly begin to drag still has forward momentum and can't put on the brakes quickly enough. What happens is that the trout splashes at your fly with its mouth closed. We call this a refusal, and it means you were close but not close enough. Change your casting angle to avoid drag or try a fly one size smaller if you think you are getting refusals.

Trout also chase streamers, and sometimes seem only to want to move that obnoxious, gaudy thing out of their territory. They sometimes just bump the fly or even throw a cross-body block at it without connecting. Try fishing the same fly slower or faster, which seems to be more productive than changing flies.

Setting the hook on trout is a matter of just lifting the tip of the rod enough to tighten the line.

What do you do if a rising trout won't take your fly?

YOU'VE FINALLY FOUND A STEADILY RISING TROUT, AND DESPITE YOUR BEST EFFORTS, you can't get it to take your fly. Congratulations! At least you have not spooked the fish, and that's more than half the battle. Many anglers prefer trout that are tough to catch on a dry fly because they love the challenge of matching wits with an animal whose brain is smaller than your thumbnail.

More than half the time, a trout will refuse your fly not because the fly was wrong but because it was not behaving naturally. Because your fly is connected to a line and leader that drift at different speeds than the fly, and often land in currents of different velocities, it's very difficult to get a float free of drag for very long. Sometimes just a change in position will give you a longer float. A longer, lighter tippet can also help—if your tippet is twenty-four inches of 5X, try thirty inches of 6X instead. You can also try casting a lot of slack, which will prolong the natural drift of your fly before drag sets in.

If a fish keeps rising but ignores your fly, often a smaller imitation will do the trick.

If you're sure that your presentation is good, then it's time to try a new fly. I've found that the best approach is to try a fly one size smaller with a slightly different profile. For example, if you see the fish taking what looks like a size 16 cream-colored mayfly and you've been fishing with a size 16 Pale Evening Dun, try a size 18 Sparkle Dun. And if that doesn't work, the fish may be taking the emerging mayflies just under the surface, so try a cream-colored emerger.

What do you do if the water is dirty?

REALLY FILTHY WATER THE COLOR OF COFFEE WITH CREAM, WITH VISIBILITY OF less than a couple inches and lots of debris floating down a river, usually means you should read a book or head to the nearest establishment that serves fine food and drink. Sometimes, if you catch rising water when it first begins to get dirty a streamer will draw very aggressive strikes from fish that are on the prowl for disoriented baitfish, but once the water has been dirty for over an hour it's going to be slim pickings and I really can't offer you much solace.

However, dirty water with visibility of ten inches or more can actually work in your favor, because trout lose a lot of their caution when they can't see out of the water very well. In this situation, look for trout in slower, shallower water where they can still find food in the slower, less turbulent current of a still pool. Dry flies, nymphs, and streamers all work well in slightly dirty water, especially if it is in that optimum temperature range of 55 to 65 degrees farenheit.

In dirty water, a big streamer may be the only fly a trout can see.

70

What do you do if you don't see any trout?

TAKE HEART. JUST BECAUSE YOU don't see any trout in the water does not mean a river is lifeless. Unless trout are obviously feeding on the surface, you may not see any, because they are very well camouflaged; otherwise, they would not survive. The best place to see trout in a river is from a high vantage point where you can creep up to the edge without spooking them, but even in perfectly clear water you can stare at the bottom for many minutes before you finally pick up the shape of a tail or a shadow that moves sideways. In some rivers, trout are relatively easy to spot, but in most you can fish all day long (and catch a dozen) without ever seeing one in the water. If you know the water holds trout, fish a streamer or a nymph over places you think will hold fish.

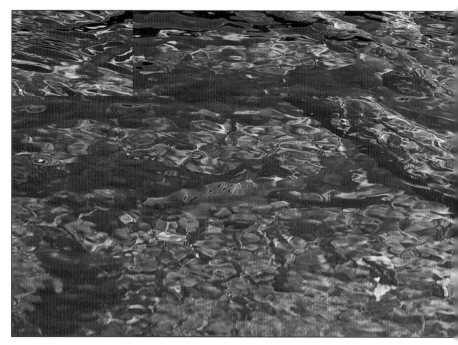

If you don't see any trout in the water, take heart. Even from a good vantage point looking down into the water, this brown trout (in the center of the photo) is so well-camouflaged it is nearly invisible.

What do you do when you scare all the fish?

TROUT ARE VERY GOOD AT SEEING US, AND WE'RE PRETTY BIG AND CLUMSY critters in their world. You will scare fish. In fact, I believe that even the best fly fishers scare over half of the fish in a pool before ever getting a cast over them. You probably won't see many trout bolting for cover in fright, either, because they are good at sneaking away before you can spot them, unless the water is very low and clear and the sun is directly overhead.

You may *suspect* that you're scaring fish when you never seem to catch any, and this is especially common in small streams, where the fish aren't terribly picky about flies but are very wary of predators. There are many tricks to help you fish without scaring the fish.

- Fish can see out of the water, and the deeper they are the better they can see you. They do have a blind spot directly behind them, so working upstream helps. Just be careful of fish in whirlpools, as some of them may be facing downstream.
- Keeping your profile low is especially important when not fishing upstream. Objects close to the ground or surface of the water are tougher for a trout to spot.
- Objects that move are immediately spotted by all animals. Try to keep your movements slow, and keep a high bank or trees behind you so your silhouette does not stand out against the sky.

Skinny Water

- Fish can't see very well into the sun but are very frightened by sudden shadows on the water. Try to keep the sun at your back but avoid letting your shadow fall on the water.
- Fish are equally sensitive to vibrations, which travel a long way underwater. Tread lightly on the bank, try not to roll rocks with your feet as you wade, and don't slap your fly line on the water.
- When fishing in a still pool, don't create a wake when you wade. Sudden waves across the still surface of a pool can send every trout within fifty yards bolting for cover. This sometimes means moving excruciatingly slowly, but it will be worth the effort.

What is a mend and when should you do it?

IN MOST DRY FLY AND NYMPH FISHING, THE BEST PRESENTATION IS A DEAD drift, which means the fly moves at exactly the same speed as the current, no slower and no faster. When swinging a wet fly in the current for steelhead, salmon, or trout, the best presentation is usually obtained by having the fly line in a straight line as it swings in the current. And when fishing a sinking-tip fly line, it's important to keep the floating portion of your line from pulling on the weighted part because the floater will draw the sinking part back to the surface. Forty feet of fly line cast across several different currents never behaves the way you want it to, and this is where mends come in handy.

Making a mend is easier than deciding when and where to use one. If you make a cast straight across a uniform current, you'll see that the line in the middle of the cast begins to move downstream faster than the line that is held close the rod tip, and faster than the fly and leader, which are slowed down by resistance to the water. As a result, as the line swings round, the fly begins to accelerate like the end of a whip. A little acceleration at the end of a swing is sometimes desirable, but left unattended it's too abrupt to appeal to most fish. By reaching out with the rod and making a quick flip upstream, you

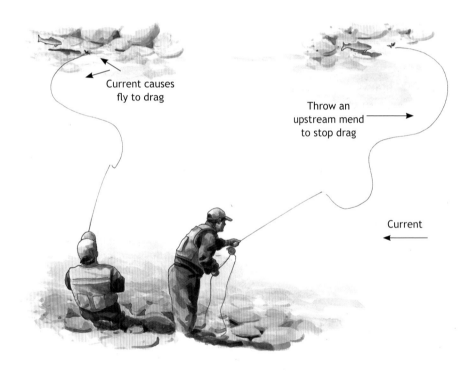

Current causes fly to drag

Throw an upstream mend to stop drag

Current

can straighten the fly line, or actually move the arc upstream in a mirror image of itself, depending on how much you want the swing to slow down or how deep you want your sinking-tip fly line to descend.

There may be times when you want a downstream mend, especially when your fly lands in fast water and the current between you and the fly is slower. In this case you mend in the opposite, downstream direction. Mends can be done with a stiff arm, a quick flip of the wrist, or a combination of the two. The more line you have to mend, the longer your rod should reach and the higher you'll have to reach with the rod. It doesn't matter how you do it as long as you move the line without moving the fly.

73

What is an emerger fly and when should you use one?

A NATURAL EMERGER IS AN AQUATIC INSECT AT THE MOMENT IT REACHES THE meniscus. The surface is quite a barrier to emerging flies, and they often struggle against it, more helpless than they are at any other time in their short life spans. Trout recognize this easy meal and go out of their way to prey on emergers. If you see trout rising but they keep refusing your dry flies or seem to be swirling in the current without breaking the surface, they may be taking emergers.

An emerger fly is a dry fly that doesn't float well or a nymph that doesn't sink. Take your pick on the definition. Emergers are tied with light wire hooks but with materials that don't float well, so they hang just below the surface or right in the film. Sometimes a bit of fly floatant helps keep them suspended, but often just a few false casts will keep them right where they should be. Fish an emerger just like you would a dry fly, and strike to the rise the same way you would a dry, because even if a trout takes your fly just under the surface it will still produce a swirl when it eats.

Emerger flies float right in the surface film.

74

When is the best time of day to go trout fishing?

THE BEST TIME TO GO FISHING FOR TROUT IS WHEN THEIR FOOD IS ACTIVE. IT'S typically also the most pleasant time of day for humans. So in winter and through the beginning of May at lower altitudes and through June at higher altitudes, the best time to go fishing is in the middle of the day, when the water warms up enough to stimulate insect hatches and get a trout's metabolism moving. As summer progresses and the weather gets hotter in the middle of the day, the best time to go trout fishing is at dawn and dusk. In fall it reverts back to mid-day.

There are a few caveats to this rule. Dawn and dusk are nearly always worth trying, unless the water is below 50 degrees, because although insects may not be hatching, trout may be prowling the shallows for minnows and crustaceans when light levels are low. Also, late morning through late afternoon can be good for trout fishing as long as the water does not rise above 65 degrees, because ants, beetles, grasshoppers, and other land insects are more active in the hot parts of the day and fall into the water, especially on windy days.

And, of course, the answer you'll get from many authorities on the best time to go trout fishing is, "When you can get away."

In the warmer days of the season, dawn and dusk are the best times for trout fishing.

75
When to fish streamers

THERE IS SOMETIMES ONE streamer pattern that out-fishes others, and frequently the speed you strip line when fishing a streamer is important. But I've found that it's more a matter of timing and location in a river, and when trout are really pounding streamers it's hard not to catch them. First, streamers are always productive when the light is low, when predatory trout have an advantage over the faster, more maneuverable baitfish. Dawn, dusk, after dark, and during rainstorms are the best times to catch trout on streamers.

Water temperatures in the prime range for trout, 55 to 65 degrees, also make them more aggressive for streamers, because a trout will often chase a streamer eight to ten feet before grabbing it, and they just won't move that

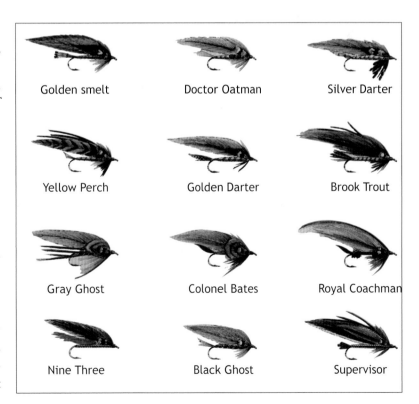

Golden smelt   Doctor Oatman   Silver Darter

Yellow Perch   Golden Darter   Brook Trout

Gray Ghost   Colonel Bates   Royal Coachman

Nine Three   Black Ghost   Supervisor

far for a fly when the water is too cold or too warm. Water that is just starting to get dirty after a sudden rainstorm is one of the best times, as dirty water disorients baitfish and trout will begin feeding on baitfish like someone threw a bucket of chum in the water.

Trout can be caught on streamers in the middle of a bright, sunny day. It seems like about 5 percent of the trout in any given stretch of water can be induced to chase a streamer in bright sunlight, and this is why fishing streamers from a drift boat is so productive—you cover so much water that you're bound to put your fly over one of those takers. The best places to catch fish on streamers in the middle of the day are stretches of fast, heavy water and deep water around logs and big jumbles of rocks, where large trout wait in ambush.

76

Where will you find trout in a lake?

WHEN FACED WITH A FLAT EXPANSE OF WATER WITH NO CURRENT, EVEN experienced fly fishers panic. Lakes are not as easy to read as rivers, trout can be anywhere because there are no currents to keep them pinioned to one spot, and in lakes you have both geography and depth to worry about. Local knowledge is best, but there are a few tips that can help you narrow down the possibilities.

- Scan the lake surface with binoculars for rising fish early in the morning or right before dark. Chances are any trout that are hungry will come to the surface then looking for hatching insects.

On Secret Pond

- Inlets and outlets are always hotspots in lakes. Trout spawn in moving water in spring and fall, and inlets bring in hatches of insects.
- In the cold water of early and late season, look for trout in shallows where the water is warmer than the depths.
- Springs coming into a lake will attract trout in both cold and warm water, as springs are warmer than lake water in the early spring and colder during the summer. If springs aren't obvious, put a thermometer on a long string and take temperatures close to the bottom at various places.
- Submerged weed beds hold more insect life than sand or rock bottoms, so look for trout close to aquatic vegetation.

Warmwater Fly Fishing

Flies to use for smallmouth bass in rivers

The Woolly Bugger is one of the best flies for river smallmouths.

SMALLMOUTH BASS EAT INSECTS AND baitfish just like trout, and you can fish for them with your standard trout flies. But that's not as effective and certainly not as much fun as getting them to chase bigger bugs. A smallmouth's number one prey is crayfish; thus any streamer with lots of action and stuff wiggling at all angles to look like the claws and legs of a crayfish will drive them wild. Bead-Head Woolly Buggers with rubber legs, Yellow Muddler Minnows, and patterns with rabbit strips all appeal to smallmouths. Throw in a few patterns that look more like a baitfish, such as a Clouser Minnow or a White Zonker, and you'll have the streamers covered.

Another favorite smallmouth food is the hellgrammite, a large black larva of the dobsonfly. A black Woolly Bugger or large black stonefly nymph with rubber legs will do for them. Fish these dead drift, with or without a strike indicator, especially on days when smallmouths aren't aggressive and inclined to chase streamers.

Don't rule out surface poppers, though. Smallmouths will investigate small bass bugs, often hanging back for a full minute before smashing them, but there is nothing more thrilling than catching a frisky smallmouth bass on a bug. Even if you come upon a smallmouth sipping delicate mayflies on the surface, you can often convince it to go for a bigger mouthful and inhale a bass bug that is ten times the size of the mayflies it's eating. And there is no better surface bug for smallmouths than the cone-shaped chartreuse popper with rubber legs known as a Sneaky Pete.

Smallmouth Bass

How to find a bass and panfish pond close to home

IT'S SILLY TO WAIT FOR A TRIP TO Montana or Alaska to enjoy some fly fishing. Anglers who have fished throughout the world still thrill to the dawn rise of a largemouth bass to a popper in a suburban golf course pond. And the many species of sunfish swirl eagerly to small poppers and regulation trout flies, making you feel like a hero. I would be willing to bet there is a pond within five miles of your house that holds some bass and panfish, no matter where you live. Even the ponds in Central Park are packed with eager bass and panfish just waiting to inhale a fly.

Here's how to find one: Pick the pond closest to your house that is *reasonably* accessible. ("No fishing" signs on golf course ponds are only meant to be obeyed during the day, and dawn raids on these places will evoke thrills you forgot when you reached puberty.) When spring flowers begin to bloom (this might be March in Florida or May in North Dakota), begin scouting the shoreline for saucer-shaped nests made by bass and panfish as they clean a place on the bottom prior to laying eggs. The spots typically show up as a light spot or a clean area of gravel in an otherwise muddy bottom. Now you know fish live there. Catching them is simply a matter of trying a small surface bug or a size 10 Hare's Ear Nymph.

After spawning is over in a few weeks, the fish will stay close to the shallows, but in mid-summer they might spend most of their time deeper, in the middle of the pond. But don't worry. They still come close to shore to feed at dawn and dusk, when you can sneak in without getting caught.

Chances are you won't have to travel far to find a pond filled with bass or sunfish.

Small Fry – Largemouth Bass

How to find bass in
a pond or lake

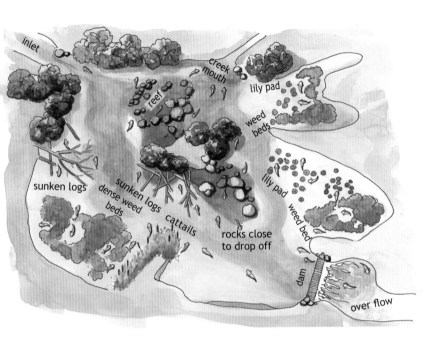

YOU *CAN* CATCH LARGEMOUTH and smallmouth bass anywhere the Bassmaster folks can catch them with conventional tackle, but you probably won't bother, because catching bass with a fly sometimes involves fishing a sinking line in twenty feet of water. Most of us prefer to catch our bass on the surface or close to it, where we can fish a floating line. Casting and picking up a floating line is a pleasure instead of a chore. Bass ambush their prey, so when fishing for them in shallow water you will seldom find them far from dense weed beds, logjams, piles of big rocks, or docks. Largemouths prefer dense mats of lily pads, cattails, and other aquatic weeds, and they will be *in* the weeds, not just close to them. A weedless fly helps. Sometimes they won't move more than a few inches from their ambush point, so you should cast right into the nasty stuff. Smallmouths prefer rocky bottoms. Look for them close to submerged logs and large boulders, especially close to a place where shallow water quickly drops off into the depths.

80

How to fish a bass bug

WHETHER FISHING FOR LARGEMOUTH BASS, SMALLMOUTH BASS, OR SUNFISH, YOU should begin by fishing a surface bug slowly. Slow enough that you get impatient. Bass are infinitely more patient than you. The natural tendency is to cast the bug and begin moving it as soon as it hits the water, like something trying to get away. Bass prefer prey that is struggling, and most animals that struggle twitch a few times, then rest motionless.

So cast your bug and don't move it. Strip in enough line to come tight to the fly but not enough to move it. Then wait until all the rings around the fly disappear. Don't worry about a bass losing interest, as they often approach potential prey and eyeball it for a full minute before making a decision.

Time and again, a bass will wait until everything gets quiet and then suddenly pounce on a fly that is totally motion-less. After you've waited so long you can't stand it, give the fly a single twitch. Move it about an inch. Then wait again. Continue this way until the fly is close enough to pick up for another cast.

This twitch-and-wait strategy is by far the most productive way to fish a bug, but if it doesn't work, by all means try others. If the water is deep, sometimes three or four abrupt twitches followed by a long pause bring bass up from deeper water when they hear the commotion. You can also try a steady retrieve, where you keep the fly moving and never let it pause. Experiment until you find the right formula, and it will work for you throughout the day.

A deer hair mouse and a cork popper, two very popular bugs for largemouth bass

81

How to fish a bass streamer

LARGEMOUTH BASS SELDOM CHASE A FLY AGGRESSIVELY AS THEY ARE AMBUSHERS— sprinters, and not long-distance runners. When you fish a sinking bass fly, move it slowly and steadily, and when presenting a subsurface fly to bass try to position your cast so that nearly your entire retrieve moves the fly along near cover. In other words, if a big log sticks out into a lakeshore, don't make a cast at 90 degrees to the log, because only the first foot or so of your retrieve will be appealing to bass lying in ambush. Instead, position yourself so that your fly will swim along parallel to the log, presenting a tasty morsel to a lurking bass throughout its progress.

Get that streamer in the middle of the thick stuff, too, not just along the edges. Cast your streamer right into the lily pads, drawing it over the surface of the pads, letting it sink into the holes between them. Even with a weedless fly you'll get frequent snags, but if your fly is not in deep cover it won't be fishing where largemouths feed.

Smallmouth bass are found more often amongst rocks and logs than weeds, so here you should try to fish your fly so that it rides just above piles of large rocks on the bottom, or off rocky points and cliffs. A weighted fly like a Clouser Minnow is deadly on smallmouths, and these heavy flies should be fished with a strip and then a pause that lets the fly sink. Smallmouths usually pounce on a fly that is sinking or just beginning to rise after it has sunk, so watch your line for any twitch or pause because a big smallmouth may have just inhaled your fly.

Typical subsurface streamers used for bass

82

Picking the right leader for warmwater fly fishing

BASS ARE NOT LEADER-SHY, AND EVEN A FLY LINE LANDING ON TOP OF ONE seldom spooks it. For largemouth bass, the leader should be as heavy as you can find, and if you can

Musky Moon

get the leader through the eye of the fly you've gone as light as you need to. Big bass flies are very wind-resistant, and a short, stiff leader helps turn them over, so a leader of between six and seven and a half feet long with a breaking strength of fifteen to twenty pounds is about right. You'll appreciate that heavy leader when yanking a big largemouth out of aquatic salad, too. Smallmouths live in clear water and are slightly spookier than largemouths, so a nine-foot leader that breaks at twelve pounds will straighten the smaller flies used for them and will land even a world-record smallmouth with ease.

83

When and how to catch carp on a fly

CARP CAN THRIVE IN ALL KINDS OF WATERS, FROM LARGER TROUT STREAMS TO THE most polluted urban lakes. Although some consider them to be pests, carp are highly prized in Asian and European countries and were originally introduced into North America as a food fish. Fly fishers have discovered that carp are stronger fighters than many celebrated gamefish, and are just as difficult to catch as a spring creek trout or a tropical permit.

Carp are best on a fly rod in spring, when they cruise shallow water to seek warmth, look for mates, and lay eggs. Fishing for carp in deeper water where they can't be spotted is nearly fruitless, because a successful presentation must put the fly right in front of a carp's nose. Carp cannot see very well and find much of their food by smell, but they will pounce on an object moving just a few inches away that looks like a crayfish, insect larva, or minnow. However, just because they can't see well does not mean they are easy to approach. Carp are extremely cautious of vibrations in the water, so sloppy wading, noise from a boat, or the splash of a fly line landing close is a sure way to send a school of them dashing for cover.

Look for carp in shallow water with a silt or sand bottom, along the edges of weeds. If present, they'll give themselves away by rolling, waking, and even jumping clear of the water. Try to determine which way a fish is moving and throw a weighted nymph or small streamer two to three feet ahead of the fish so that the sound of the fly and line hitting the water don't spook the fish. When you think the fish is close to your fly, begin moving it slowly and steadily, close to the bottom, like a crayfish or insect larva that has been dislodged by the rooting carp and is trying to get away. If you feel resistance, set the hook with a long and brisk strip rather than lifting your rod, because if you miss the fish it might follow the fly and give you a second chance.

Mirror carp

Don't be discouraged if you spook many of the fish and if they ignore your fly. Carp may not be pretty and glamorous, but they are some of the smartest, most wary fish in fresh water. The fact that they are so abundant gives you plenty of opportunities to try again!

84

Where to find smallmouth bass in a river

BECAUSE SMALLMOUTH BASS ARE NOT AS STREAMLINED AS TROUT AND WILL PURSUE and ambush their prey as opposed to lying in the current waiting for food to drift by, they are commonly found in slower water than trout. Look for smallmouths in deep eddies at the heads of pools, in rock piles at the tails of pools, and halfway down large pools, along the deeper bank especially if it is lined with ledge rock, big boulders, or fallen logs. Smallmouths will also lie on the outside edges of weed beds in large, warm rivers, waiting to ambush baitfish that use the weeds for protection.

Smallmouth bass prefer rocky streams and lakes.

PART

VIII

Saltwater Fly Fishing

How do you catch fish on a fly in the surf?

FLY FISHING IN CRASHING SURF SEEMS AT FIRST TO BE A DAUNTING PROSPECT, but many saltwater gamefish like striped bass, bluefish, sea trout, surf perch, and corbina prey on baitfish and crustaceans that get disoriented and corralled along the shoreline in rough weather. The most important aspect of surf fishing is line control. Tony Stetzko, known as "Striperman" on Cape Cod, specializes in fly fishing the big surf along the National Seashore, and taught me to take a cast and then take three steps backward. You must come tight to your line quickly when fishing the surf; otherwise, the incoming waves put too much slack in your line. Sinking or intermediate weight lines are usually best in the surf. By getting just below the surface currents, you'll retain a better connection to your fly as the sinking line somewhat counteracts surface turbulence.

The best presentation in the waves is to wait for a big wave to break, and then cast your line as far as you can beyond the wave in the slick behind it. This will give you an expanse of relatively calm water to strip your fly through, ensuring that the fish see it better and that your line does not get pushed around by too many waves. Don't always cast directly into the waves. The tide will usually be moving one direction or another along the beach, so try some casts both "down-tide" and "up-tide" so that your fly runs parallel to the beach, which mimics the behavior of baitfish.

When fishing the surf, line control is important. Wearing a stripping basket and taking three steps back after every cast will help.

A stripping basket is essential when fishing the surf. You often need to strip line quickly, and if you strip line at your feet it will swirl around your legs and tangle in them, and will also pick up bits of weed and debris. A stripping basket keeps fly line coiled and ready for the next cast.

Finally, when landing a big fish in the surf, play it close to the surf line and then hold it in place until the next big wave. Just before a big wave breaks over the fish, walk backward quickly and use the power of the wave to roll your fish up onto the beach, where it will be left sideways in shallow water, ready for you to dash to it before the next big wave breaks. And when admiring your fish or holding it up for others to see, remember—never turn your back to a wave!

Which tide is best for saltwater fly fishing?

THERE IS NO "BEST" TIDE FOR SALTWATER FLY FISHING, AS THE RIGHT TIDE TO FISH varies with each location. When fishing beaches or estuaries, the first stage of the tide, when water reverses direction and begins to move, is usually best, but I know of some places when the last hour of an incoming or outgoing tide offers the best fishing.

In general, an outgoing tide is best on the outside of an estuary or tidal marsh, where it hits bigger water, because baitfish and crustaceans from the food-rich shallows get washed into deeper water, where bigger fish lie in ambush. On an incoming tide, fish move with the rising water back inside estuaries when more water allows them to cruise food-rich areas, so on a rising tide you may find more gamefish up inside a tidal marsh or salt pond.

On most shallow sand and coral flats the best fishing is on an incoming tide. The rising water exposes productive feeding areas that have been inaccessible to the fish, as shallow water always hosts more baitfish and crustaceans than deep water. And when sight fishing on the flats, the fish are a lot easier to spot in skinny water than they are when the flat is covered with four of five feet of water. High tide is difficult for flats fishing, as the fish are not concentrated on deeper, narrower channels and can be almost anywhere, plus they're difficult to spot. The best advice at high tide is to fish very close to the shoreline or up against coral heads or in the mangroves. On a falling tide, fish don't feed as aggressively and are often just migrating back to deeper water, but if you can find the channels they use to move into the depths you may be able to induce them to feed.

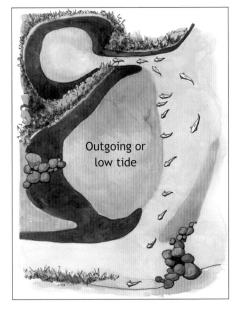

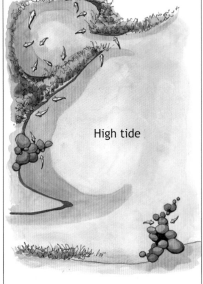

Outgoing or low tide

High tide

Estuary

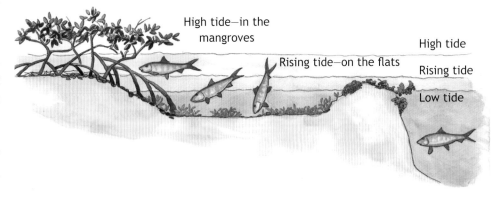

High tide—in the mangroves

Rising tide—on the flats

High tide

Rising tide

Low tide

Shallow sand and coral flats

87

How to get started with redfish and sea trout on the fly

SMALL SEA TROUT AND YOUNG REDFISH OR "PUPPY DRUM" ARE SOME OF THE EASIEST fish to catch on a fly from New Jersey south to Florida on the Atlantic Coast and along the entire Gulf Coast. These fish are always hungry, relatively easy to please, and stay in shallow water throughout the season—although during strong winter cold fronts they may move to deeper holes until the water warms. Thus they are perfect fish to hone your technique and build up some confidence for saltwater fly fishing.

Both species are found in shallow water, from one to four feet deep, and are especially common over weed beds and above oyster bars. Any kind of discontinuity in the shoreline—whether a creek mouth, dock, jetty, or point—will attract them, but they can also be found along beaches on a sandy bottom. The best fly for both species is a Clouser Minnow in bright colors like chartreuse or orange, but any fly from one to three inches long that imitates baitfish, shrimp, or crabs will interest them.

Because they typically run from one to four pounds, there is a natural tendency to use a light 6- or 7-weight fly rod for small sea trout and redfish. However, the best flies for these species are weighted, and you'll often encounter wind along the shore, so if you're starting out, an 8- or even 9-weight rod is a better choice. Besides, in the fall and early winter you may encounter larger "bull" redfish of twenty or thirty pounds in the same shallow water, and if you do you'll be happy you have the heavier rod.

The most exciting fishing for redfish is on a calm, sunny day when you can spot them tailing or cruising in very shallow water. Not only is sight-fishing for them more fun, you'll learn a lot about their behavior and reaction to your fly presentations when you can see every move they make.

Redfish and Sea Trout

88

How to get started with stripers on the fly

STRIPED BASS ARE EXTREMELY COMMON ALONG THE ATLANTIC COAST FROM Maine to North Carolina and can be found as far south as Florida. They are also found in the Mississippi Delta and were introduced over one hundred years ago to the West Coast, where they are abundant in estuaries from San Francisco Bay north to Oregon. "Schoolie" stripers from eight to twenty-four inches are very common, often traveling in schools of hundreds of individuals. These juvenile striped bass are very aggressive and seldom pass up a streamer, bonefish fly, or popper. When even a sixteen-inch striped bass takes a popper, you'll think a fish three times its size has crashed your fly.

Schoolies tend to concentrate inside harbors and along beaches, often moving far inside tidal creeks and salt ponds. Look for them at the mouths of creeks, around jetties, near docks, and on shallow sandy flats, especially in early spring when they're more comfortable where the sun warms the bottom. Schools often move quickly, so you should cover a lot of water, stripping a small weighted baitfish pattern with aggressive short, quick strips. If there are any small stripers around, they'll quickly pounce on the fly, and once you find a concentration of them, it's fun to put on a surface fly and watch them smash it.

Schoolie stripers are always eager to take a fly—and they fight hard!

89

How to set the hook on bigger saltwater fish

FOR MANY SALTWATER SPECIES LIKE BONEFISH, STRIPED BASS, AND SMALL REDFISH, a simple strip strike is enough to penetrate the jaw and secure the hook firmly. However, for large bony-jawed fish like tarpon, tuna, sailfish, trevally, redfish over twenty pounds, and even large freshwater species like pike and muskellunge, you need more force and a wider arc in your strike, plus you should strike using the butt of the rod instead of the tip. With the bigger species, strikes should be long and low. You can't do this by raising the rod tip straight in front of you because your body blocks the butt of the rod from moving past the vertical. So to strike them, jab your rod down and off to one side, using your stronger forearm and shoulder muscles instead of your wrist, which should remain locked throughout the strike. If there was any slack in the line or if you don't feel a very firm pressure when you set the hook, make another sideways jab with the rod and also make a hard strip strike by yanking the line away from the rod, just as if you were making a double haul. To be absolutely sure, some fly fishers make yet another strike after the fish has made its first run and has paused before trying its next move.

The best way to strike larger saltwater fish is to strike to the side with a low rod, sometimes using the line hand for added pressure. ▶

Preparing for your first bonefishing trip

MOST PEOPLE TRAVEL A LONG WAY AND SPEND A WEEK'S PAY OR MORE FOR a bonefishing trip. I've watched even experienced trout anglers get frustrated, angry, and even embarrassed on bonefishing trips because they weren't ready for the wind, difficult fish spotting, and unfamiliar directions given by a guide. Just a little preparation will make your first trip a lot more fun.

First, practice your casting. Most bonefish are caught within forty feet, but that forty-foot cast must be made quickly, under pressure, with deadly accuracy, and with the good chance of a stiff breeze. Being able to get forty feet of fly line outside the rod tip is not enough. Pace out forty feet and make sure you can hit a target the size of a hula hoop with reasonable consistency, with a wind coming from any direction, and be able to change directions to cast to another hula hoop with just one false cast. Bonefish are spooky critters and too many false casts will ruin your chances.

Either before your trip or just after you arrive, take a heavily weighted, lightly weighted, and unweighted bonefish fly to some shallow water where you can see the fly sink. Watch how fast each fly lands, as having different sink rates in bonefish flies is far more important than having the favorite fly on the island. Over sand and mud bottoms you want the fly to sink to the bottom and make little puffs of silt when you strip, because these plumes attract the attention of a bonefish looking for a crab or shrimp trying to escape. Over weedy and coral-covered bottoms, a bonefish can't see a fly that sinks down into the debris (and you'll get hung up), so you'll begin to strip your fly before it hits bottom. And you never know beforehand how deep the water will be on a given flat, so you must have some idea of how fast your fly will sink.

No matter how good you are at spotting trout or steelhead, you will have trouble seeing bonefish in the water, at least for the first day and probably for a couple days. Count on it. Bonefish are nearly invisible underwater because their shiny sides reflect the bottom, and without a shadow to pinpoint their position you'll have a very difficult time. If you are unlucky to have a week of cloudy weather you may see very few of them unless they are tailing in shallow water. Some guides are excellent at helping clients learn to spot bonefish. Others, because of a language problem or reticence, just tell their anglers where to cast and forget about trying to teach them. Try to discipline yourself to see through the water, not at it, and remember that bonefish hardly ever stop moving, so look for shadows and grayish indistinct shapes that don't stay put.

Once you get onto a boat with a guide, remember that he will be giving you directions to cast by the hands of a clock *in relation to the boat*. Twelve o'clock is always directly in front of the boat, not where you are looking. And you will get befuddled—guaranteed. I don't know how many times I've had a guide say, "Cast thirty feet at nine o'clock. *Sigh*. No. The other nine o'clock." I even saw an enterprising young Bahamian guide on my last trip who had painted the hands of the clock, including the numbers, on the bow of the boat, just for clods like me.

The other miscommunication with guides and clients is distance. Different people have different ideas of what forty feet is, especially in the heat of the moment. Make a short and a long cast before you start and ask your guide how far the casts were. If you're traveling to Mexico or Central America, it's not a bad idea to learn the Spanish words for twenty, thirty, forty, fifty, and sixty feet before you leave.

Finally, the strike is the bane of all trout anglers. You should never strike a bonefish (or any saltwater fish) with the rod tip, but by making a long, firm strip with the line while the rod is held low. Raising the rod tip lifts the fly out of the water, and if a bonefish hasn't really taken it or misses the fly, it may come back to a fly that just makes a long dart through the water rather than one that goes airborne. (Many guides, when they see a bonefish take a fly, will instruct the angler to "make a long strip" because they know if they say "strike," up will come the rod tip.) One of the best suggestions I've heard for people who cannot modify their reflexes to strip strike is to retrieve a bonefish fly with the rod tip help a few inches underwater throughout the retrieve. With the tip underwater, the line stays in excellent control and it's almost impossible to make a "trout strike."

A Short Cast

Tackle Care

Do you need to clean your gear after each trip?

MODERN FLY-FISHING TACKLE IS INCREDIBLY RESISTANT TO THE ELEMENTS. AFTER most fishing trips, you can put away all your gear without a care in the world. Graphite rods are totally resistant to dirt and moisture, reels are anodized to prevent corrosion and rust, and lines don't need to be dried. For nearly every piece of tackle you own, a little soap and water is all you need. Here are some tips to help keep your gear in perfect shape for many years to come:

- Your rod should not be put away in a rod tube wet, because the cloth sack can develop mildew. Just let your rod and its sack dry before putting them back in the case. Although saltwater reel seats are anodized to prevent corrosion, salt crystals can build up on a reel seat, so wash the seat with fresh water and dry before putting it away.

- Reels should also be rinsed in fresh water after a day in the salt. Some anglers strip all the line off the reel and spray some water inside to prevent salt crystals from building up on the line and backing. If any mud or grains of sand have gotten inside the reel, remove the spool and clean them with an old toothbrush. A sparse application of light machine oil on all the moving parts of a reel except the drag surfaces is a good idea several times each season.

- Lines need no maintenance besides keeping them out of the hot sun for extended periods. However, if you fish in areas with high salinity or profuse algae, it's a good idea to clean your line with soap and water after every trip.

- Waders don't need any cleaning to prolong their life, but the soles of waders should be cleaned thoroughly with hot water and soap and a scrubbing brush whenever you move from one watershed to another. Then dry the soles and inspect them for any debris. Spores and eggs of invasive species like didymo algae, mud snail, whirling disease, and others not yet identified can become aquatic hitchhikers, and we all need to do our best to prevent their spread.

- Never put flies away wet or they will rust and get matted out of shape, and the dyes used in some fly-tying materials may run and spoil the colors of other flies in your box. Leave your fly box open on a sunny table or on the windshield of your car—but not exposed to the wind or you might return to a nearly empty box!

Midwinter Daydreams

How to keep your rod from breaking

MODERN GRAPHITE FLY RODS HAVE INCREDIBLE TENSILE STRENGTH, BUT THE TREND toward lighter rods has given us tools that don't have the crush strength of older graphite or fiberglass rods. You can land a 150-pound tarpon with a rod that weighs a few ounces, but that same rod won't survive even a glancing encounter with a ceiling fan or car door. To avoid breakage by fans and screen doors never put a fly rod together indoors. Never lean a rod against a car because the chances are good that it will either get slammed in a door or the wind will blow it over and someone will step on it. Always lean your rod up against a tree, rather than laying it flat on the ground, because those thin black tubes just disappear amongst the brush.

When transporting rods in a car or boat, resist the temptation to keep your rod strung up and banging around the deck of a boat or extending throughout the length of a compact car, bent against the windshield. We all do it, but you're just asking for trouble. If you want to transport your rod still strung with a leader and fly, use a rod-and-reel case that protects the rod during transit.

When stringing up a rod before fishing, don't pull the leader through the guides and then yank down on the leader to get the fly line out of the guides. Many rods are broken this way, and a better method is to pull the leader and some of the line straight out from the tip of the rod while the rod is placed on a safe, flat surface or held by another angler.

Many more rods are broken through carelessness when playing a fish, but one real danger area is when a fish is close to a boat, especially one that has sounded under the boat or at its side. Lifting straight up, with the rod tip in a near-vertical position, is a sure way to break a fly rod because the stress is concentrated at the fragile tip of the rod rather than using the more powerful butt. When a fish sounds near the boat, always try to play the fish at a sideways angle so you can use the lifting power of the boat. This may entail moving around the boat or asking the captain to back off a bit with the motor, but it will save you a broken rod.

Finally, be careful when using split shot or flies with heavily weighted eyes. Always try to cast a more open loop with these rigs and keep the weight away from yourself for safety reasons and from your rod for durability. A heavily weighted fly going well over a hundred miles per hour can fracture the graphite if it hits the thin walls of a light fly rod. Even a glancing blow from a weighted fly can weaken a rod, resulting in a fracture on the next long cast or big fish. When investigating the "I was just casting and the rod suddenly broke" scenarios, the Orvis rod repair department inevitably finds that the angler was either fishing a Clouser Minnow or a big glob of split shot.

Trying to get the fly line out of the rod by pulling straight down on it is a fast track to a broken rod. ▶

How to find leaks in your waders and how to patch them

YOUR WADERS WILL EVENTUALLY DEVELOP LEAKS. MOST LEAKS ARE EASY TO FIND and repair. The resulting patches give the waders character, and you'll avoid being tagged as a rookie. Of course, the surest way to find leaks is to fill the waders with water and see where it leaks out, but not only is this a major project and a major pain, the weight of all that water inside a pair of waders can put additional stress on the seams.

The first thing I try is to run a strong flashlight inside the suspected area in a dark room. Leaks show up as bright specks of light, and it's then easy to mark them with a marking pen. This works fine for wear spots and punctures, but seam leaks won't show up. For seam leaks, you can try holding the waders underwater in a bathtub and constricting the open part of the waders with hand pressure so you compress air against the seam. You can also try blowing up the waders with a shop vacuum that has a reversing feature. I've often used the vacuum-cleaner method after brushing the waders with a combination of dishwashing soap and water, because the leaks will show up as bubbles emanating from the seam.

In the Canyon

Once you find a leak, clean the area with rubbing alcohol and let it dry. The best material for patching waders is special glue called Aquaseal that works on nylon, rubber, or polyester fabrics. For small punctures, seam leaks, or wear spots you simply brush some on and let it dry overnight. For large tears, you might have to apply the Aquaseal first, then slap a piece of old discarded wader fabric (many waders come with a piece of material for patching) over the tear, and then coat the surface of the patch, allowing some overlap. I've found that repairs using Aquaseal will outlast the rest of the wader, and I've never found glue that works as well.

You can patch your waders on the inside or the outside. The inside is neater and the patch is less subject to abrasion. But patching on the outside makes you look cool.

Advanced

How to fish small dry flies

MOST FLY FISHERS REGARD FISHING SMALL DRY FLIES WITH THE SAME ENTHUSIASM as preparing income tax records. An enlightened minority relishes the opportunity because they know trout are less suspicious of artificial flies smaller than size 20, and since the fish have to eat a lot of the tiny stuff before getting full, there are more chances to fool them.

These tiny flies are perfectly capable of hooking and holding large trout.

Don't let the thought of light tippets scare you away. Modern nylon and fluorocarbon tippets in 6X and 7X diameters are very strong, and can easily handle trout of twenty inches if you play the fish with a light touch. Small flies are more difficult to thread, but tying one on is not a major project as long as you are prepared with a pair of 4X or 5X reading glasses and/or a tool for threading small flies, of which there are dozens on the market.

Seeing a small fly in the comfort of your own hands is not the same as seeing one fifty feet way in dim light. What most anglers don't realize is that even people who fish tiny flies all the time have just as much trouble as you do seeing a size 22 Griffith's Gnat on the water. They compensate by estimating where the fly is on the water, and when a fish rises anywhere near where they suspect their fly is drifting, they gently tighten up on the line. This seldom spooks a rising fish, and it takes very little pressure to set the hook with a small dry.

You can also fish a tiny fly as a dropper behind a bigger fly to help track its progress. Tie on a size 14 Parachute Adams, then tie a twenty-inch piece of 6X tippet to the bend of the bigger hook and the tiny fly of your choice on the end of this dropper. Or you can add a very tiny strike indicator or a piece of strike putty to your tippet—there is no law stating that strike indicators may only be used with nymphs.

Hooking fish with tiny flies is no problem, as penetration of the jaw is easy and once the hook is set it's very hard to dislodge it. You can take this on faith or you can stick a size 24 Blue Wing Olive into the tip of your thumb (similar to a trout jaw) and see how easy it is to dislodge.

95

Taking better fish pictures

WANT BETTER-LOOKING FISH pictures? Keep your fish in the water. The color and movement of the water add drama and maintain the color of a fish better, plus it's better for catch-and-release fishing. And there is nothing more boring than a fish held at arms length out of the water in an unnatural pose, rather than half submerged in its environment. Whether it's a tiny jewel of a brook trout sparkling above the streambed or a giant tarpon held alongside a boat, I guarantee your pictures will be more interesting to you and your friends.

Prepare for the shot. Teach your fishing buddy or your guide how to use your camera before you start fishing. Make sure the camera

You'll get more interesting pictures and release fish in a safer manner if you take photos of fish close to the water.

is set on auto-focus and program or full-auto mode if someone unfamiliar with the camera is using it. And have them get the camera out well before you land the fish, discussing how you want the shot and planning the angle of the shot in relation to the sun and background as you are playing the fish.

Set the zoom, if you have one, to as wide as possible so that you make sure to get the whole fish and yourself (if you want to be in the picture) in the frame. You can crop away unwanted background easily, but you can't create image data where it's missing without some serious Photoshop work. Besides, with your zoom set on wide angle, your depth of field will be deeper, ensuring that if the camera does not focus perfectly most everything in the image will still be sharp.

Fish are about as cooperative as four-year-old boys during photo sessions, and you'll need to freeze the action by using a fast shutter speed or flash. If your camera has manual settings or program shift, set it to a shutter speed of at least 1/250th of a second with natural light, or force the camera to flash by setting the flash to fire regardless of light conditions. Fill flash tends to make better fish pictures, even in bright light, because it freezes action and fills in shadows you may not notice in the excitement.

96

Spotting fish in the water

TROUT WON'T ALWAYS COOPERATE BY RISING AND BONEFISH WON'T ALWAYS STICK their fins or tails above the surface. In clear, shallow water, however, fly fishing to sighted fish is one of the most fascinating ways to catch them. Bright light and elevation always help in spotting fish. You usually can't do much about the amount of sunlight, and when fishing from a boat you already have some elevation, but

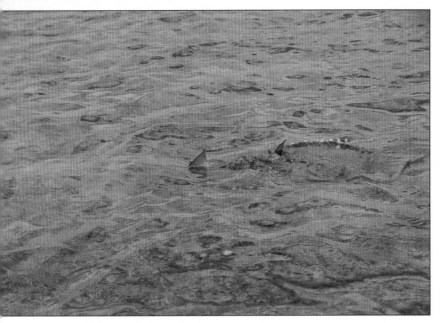

If you're fortunate, you'll see bonefish tailing in shallow water, where they are much easier to spot.

you can often get just an incremental increase in height when wading or fishing from shore by backing up a bit, staying shallower than you might normally wade.

In bright sunlight, your best approach is to look for a fish's shadow. Fish are well camouflaged and reflect their background, but they present a solid block to sunlight and will cast a shadow that is nearly always more visible than the fish themselves. Also look for movement. Bonefish, striped bass, and redfish in shallow water are always moving, so if you are wading slowly and you think you've spotted a fish, stop for a moment, as it's more difficult to perceive movement in other objects when you are moving.

You will probably spot just a piece of a fish first and your brain will have to fill in the rest of the fish from memory. This is why people with more experience spotting fish are always better than those with less experience, even if the novice has sharper eyesight. A bonefish guide may only see the tail or a single fin of a bonefish, but the thousands of hours he's spent looking into the water help his brain make the connection quickly. You'll also learn to look for the unique colors of various fish, so you can automatically eliminate objects that don't fit into the right color scheme: bonefish are light gray/green, striped bass are gray/blue, redfish are a coppery color, brown trout are pale yellow/brown, and rainbow trout are blue/green.

Finally, polarized glasses are not just snake oil invented by a marketer. They truly remove glare from the water's surface, and those with an amber tint also enhance contrast in shallow water. Combined with a long-brimmed hat that keeps flare away from your sunglasses, polarized glasses won't make up for a lack of experience but they sure give you a jump start.

97

How to catch trout in the summer when the water is low and clear

TROUT ARE MORE DIFFICULT TO CATCH DURING LOW, CLEAR SUMMER FLOWS, BUT this type of water can offer the most interesting fishing of the season. Fish will be spooky. Keep your profile low and your movements slow. Stay in the shade if possible, especially if you can keep your profile close to streamside brush, where your movements will be less noticeable. Wear drab olive or even camouflage clothing—lightweight cotton shirts made for dove hunting are perfect.

Summer means water temperatures that may reach the upper avoidance level for trout because warm water holds less of the life-giving oxygen they need than colder water. Look for fish in fast riffles or boulder-lined pocket water where the water gets more oxygen exchange, or fish below small tributary streams or close to springs trickling off rocky banks. Trout will be more active in the morning than in the evening, because a trout stream is coldest just after dawn.

Unless grasshoppers are abundant, summer means tiny flies and light tippets. Most of the insects that hatch in the summer are small, and even the ants and beetles that fall into the water are seldom larger than a size 18, so stick with smaller flies and 6X or 7X tippets because not only will they look less suspicious, but tiny flies on light tippets land with less of a splash and won't spook wary trout. You may have to scale down on your fly rod as well. That 5- or 6-weight line that worked fine in June could make too much commotion in July and August.

In the low-water conditions of summer and early fall, keep a low profile and wear drab clothing.

Low and Clear

98
How to fish dry flies when nothing is rising

YOU DON'T HAVE TO WAIT FOR A HATCH TO FISH WITH DRY FLIES. ALTHOUGH TROUT won't come to the surface under all conditions, there are certain times when you can fish a dry fly in a fishy-looking place even if you have not seen a fish rise all day. The fly pattern you use is not as critical as during a hatch, as long it is close in size and shape to something the fish eat on a regular basis. So if you see

Riffled water is the best place to fish dry flies when nothing is rising.

size-14 caddisflies clinging to brush along the riverbank, or if meadows surrounding a stream are full of grasshoppers, you have a pretty good idea of what fly pattern to use.

The conditions that favor "blind fishing" a dry fly include:

- Water temperatures when trout are most active, between 55 and 65 degrees.
- Water less than two feet deep. Trout are reluctant to come to the surface when lying in deep water. Dry flies are deadly in small streams nearly all the time because the fish are never in deep water.
- Flow of one foot per second or less, about the speed of a slow walk. Trout have a tough time coming to the surface in fast current, but don't overlook pocket water with lots of rocks, because although the water looks fast, it holds many small eddies with slower current.
- Water with a slight chop. Gentle riffles are always better than flat water for blind fishing because the fish are less selective about what they eat and don't get as good an inspection of your fly.

99

How can you get started in fly tying?

IF YOU'RE INTERESTED IN TYING YOUR OWN FLIES, IT DOES REQUIRE A COMMITment of time but little else. You don't have to have patience. (I've been tying flies for forty-five years and patience is not my strong suit.) You don't have to have tiny, nimble fingers. (The best tier of small dry flies I've ever known has fingers the size of bratwurst and drives an earth mover for a living.) You don't need superb eyesight. (Get plenty of light and a pair of 4X reading glasses and you'll do just fine.)

Begin by taking fly-tying classes if possible. Most fly shops offer them, and there is no substitute for someone looking over your shoulder as you tie. If you can't attend a class, buy a good basic fly-tying kit, one with a detailed book or manual. Make sure all the materials in the kit are labeled, as there is nothing more frustrating than reading instructions telling you to "tie in a six-inch piece of yellow chenille" when you don't know chenille from hackle. A good kit

◀ *Fly Tying Legacy*

will include a decent vise and materials. There is nothing more frustrating than a vise that won't hold a hook or a pair of scissors that doesn't cut cleanly. You can also get some great help from free videos on the Web, or from basic fly-tying DVDs. If you can't watch over someone's shoulder, a close-up video is the next best thing.

Start by tying Woolly Buggers and tie a dozen of them before moving on to something else. A Woolly Bugger teaches you many of the basic fly-tying skills—including applying a feather tail or wing, winding hackle, winding a body material, and whip finishing—in addition to the basic thread manipulation procedures. Besides, you can catch nearly any fish that swims on a Woolly Bugger, so your first efforts will begin to fill your fly box with an effective pattern.

100

Can you catch trout on a fly during the winter?

IT'S LEGAL TO FISH MANY TROUT STREAMS TWELVE MONTHS A YEAR. THUS IF YOU GET addicted to fly fishing, there is no reason to suffer withdrawal or cabin fever just because it's January instead of June. Most of the best winter fishing is found in "tailwater" rivers or those influenced by stable releases from large dams. These rivers stay closer to optimum trout temperatures than runoff-influenced streams because most flow out of dams at about the temperature of ground water regardless of air temperature. Some of the best winter fisheries are in southern tailwaters like the Chattahoochee outside of Atlanta, the White and Red rivers in Arkansas, and the San Juan River in northern New Mexico. However, if you can wade through the snow to get to the river, all of the Rocky Mountain states have tailwater rivers with excellent winter fishing, such as the Bighorn and Madison rivers in Montana or the South Platte and Frying Pan in Colorado.

Winter fly fishing is mostly nymph fishing and dry-fly fishing with tiny midge imitations. Few mayflies, caddisflies, and stoneflies hatch during the winter, but midges will hatch on warmer days, especially during heavy cloud cover. Fish eating below the surface won't move far for a fly during the winter, either, so most of the fishing (save for the lucky circumstance of a midge hatch) is with a nymph, weight on the leader, and a strike indicator. Midge nymphs are the best flies in most rivers because midges are the only active aquatic insect.

Fish will usually be found in deeper, slower water, often in the middle of large pools. They seem to "pod up" in groups—I hesitate to use the word "school" because that implies a bunch of fish milling around in circles, while winter fish stay glued to the bottom in most rivers. So if you catch one trout, chances are you'll find more of them close at hand.

With the right tackle and a little sun to warm the water, you can catch trout even in the dead of winter.

A dozen fly-fishing books you should not be without

THE FOLLOWING DOZEN ARE THOSE FLY-FISHING TECHNIQUE REFERENCE BOOKS I would not be without. In addition, if you want if you enjoy the more literary side of fly fishing, read anything related to fly fishing by Jim Babb, Bill Barich, John Gierach, Jim Harrison, Ted Leeson, Nick Lyons, or Tom McGuane.

Brown, Dick. *Fly Fishing for Bonefish*. **Connecticut: The Lyons Press, 1993.** Bonefishing techniques from a master, with emphasis on Florida Keys and Bahamas techniques.

Weathered In

Caucci, Al, and Bob Nastasi. *Hatches II*. **New York: The Lyons Press, 1986.** There are hundreds of books on fishing hatches, but I keep coming back to this one for solid information. **Combs, Trey.** *Steelhead Fly Fishing*. **Connecticut: The Lyons Press, 1991.** The bible of western steelhead fly fishers, from the sport's colorful history to tackle, fly selection, and fly presentation. **Deck, Tom.** *The Orvis Fly-Casting Guide*. **Connecticut: The Lyons Press, 2003.** Based on the methods used by the Orvis Fly-Fishing Schools, the oldest and most comprehensive fly-fishing schools in the world. **Humphreys, Joe.** *Joe Humphreys's Trout Tactics*. **Pennsylvania: Stackpole Books, 1989.** Great insight on small stream fishing and nymphing by a master of fly presentation. **Kaufmann, Randall.** *Bonefishing with a Fly*. **Oregon: Frank Amato Publications, 1992.** A great overview of bonefishing, with excellent diagrams and text on the life cycle of the bonefish and life on the flats.

Kreh, Lefty and Mark Sosin. *Practical Fishing Knots*. **Connecticut: The Lyons Press, 1991.** Pretty much the bible on knots for fly fishing as well as conventional fishing knots.

Krieger, Mel. *The Essence of Fly Casting*. **San Francisco: Club Pacific, 1987.** A complete guide to learning to cast, improving your cast, and identifying problems, by one of the most talented and generous mentors in fly casting.

LaFontaine, Gary. *Caddisflies*. **Connecticut: The Lyons Press, 1994.** Caddisflies are more important than mayflies in many rivers, and if you want to learn more about their habits, this is the bible.

Rosenbauer, Tom. *Prospecting for Trout*. **Connecticut: The Lyons Press, 2000.** You don't always see hatches on a trout stream, and this book helps you understand the techniques used to catch trout when they aren't rising.

Supinski, Matt. *Steelhead Dreams*. **Oregon: Frank Amato Publications, 2001.** Great Lakes steelhead biology and life cycles, fishing all four seasons, fly selection, playing and landing fish, and much more from one of the most experienced Great Lakes steelhead guides.

Tapply, Bill. *The Orvis Pocket Guide to Fly Fishing for Bass*. **Connecticut: The Lyons Press, 2003.** Fly-rod bass fishing is not that technical, and this complete little pocket guide tells you all you need to know.

THE ORVIS
— GUIDE TO —
BEGINNING SALTWATER FLY FISHING

101 TIPS for the absolute beginner

Conway X. Bowman

Foreword by Kirk Deeter

Illustrations by Bob White

Skyhorse Publishing

Contents

Foreword

WHEN YOU PLAY WITH SHARKS FOR FUN—USING FLY TACKLE, NO LESS—PEOPLE ARE BOUND to assume you're a little twisted.

That's certainly what I expected of Conway Bowman, the world's best-known "fly fishing for mako sharks guy," when I set out to write a story about his exploits for *Field & Stream* magazine several years ago. (The story, by the way, culminated with Conway fighting a 150-pound mako, twenty miles off La Jolla . . . from a kayak).

I've since learned, however, that the man known best for operating on the angling world's ragged edge is also one of the most grounded, meticulous, and passionate fly fishers around. Conway would be just as enthralled with the challenge of presenting tiny flies to sardines as he would be casting bunny flies at laid-up tarpon, or teasing mako sharks to bite on fleshy flies. Well almost, anyway.

Conway is a problem solver, which is essential to being an effective fly angler, especially in the salt. Of all the anglers I've fished with in salty places, Bowman is the best, bar none. He's in a league of his own. He has respected his elders, and embraced the traditions of this sport. By the same token, he's pushed boundaries far beyond where others (old and young) are willing to dabble.

When fishing with Bowman, one gets the sense that his acumen has less to do with the beautiful loops he tosses from a nine-foot rod and more to do with the intangibles. All of that starts with passion.

Conway's passion is rooted in fly fishing for sharks. He first got into the sport to satisfy an itch to tangle with the biggest, fastest aquatic creatures a young guy from San Diego with a fly rod might encounter. He spent hours and hours on the sharking grounds, learning about the fish, their habits, their moods, what they would take, and why. In time, Bowman molded himself into a superlative fly fisherman.

His passion has taken him fishing all over the world, from the Louisiana marshes to Belize, Florida, the Baja Peninsula, and other salty places that many anglers can only dream about. Along the way, he has caught all sorts of species, including the world record for redfish caught on the fly.

In this book, Conway has taken all he has learned on the water and presented it in a straightforward manner. He's done this without focusing so much on the "what" or the "where," but rather on the "how" and "why." Lefty Kreh once said that the mission of a great guide isn't to demonstrate his knowledge; rather, it's to *share* it in a way that other people can grab onto and understand, then use themselves. In *The ORVIS Guide to Beginning Saltwater Fly Fishing*, Conway has done just that.

Reading through the pages of this book, I felt as if I were right there with Conway, in a flats skiff, or wading in skinny water . . . and I could hear him talking. I'm lucky to count such experiences among my favorite real-life saltwater memories. And I'll gratefully take these book lessons with me (new wrinkles included) wherever I fish.

The highest praise one writer can give to another is to say he hears the voice, feels the essence, and learns from the experience of reading the words on written pages. That's what I'm saying here. Conway has poured it all out . . . gracefully, eloquently, and honestly. I am grateful that he has done so. And I am sure you will feel the same way.

—**Kirk Deeter**
Editor-at-Large, *Field & Stream*
Coauthor, *The Little Red Book of Fly Fishing*

Introduction

WHEN TOM ROSENBAUER AT ORVIS ASKED ME TO WRITE *THE ORVIS GUIDE TO BEGINNING Saltwater Fly Fishing*, I was honored. An opportunity like this does not present itself very often—so I accepted with excitement and some anxiety. I went for it! I have never considered myself a writer. Yes, I've written articles for various fly-fishing magazines over the past fifteen years or so, but to write a book on the how-tos in fly fishing seemed daunting at first. I've been guiding fly fishers for the better part of thirty years, cutting my teeth as a kid taking family members, friends, and anyone else who wanted to fish on the many creeks and rivers in Idaho's Sawtooth Mountains. After that, I logged many years on my home waters off the San Diego coast, searching for tuna, yellowtail, and mako sharks from the deck of my sixteen-foot skiff. It was on these deep Pacific trips that I realized I had a talent for grasping and understanding the ocean environment and the fish that lived there. From fishing with other people, I also realized that I had the ability to communicate the basics of fly fishing.

This book follows in the giant footsteps of the true pioneers of this wonderful sport. And no one has left a bigger footprint than has Lefty Kreh. I believe that much of what we know today about saltwater fly fishing comes from the pages of Lefty's many books, and from his dedication and unselfish sharing of his knowledge with all fly fishers, veteran and novice alike.

I place much of the blame for my "addiction" to saltwater fly fishing on a friend and mentor, Nick Curcione, another saltwater fly-fishing icon, who kindled my interest in the pursuit of the shortfin mako sharks close to my home in San Diego. Nick, like Lefty, has authored many books on the subject over the years, but none as important to me as *The ORVIS Guide to Saltwater Fly Fishing*. That book led to my becoming a saltwater fly fisherman and one of the most vocal proponents of the sport. It didn't take me long to realize the fly-fishing potential that lay but a double haul from my back porch. Nick's progressive casting techniques with shooting heads, and his mastery of fighting big fish on the fly, have had a big influence on me.

I can remember as a youngster (eight or nine years old) sitting on the floor of my father's study, thumbing through books by Lefty, Nick, and Stu Apte, my eyes riveted on pictures of giant tarpon, snook, and sharks that these master anglers had caught on flies. I was fascinated by the environments they were fishing, tropical places like Belize, Florida, and Costa Rica, destinations that offered anglers the opportunity to fish waters that were a far cry from the trout streams most fly fishers were used to. That's what attracted me: This was fly fishing on the ragged edge! Even way back then, I knew that I wanted to catch big fish on the fly rod in exotic locales.

My conversion into a saltwater fly fisherman did not happen overnight—it was a slow process. I was born and raised in San Diego, California, a city long known for its temperate climate, as well as its proximity to Tijuana, Mexico. For anglers, it offered access to some of the best saltwater fishing in the United States. My buddies and I spin-fished or fished from half-day boats in the kelp beds for bonito, yellowtail, and barracudas, or hit local lakes and ponds for largemouths, crappies, and bluegills. A few locals fly-fished for these freshwater species—only one man, Sam Nix, used a fly rod for fishing salt water. Nix, an older man who had fly-fished San Diego's bays and jetties since the 1930s, was a legend to some folks, but to many fishermen he was an eccentric. One thing is a matter of record: He caught saltwater fish with a fly rod, a practice that was practically unheard of back then. In 1977, however, something happened that helped me see the light.

That summer, my father was hired to work as a fishing guide at a lodge in Idaho's Sawtooth Valley. Each summer for four years, Dad and I would spend two months living in a house trailer on the shores of Redfish Lake, just a short drive from classic trout streams in Idaho, Montana, and Wyoming. With an inexpensive fly rod and reel, I caught my first fly rod fish, a rainbow trout, out of the spring-fed waters of Silver Creek, only a few miles from Sun Valley. I was six and, like the 'bow, I was hooked. Enter Bill and Eileen Stroud.

Bill and Eileen Stroud, my surrogate uncle and aunt, owned and operated the only real fly shop in San Diego. When not fishing or duck hunting, my father and I would hang out there, rummaging through trays of flies or just talking fly fishing with this wonderful couple. They were the ones who first took me out on a "cattle boat," where they taught me the finer points of saltwater angling. More important, they introduced me to the world of saltwater fly fishing.

Years later, as a young man, I began walking the local beaches, fly rod in hand, casting flies to corbina and surf perch feeding along the surf line. Then, in my early twenties, I bought a sixteen-foot aluminum boat with a tiller-controlled twenty-five-horsepower motor and began venturing offshore in search of sharks, bonito, and yellowtail. Those early journeys helped me learn about the ocean, and eventually led me to a career as a fly-fishing guide.

No matter where you are, be it a distant tropical location or a beach or estuary close to home, or what you're fishing for, from snapper to bluefish to gigantic blue marlin, you'll find that fly fishing saltwater is an exciting, challenging, and rewarding sport. It's my hope that this book will help you along your journey.

Great tides . . .

—**Conway X. Bowman**

PART
1

Getting
Started

1

Learn from the conventional fishermen

YOU CAN LEARN A LOT ABOUT CATCHING FISH ON THE FLY FROM THE CONVENTIONAL spinning and casting rod anglers. The spin-and-cast guys are just as hardcore and passionate about saltwater fishing as fly fishers. These folks can teach you something about what types of flies to select, how to fight fish, how to read the water, the best knots to tie, and what to look for when you're fishing. If you don't come off as an elitist, as some fly fishermen do, one of these guys may even invite you to go out on his boat for a day of striper fishing, or to go check out one of his favorite surf-fishing spots. Pay attention, because you'll learn things that you will never find in a book. Remember the adage that "Experience is the best teacher."

Many of the most skilled and knowledgeable saltwater fly fishermen are also outstanding spin-and-cast anglers, people who have honed their skills by casting with a surf rod and/or jig fishing from a boat. Learning to cast a spinning outfit well will also make you a better fly caster. Why? Because being able to cast a small jig accurately into a small space, like a mangrove or along a shoreline, will help you refine your fly-casting abilities.

Another example of learning from a conventional guy: The "old salt" you routinely find hanging around the local dock or tackle shop is a wealth of information, even if he has never held a fly rod. There's a good chance that he has logs of his countless hours spent fishing the salt, and has probably caught more than his share of saltwater gamefish. Many of these guys love to talk about fishing in the "good ol' days." Get them started and stand by—they will regale you with tales about the old days that are not only interesting, but also educational.

The beginning fly fisherman can learn a lot from a guy like my father, who's been fishing most of his life.

Fish with a buddy, find a mentor, go to a trade show

FISHING WITH A FRIEND IS ONE OF THE GREATEST JOYS OF BEING OUT ON THE WATER. YOU can share the experiences of catching your first redfish, hooking the first bonito of the season, or finding that flat or beach that has never felt wading shoes. Often, it's not even about the fish or fishing, but about appreciating the surroundings and sharing a few laughs. Perhaps you can share knowledge about knots and flies, or critique each other's casting skills. If so inclined, the two of you can join a local fly-fishing club or fly-tying class, where you can absorb and share all sorts of information with other saltwater fly enthusiasts.

If you are a newcomer to saltwater fly fishing, find a mentor who will take you under his wing and teach you everything that's important to becoming a proficient saltwater fly angler. There's a given about fly fishers, no matter if they prefer salt or fresh water: They are not loners. They love fellow fly anglers, especially those folks just entering the sport, and will gladly jaw with you for hours about fishing, sharing their experiences. Where does one find a mentor? Visit your local fly shop or join a fly-fishing club.

Another great source for learning is the fishing trade show. In fact, trade shows are where I began gathering information about fly fishing the salt. A Southern Californian by birth, I had the chance to speak with the pioneers of saltwater fly fishing only at the West Coast fishing trade shows. It was at these shows that I had the chance to speak with my childhood saltwater fly-fishing heroes such as Lefty Kreh, Nick Curcione, Flip Pallot, and Dan Blanton. Every year, I looked forward to these shows and the opportunity to speak with and learn from these outstanding anglers.

Good friend. Good fishing. Great times!

PART
2

Equipment

3

How to choose a basic saltwater outfit

GETTING STARTED IN SALTWATER FLY FISHING CAN SEEM LIKE AN OVERWHELMING TASK, but it isn't complicated. It's most important to buy the right rod and reel for the type of fishing you'll be doing. The East Coast striper fly fisherman will require a very different outfit from what a West Coast surf perch fisherman needs, and the guy interested in catching redfish in the Louisiana marsh will need a vastly different rig from the angler casting to bonito off a jetty in Southern California. Here are my suggestions:

The Rod

Choose a seven- or eight-weight rod. This is the perfect starter rod for the beginning saltwater fly fisher, heavy enough to punch a fly into a stiff wind, yet light enough to cast all day. Technically, you could use a heavy trout rod, but ideally you want to use a saltwater rod because it's made of materials that can handle salt, sand, and generally tough conditions.

The Reel

A good direct-drive reel that can hold a minimum of 200 yards of thirty-pound Dacron backing will work well in most saltwater fly-fishing situations. Currently, fly reels designed for saltwater fishing are more than adequate in handling fish up to fifty pounds. Buy an extra spool to hold your shooting head.

Fly Lines

Here is what you'll need:

A basic rod matched with a quality reel is a good starting point for a beginner.

1. A basic weight-forward (WF) floating line matched to the weight of your fly rod. The WF floating line is a great all-around fly line for sight-casting in shallow water. Don't get confused by all the marketing of "saltwater tapers," "bonefish tapers," or "redfish tapers." Such lines are for more advanced, specialized fly fishers, not beginners.

2. A weighted shooting head. A combination of a weighted front taper and an intermediate running line, this is ideal for subsurface fishing or fishing rip currents from the beach. When fish are feeding below the surface, the shooting head will keep your fly in the hit zone longer. A 250- to 300-grain should be sufficient for most situations. The grain weight equals the sink rate of the fly line, so a 250- to 300-grain line will sink between five and eight inches per second. This is plenty of sink rate to get you down to feeding fish.

4

Saltwater fly rod length

THE STANDARD NINE-FOOT FLY ROD WORKS BEST IN MANY SALTWATER FLY-FISHING situations. It provides the angler with enough length to keep his fly line high off the water while backcasting and is effective when fighting fish in shallow water.

Many beach fly fishermen prefer a longer fly rod, something in the ten- or eleven-foot range. The added length assists in keeping the fly line safely above the shoreline structure on the backcast. This also allows for the shooting and/or weight-forward section of the fly line to extend beyond the rod's tip section, providing much-needed assistance in shooting the fly line as well as extending the length of the cast.

For bluewater fly fishing, a shorter rod (eight to eight and a half feet) works best when fighting a fish in deep water. A stiff butt section is especially important for putting pressure on a fish when reeling it in from deep water. It also saves the angler a trip to his chiropractor for an adjustment on his sacrum.

A shorter rod is best when you're fishing for bluewater fish such as tuna, sharks, and billfish.

5

What makes a good saltwater fly reel?

A quality saltwater fly reel is a smart investment.

A GOOD SALTWATER FLY REEL SHOULD BE MADE FROM FIRST-grade aluminum bar stock, have a slightly oversized handle that can be easily cranked while fighting a fish, and, most important, have a strong drag system.

The drag system is the heart of a good saltwater reel—it is essential in controlling the powerful surge of a gamefish that's determined to escape. A disk drag system of cork, Rulon, or graphite will stand up to the long, strong fights of saltwater gamefish. Many of the stacked-disk-drag fly reels on today's market are outstanding and require little special maintenance. The cork-drag reel has the most powerful drag system; however, such reels require a bit of TLC. Oiling and lubricating the cork drag are essential to retaining its excellent action.

For both synthetic and cork fly reels, back off the drag at the end of each fishing day or if the reel is not to be used for a long time. This will help preserve the drag and keep it working in top form on future trips.

6

Drag setting for saltwater fly fishing

PROPER DRAG SETTINGS ARE ESSENTIAL FOR SALTWATER FLY FISHING. A PROPER SETTING CAN spell the difference between landing and losing the fish of a lifetime. Unlike conventional or spinning reels—on which the drag is usually preset and not adjusted during the fight—the fly reel drag can be manipulated by applying pressure to the reel with palm or fingers, giving the angler more control over the amount of pressure needed throughout the fight.

Palming the reel gives the angler more control when fighting a fish.

To set the drag, take your fly reel and tighten the drag so there is only light tension on the reel as you pull off line with your free hand; then tighten the drag until you feel resistance.

Begin fishing using a light drag. Once you have a fish on and the fight has begun, apply needed pressure by palming your reel—however, apply the pressure carefully so you don't break the tippet. Don't be surprised if you lose a few fish as you learn this method. It takes time and practice. Eventually, though, knowing when and how to apply pressure will become instinctive.

7

Using intermediate lines

INTERMEDIATE LINES DON'T FLOAT AND THEY DON'T SINK rapidly. When you cast them out onto the water, they will sink very slowly, which makes them perfect choices when casting to fish feeding just below the surface (one to five feet) or in slightly deeper channels. You can use these versatile lines in situations as varied as casting to bonefish feeding off a reef in a channel or to West Coast yellowtail feeding just below the surface in the middle of the ocean.

When choosing your rod and corresponding fly line, base your choice on the type of fishing you intend to do, as a heavier intermediate line, such as an eight, will sink faster than a lighter line, such as a five.

In addition to getting the fly in the hit zone, the slick coating on an intermediate line will let you put extra length in your cast.

An intermediate fly line is perfect for fishing along reef channels.

8

Using a sinking line

THE BEST SALTWATER FLY FISHING USUALLY TAKES PLACE BELOW THE SURFACE, WHETHER you're fishing near shore or offshore. Fish such as tuna, dorado, bluefish, and stripers will often feed in deep water, requiring anglers to get their flies deeper into the water column. This requires the use of a full-sinking line or sinking shooting head.

Full-Sinking Line

Full-sinking lines are rated Types I through V, I being the lightest and V the heaviest. If you are casting to fish only a few feet below the surface, a Type I or II shooting head will work fine. However, if the fish are feeding twenty feet down, the Type V would be your line of choice. The entire fly line is weighted, and is approximately one hundred feet long.

Once mastered, the integrated shooting/sinking head is a joy to cast. ▶

Integrated Sinking Shooting Head

These are my favorite sinking fly lines. The first twenty-six feet of these lines are weighted, and the rest is mono-core running line. Due to the slick surface of the monocore running line, these fly lines cast like a dream. Additionally, since all the weight is loaded at the front end of the line, the momentum of the weighted section helps extend the distance of your cast. These lines are rated in grains, from 150 to 800 grains—150 is the lightest, 800 the heaviest. An 800-grain line will work most effectively to fish to thirty feet.

Lead-core Line

In depths over twenty-five feet, lead-core lines are usually the best choices. Because they sink so quickly, they work well when you're fishing from a drifting boat and when you're dealing with strong currents. They are typically twenty feet long, and are attached with a loop-to-loop connection to a monofilament running line. The weight of the lead-core line and the thin diameter of the mono running line allow these lines to get down faster when compared to the other types of sinking fly lines. However, they can be difficult to cast—not only that, but the mono running line has a tendency to coil while casting.

9

Does fly line color matter in salt water?

Fly lines in light blue, tan, or light green are good choices for salt water.

TODAY'S FLY FISHERMAN CAN BUY FLY lines in a wide variety of colors. Before settling on a color, consider its advantages and disadvantages. If you buy a brightly colored line, for example, you'll be able to follow a hooked fish's position in a fight. On the downside, many fish, especially those found in shallow, clear water, are skittish and easily spooked by brightly colored line.

Fly lines in natural colors (light blue, tan, or light green) are wise choices in most situations. Such colors make it easier to match the line color to the surroundings in which you plan to fish. On overcast, low-light days, gray and green lines are good choices; clear, sunny, blue-sky days seem best served by light blue lines; in rocky areas or light brown sandy waters, tan should be considered. Remember that one color does not suit all conditions.

10

Backing: weight and quantity demands

LOSING A BIG SALTWATER GAMEFISH AFTER IT IS HOOKED AND decides to head for the horizon is, in many instances, the result of filling your reel with backing that is either too short or too light.

Twenty-pound backing is a good choice for most inshore saltwater fly-fishing situations, while thirty-pound backing is better suited for larger bluewater gamefish.

Since many inshore saltwater gamefish will make initial runs of seventy-five to one hundred yards before they turn and settle into fighting mode, your fly reel should hold a minimum of 175 yards of twenty-pound Dacron backing.

For bluewater fly fishing, a minimum of 300 yards of thirty-pound Dacron or gel-spun polyethylene is standard. Big bluewater gamefish such as tuna and marlin will run off 200 yards of backing before you have time to say, "Come back and fight like a man!" These fish can also dive to great depths, thus making essential an abundant supply of backing.

Twenty- and thirty- pound Dacron backing are good choices for a saltwater fly reel.

11

Best color for backing?

THE PHRASE "GETTING INTO YOUR BACKING" AROUSES EXCITEMENT through a saltwater fly fisherman's being each time he hears it. There is nothing more exciting than witnessing one hundred yards of backing slicing through the water, pulled by a bonefish, tarpon, sailfish, or marlin. When this happens, the color of your backing is essential for tracking the fish's direction: Is it swimming at an angle, or is it sounding? Sooner or later, every saltwater fisherman is going to experience this.

High-visibility backing will help you determine how to fight a fish. For instance, when tarpon fishing it is important that you are able to turn a fish's head during the fight, a move aimed at keeping the tarpon off balance and assuring that it is brought quickly to the boat. Just as important, high-visibility backing allows the angler to track the fish's direction and keep applying pressure in the direction opposite from where it wants to go.

The best colors? I prefer bright yellow or bright orange, both highly visible backings regardless of weather conditions or water color.

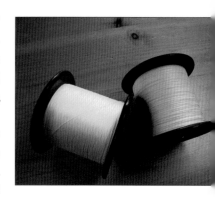

Bright colors allow you to see where your fish is going during the fight.

Tying the backing to the fly reel

MANY FLY FISHERS DON'T KNOW HOW TO TIE THE BACKING TO THEIR FLY REELS. AND WHY should they? Isn't backing usually wound onto your fly reel at the time of purchase? We have come to expect this courtesy from fly shops after buying a reel. However, if you ever need to change your fly line and attach new backing to your reel and find yourself miles from the nearest fly shop, being able to do it yourself will not only save you a lengthy trip to town but will also afford you more fishing time.

Gel-spun and Dacron backing have a tendency to slip once they are connected to the fly reel's arbor. A good way to avoid this problem is to wrap a strip of blue medical or gaffer's tape around the arbor before putting on the backing. The tape's surface will create just enough friction to prevent the backing from slipping as you wind it onto the reel.

The Arbor Knot is a good knot for tying backing to your fly reel's arbor. It is simple to tie and very low profile.

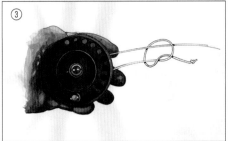

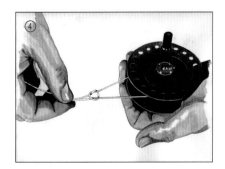

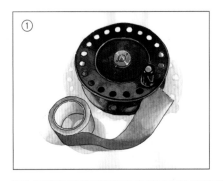

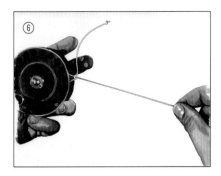

How to build a basic saltwater leader

THE LEADER IS THE MOST IMPORTANT CONNECTION BETWEEN THE SALTWATER FLY FISHER-
man and the fish. Tied incorrectly, it will place the angler at a distinct disadvantage in casting, especially under windy conditions.

Simple in its design, the saltwater fly leader can meet the demands of almost every saltwater fly-fishing situation. A leader's length varies depending on conditions, but a nine-foot leader will work in most situations; a "four-three-two combo" works well, as it allows the fly to roll over as it is cast. Creating this leader is fairly simple:

To start, tie a two-turn Surgeon's Loop of forty- or fifty-pound soft monofilament at the fly line's end; then join the sections of your leader with Blood Knots, applying saliva to the knots to guarantee a solid connection impervious to separation, taking care to test the strength of each knot as you complete it.

    ★four feet of forty-pound soft mono
    ★three feet of thirty-pound mono
    ★two feet of twenty-pound mono

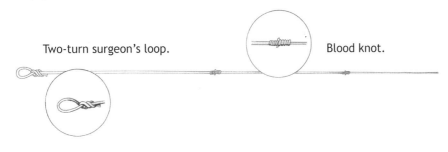

Two-turn surgeon's loop.   Blood knot.

Choosing the best material for a wire leader

WHEN YOU FLY-FISH IN SALT WATER, THERE WILL BE TIMES WHEN YOU WILL BE DEALING WITH
a toothy critter such as a barracuda, shark, needlefish, or Sierra mackerel—fish with sharp teeth capable of severing the heaviest monofilament and fluorocarbon leaders. It is the savvy saltwater fly fisherman who has learned to attach a biteproof tippet to his fly line.

There are two schools of thought regarding biteproof tippet: One school favors a soft, stainless steel leader when fishing for toothed gamefish; the other prefers a single-strand stainless wire leader. Let's compare the two.

The soft stainless steel leader is easier to tie, but not as durable as the single-strand stainless wire leader. In a lengthy battle, chances are that a sharp-toothed fish is eventually going to bite through the soft stainless steel leader and break off.

Single-strand stainless-steel wire is the best choice when targeting toothy critters such as mako sharks.

The second option, and my personal preference, is the single-strand stainless wire leader. The wire is tough, able to withstand the raking teeth of a shark far better than soft a stainless steel leader. Another advantage of this type of leader is its small diameter. Like a piece of dental floss, it fits nicely between the fish's teeth and doesn't get worn, frayed, or chewed as the battle rages on.

If you decide to use a single-strand wire leader, the most common way of attaching it to your line is with a Haywire Twist. Although there are tools to assist you in tying this knot, I recommend the old-school method demonstrated in many fishing knot books.

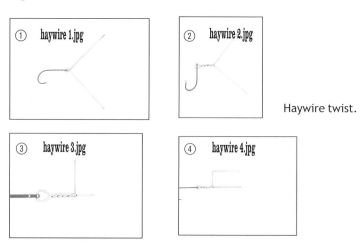

Haywire twist.

15

How long should a leader be for a sinking line?

BECAUSE WEIGHTED SHOOTING LINES AND SHOOTING HEADS SINK, THE LEADER NEED NOT be the standard nine feet. In fact, the shorter the leader, the faster the fly will sink into the fish's hit zone. Conversely, if the leader is too long, the fly will not keep pace with the line as it sinks, causing the leader and fly to end up higher in the water than the sinking line—a situation bound to create problems when gamefish are feeding at a certain depth.

Depending on how leader-shy the fish are, and to some extent which species is being sought, a single four- to six-foot piece of monofilament or fluorocarbon in twelve- to thirty-pound test will suffice for many situations.

To attach, tie a Double Surgeon's Loop at one end of the mono leader and attach to the loop at the end of the shooting head. Then tie the fly to the other end of the mono leader.

This is a simple and effective way of keeping your fly in the zone and getting more strikes.

16

How to make a redfish leader: the Half and Half

THE REDFISH IS AN OUTSTANDING FISH ON THE FLY. It's aggressive and strong, and provides the chance to experience outstanding sight-casting. This fish is not as spooky as the bonefish or tarpon, so the leader system can be very simple.

The Half and Half is a nine-foot, two-part leader system that is easy to make and casts well. The butt section should be a thirty- or forty-pound test, four-and-a-half- to five-foot piece of monofilament; attach it to a twenty-pound piece of mono, of similar length, with a Blood Knot.

In most situations, this is all you will need.

The Half and Half is the ideal redfish leader. ▶

Creating a loop on the end of your fly line

THERE ARE MANY WAYS TO ATTACH YOUR FLY LINE TO YOUR LEADER. MANY FLY LINES COME with a premade loop on the end; unfortunately, these loops tend to pull apart when subjected to heavy pressure.

To tie your own, begin by forming a strong, whip-finished loop at the end of your fly line. If properly formed, the loop will exceed your fly line's strength.

1. Fold over the end of the fly line and double the line.
2. Make the loop large enough to allow a fly to pass through it.
3. Tie three Nail Knots on the doubled-up part of the fly line.
4. Secure the Nail Knots, then test them by securing the loop around a dull object like the end of a pair of pliers and applying tension on the loop.
5. A coating of Super Glue or Knot Sense on each Nail Knot will ensure that the knots will hold and not unravel during a prolonged fight with a gamefish.

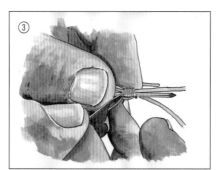

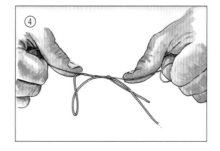

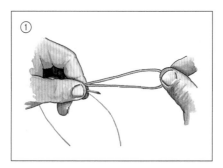

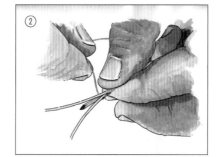

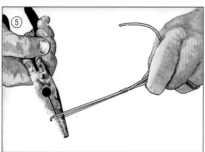

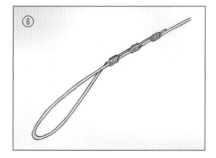

18

Attaching the leader to the sinking line

MOST SINKING LINES CONTAIN A MONOCORE (COATED MONOFILAMENT CORE). THESE LINES are strong and able to handle the demands placed upon them by hard-fighting saltwater gamefish.

These lines do have a weakness, however, in that an incorrect connection between the leader and the line, such as a Nail Knot, can cause the monocore's coating to strip off while you are fighting a fish.

A better option is the Albright Knot. It's bulky, but it's a very solid and reliable choice.

Even better, don't use a knot at all, but put a loop in the end of your sinking line. Take fifteen-pound monofilament and use two Nail Knots to create a loop in the end of the sinking line. Once the loop is made, coat the Nail Knots with Knot Sense or some other glue. If done properly, this loop will not break.

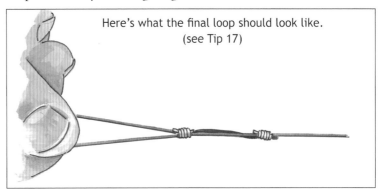

Here's what the final loop should look like.
(see Tip 17)

19

How to tie a Bimini Twist

THE BIMINI TWIST IS AN IMPORTANT SALTWATER KNOT THAT YOU SHOULD KNOW HOW TO tie. It has a high breaking strength and can be used for a variety of connections, from IGFA tippets to mono shock tippets, or even connecting mono to steel leaders.

The Bimini requires practice to master, but once you understand the process, you'll find it to be a very useful knot that you'll come to rely upon in a variety of situations. Follow these eight steps:

1. Form a loop in the line. Place one hand in the bottom of the loop and make twenty to twenty-five twists by rotating your hand.
2. Place the loop around your foot; then, with both hands, pull the two ends of the line apart, twisting the line into tight spirals.
3. Take the tag end of the line and, at a right angle, let it spin downward toward your foot. Pull up lightly on the line, letting the tag end roll down toward the loop.
4. Work the tag end all the way down to the top of the loop.

5. Hold the wraps tightly, make a Half Hitch on one side of the loop, then pull tight, which will secure all the downward wraps.
6. Take the tag end and make four to six Half Hitches around both legs of the loop.
7. Pull the tag and force all the wraps together.
8. Finally, place the loop around a boat cleat or something equally secure and pull the knot together. Trim the tag ends.

Master the Bimini Twist and you'll not only impress your fishing buddies with your tying skills, but you'll also be using one of the most important and secure knots associated with saltwater fly fishing.

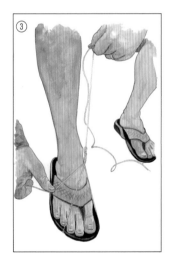
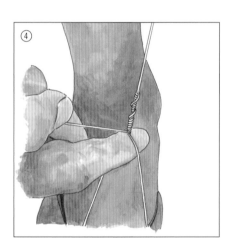
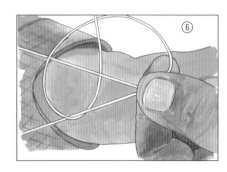
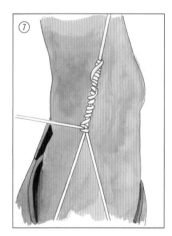
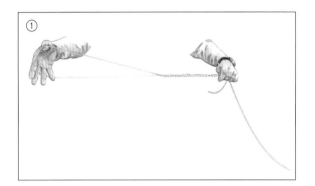
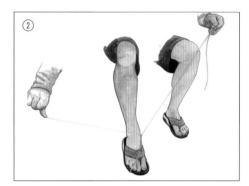
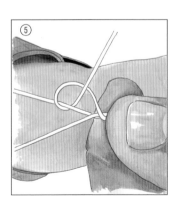

How to tie a Figure Eight Loop knot using soft stainless steel wire

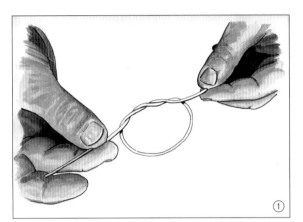

SOFT STAINLESS WIRE IS A GOOD ALTERNATIVE TO single-strand wire. It works well on the smaller saltwater gamefish, such as the Pacific barracuda and bonito, which the fly rodder will encounter in many nearshore fisheries.

The best attribute of the soft stainless wire is that you can tie a loop knot in it, thus avoiding the time-consuming process of making the Haywire Twist that is so commonly used with single-strand wire.

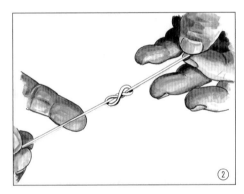

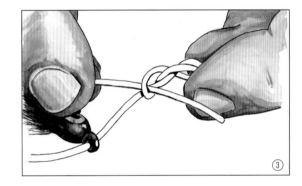

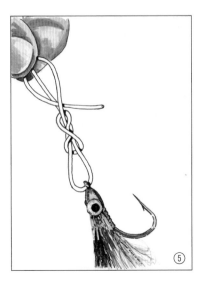

21

Coat fishing knots with Knot Sense

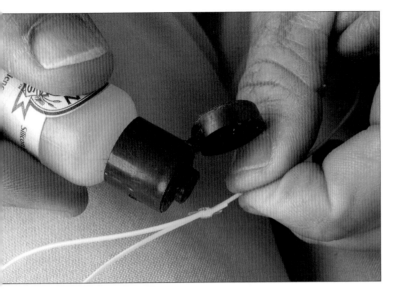

WHEN YOU'RE FIGHTING A SALTWATER GAME-fish, your leader system is sorely tested as the fish makes long, strong runs along mangrove shoots, coral heads, and rock pinnacles. There are times when it's impossible to avoid breaking off a fish; however, one way to make certain your knots can stand the stress of a long battle is to coat them with Knot Sense, a liquid that will strengthen your connections and smooth out your tag ends.

Knot Sense is a clear liquid with the consistency of household dish soap. Because it solidifies when exposed to the sun's rays, it should be applied outdoors or in direct sunlight; once dried, it creates a clear, soft coating around your leader connections. While setting, the liquid penetrates the knot's wraps, helping bond them into stronger and more dependable links.

22

Reading a fish finder or GPS

IF YOU'RE A BOAT OWNER AND YOU FLY-FISH IN SALTWATER, AT some point you'll have to read a fish finder or a global positioning system (GPS) unit. The fish finder/GPS unit is a key component to success when fishing the salt. Whether pinpointing schools of baitfish, locating structure, reading water temperatures, or getting safely back to your launching site, this unit's importance to the angler cannot be overstated. Some portable models can even be mounted on a kayak. Tackle stores and mail-order and online catalogs stock a wide variety of units; all share similar features, the most important being the following:

1. GPS for navigation
2. Water temperature
3. Bathymetry (locating underwater structure)
4. Sonar for locating baitfish and gamefish

23

Don't forget the long-nosed pliers

I CAN'T REMEMBER HOW MANY TIMES I'VE BROUGHT A barracuda, shark, or bluefish in to be released, only to realize I had only short-nosed pliers with which to remove the hook from the fish's mouth. Short-nosed pliers work well enough for freshwater fishing, but for dealing with the teeth of many saltwater gamefish, the wise angler carries long-nosed pliers. To paraphrase an old TV commercial, "Don't leave home without them."

There are two important reasons for packing these fishing aids: First, they protect your fingers, for even the smallest barracuda can take a nasty bite out of your finger, while a bluefish has the potential to sink its razor-sharp teeth clear to the bone. Furthermore, if the fish is deeply hooked in the throat, the long-nosed pliers will give you a better chance of removing the hook and releasing the fish unharmed.

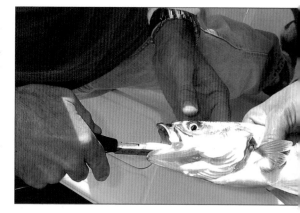

Long-nosed pliers are useful for extracting hooks.

24

Use a net in salt water

THE FISH NET IS NOT JUST FOR STREAM OR LAKE FISHING; IT'S ALSO A USEFUL AID IN SAFELY catching and releasing saltwater gamefish. It helps you control a fish, remove the hook from its tooth-filled mouth, and then release it without causing it harm.

If you are a catch-and-release fly fisherman, employing a net is easier on the fish once it is brought to boat or shore. Handling the fish can be harmful to it, as your hands tend to remove the fish's protective slime coating, leaving it susceptible to bacterial and fungal infection after it's released.

The standard trout net may be a bit small, but there are many great medium to large nets on the market. Select a net that suits the fishing you have planned. Smaller nets are suitable for Southern California's surf perch and corbina; larger nets are needed for tackling species such as Gulf Coast redfish or East Coast stripers. Use only nets that have black rubberlike webbing, as the soft, slick texture will not harm the fish. Forget about using grandpa's old aluminum net with the green polypropylene webbing. These nets do the fish more harm than good.

Using a net can help tame an unwieldy gamefish. ▶

Polarized sunglasses

WHETHER YOU'RE STALKING BONEFISH ON THE FLATS OR SIGHT-CASTING TO TUNA OFF-shore, your most important piece of equipment, next to the fly reel, is quality polarized sunglasses, which eliminate glare from the water's surface. Drugstore sunglasses? Forget them. All they do is make you look sharp. A pair of high-end polarized glasses is well worth the money.

The variety of polarized lens color choices can be confusing, so here are a few guidelines in selecting your glasses:

1. For shallow flats, beaches, and marshes: amber lenses
2. For deep water, offshore waters, and bright sunlight: gray lenses
3. For softer light, glare, and cloudy days: yellow, light rose, or amber lenses

Frame styles vary greatly, but function and coverage are the major concerns. Choose a frame that provides good coverage over the eyes, as well as in the temple area. Look for frames that do not let in light peripherally (from the side of the head), and choose a frame that will remain comfortable throughout a long day of fishing. Consider lightweight frames with arms that don't pinch behind the ears.

In the past, most anglers chose glass as a lens material. Glass is durable and relatively scratch-resistant, although it's heavy. Nowadays, outstanding synthetic lens materials such as polycarbonate and SR-91 are good alternative choices. SR-91 is strong, light, and has superior light transmission and clarity. Wearing glasses with SR-91 lenses all day isn't as much of a burden on your nose.

Eyewear is a personal choice. Whether you're a hipster or lean more toward the traditional styles, the important things to remember are lens coloration and eye coverage. Oh, and don't forget a lanyard for your glasses. It would be a shame to lose your expensive pair of shades to the deep blue sea!

Good polarized sunglasses will help you pinpoint more fish.

Proper footwear for fishing

IF I COULD FISH BAREFOOT, I WOULD; HOWEVER, THIS IS NOT PRACTICAL IN MANY SALTWATER situations. A good pair of fishing shoes is as important as your favorite fishing hat, shirt, or sunglasses. It's important that your feet are properly shod for any occasion.

On the Skiff

When skiff fishing, a firm-soled running or deck shoe works well, but with modifications. The first thing I do when I put on a pair is to tuck in the laces snugly, leaving no exposed dangling ends. Fly lines can hang up on anything, but loose laces always seem to be at the top of the list. I know some fly fishers who are so concerned with this problem that they run duct tape around their shoes to keep the laces covered. And don't forget: No black soles!

Sandals? I would leave them at home. Like shoelaces, the straps on sandals pose another problem in line hangup.

Flip-flops, if you are so inclined, are an acceptable and comfortable option, as they have no line-grabbing laces or straps. On the downside, they offer little support for your feet.

On the Beach and Flats

There are hundreds of different types of practical shoes that will fit your needs on fishing trips. Select a shoe with high ankle support, a firm and solid toe, and stiff arch support. Since you'll be wading in a variety of bottom conditions, including mud, soft sand, hard sand, and even coral reefs, select a shoe that has a thick sole to prevent punctures. If you fish with a stripping basket, you can use sandals because there is less chance of your line getting snagged on the straps of the conventional wading shoe.

Rocks and Jetties

If you fish from rocks and jetties, heavy-duty wading boots are not only comfortable, but provide great support. If you choose not to wear waders, then wear two pairs of socks in the boots for a better fit.

Proper footwear protects your feet when walking on coral reefs.

The stripping basket

WHEN FISHING FROM THE BEACH, THERE IS NOTHING MORE FRUSTRATING THAN HAVING your fly line wrap and tangle around your legs and feet, especially after you have just made a perfect cast to a school of gamefish.

The simplest way to solve this problem is to invest in a stripping basket. Made from a variety of materials and available in many styles, the stripping basket will assist you in managing your line, leaving you free to concentrate on improving your casting and distance.

The stripping basket is not limited to beach fishing. More and more anglers are also accepting the value of the stripping basket on boats. This taller, free-standing cousin to the standard wearable basket allows you to keep your line off the deck and avoid potential hangups with boat cleats, shoelaces, coolers, and other obstacles commonly found on a boat deck.

A large stripping basket on the bow of a skiff helps you avoid tangles and add distance to your casts.

Wear a wading belt when fishing the surf

THE SURF ZONE CAN BE LIKENED TO A ROUGH NEIGHBORHOOD, AN ENVIRONMENT WHERE you must exercise great caution. There are a few things that you can do to ensure your safety, however.

Since most of us wear waders when fly fishing the surf, it is important to use a wading belt, a seemingly unimportant piece of equipment that could save your life if you are lifted up and thrown into the drink by a large breaker. In the surf zone, it also isn't uncommon to have your feet swept out from under you by a rip current, leaving you in a helpless position. Even if you're a swimmer with the talent of an Olympic gold medalist, once your beltless waders fill up with water, you'll find it almost impossible to regain your footing. Without that belt tightly cinched around your middle, you are a candidate for the morning paper's obits.

The tightened wader belt creates a nice pocket of air below your waist, giving you a little buoyancy as well as saving you the problem of dealing with the extra weight of full-to-the-brim waders. To be most effective, the belt should be positioned above your hips.

For added safety, some fly fishers also wear an inflatable life vest, especially if they are not good swimmers. Most vests can be inflated with the pull of a string; many come equipped with pockets for storing fly boxes and other gear.

No matter what you wear, always remember this: Never turn your back to the surf.

A wading belt should always be worn while fishing the surf.

PART
3

Casting

The double haul

MANY BEGINNING SALTWATER FLY ANGLERS WILL INVEST A TON OF MONEY BUYING THE best equipment, and spend thousands of dollars traveling to exotic locations that offer incredible fishing for the likes of trophy tarpon or permit. Then, once they are on the bow of the boat, ready to cast to the fish of a lifetime, they're unable to cast the fly into the wind or achieve the distance required to reach the fish—a situation that is frustrating not only to the angler, but to the guide as well. The key to solving this problem is to learn to double haul: It will improve your casting speed and accuracy, enable you to cast the fly into the wind, and let you cast a weighted shooting head or sinking line. The end result is that you'll catch more fish. And you know what? The double haul is easier to learn than you might think.

Start by finding an open, grassy area (parks are great places to work on your casting, but watch for kids and dogs). Strip off forty feet of fly line, make a single forward cast, and lay out the line in front of you. Now, with the rod tip on the grass, pick up the fly line and make a backcast. Let it unfurl and lie behind you on the grass. This is a single haul.

Once the fly line is laid out behind, make a forward cast by pulling the line off the lawn with your line hand while your rod is moving forward. As you bring your rod forward, pull the line in your hand down toward your waist. You will feel the rod load up as it bends, and then the line will shoot forward. Release the line from your hand as it starts to go forward, and watch it fly forward through the guides. This is what gives you the extra distance and lets you push through the wind. This is the second or double haul.

Once you get the feel of both the single and double haul, keep the forward and backcasts off the lawn. You should be able to feel the line accelerating on both the backcast and forward cast.

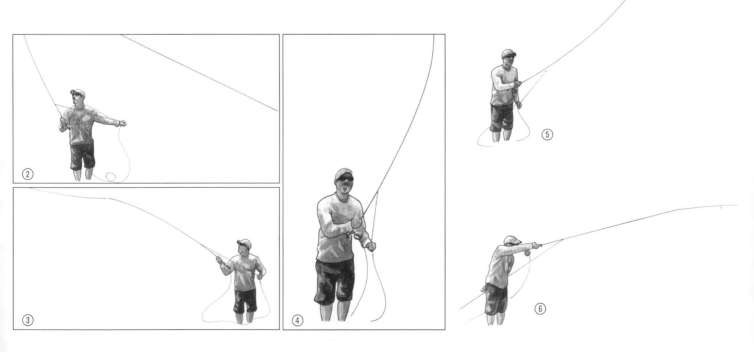

Develop a good backcast

BEING ABLE TO LAY OUT THIRTY OR FORTY FEET OF FLY LINE behind you is a skill you need to master. Fish can materialize behind you as easily as they can in front of you, and a quick, accurate backcast will improve your chances of catching them.

You can make the backcast in the same manner as the forward cast. First make a forward cast, allowing the line to lie on the water, then pick up the line and shoot it behind you. This move is called the water haul (see Tip 32); instead of coming forward with the forward cast, you now allow the fly line to lay out behind you in the area where you spotted the fish. You can proceed with stripping the line from there, just as you would if the fish were in front of you.

31

The Long Cast

FOR ALL INTENTS AND PURPOSES, THE hundred-foot cast does not exist in fly fishing. There has been much lore and myth around the need to make the "hundred-footer" to saltwater fish. Even if an angler were able to make such a long cast, seeing the take and successfully hooking a fish from that distance is extremely difficult.

A more realistic casting expectation for all fly anglers is the ability to cast fifty feet quickly and with minimal false casting. The sooner the fly is in the water and not in the air, the more chances you're going to have to catch the fish. False casting will often spook the fish, and then it won't matter how far you can cast . . . the fish is gone.

A quick, accurate, fifty-foot cast will cover most saltwater situations.

32

The water haul

IN MANY SITUATIONS, LONG (FIFTY-PLUS FEET), ACCURATE DOUBLE HAULS are required if you want to catch fish. But what happens when you're casting to fish in deep water? Or casting into the shore break as the currents from the waves are dragging your line back and forth? How about casting a 550- or 650-grain shooting head or sinking line from a tossing and pitching boat on the open ocean? This is not the place for artful double hauling. This is rock and roll fly fishing, and the name of the game here is to get the fly quickly into the water so you can catch fish.

When you're using a heavy sinking line, the water haul is usually the most practical cast. Here is how to do it:

1. Make your forward cast at a comfortable distance.
2. Once the cast is out in front of you, with the rod tip on the water, strip the line in until you get the sinking part of the shooting head at the tip of your rod.
3. Slowly lift up your rod tip and make a roll cast. This will lay the line out straight in front of you.
4. Now make a slow backcast and feel the line drag up off the water.
5. Let the sinking line fall out behind you on the water as if you were presenting a fly to a fish behind you.
6. Once the line is laid out behind you, make a forward cast and pull the line with your free hand with a downstroke toward your hip, then release the line.

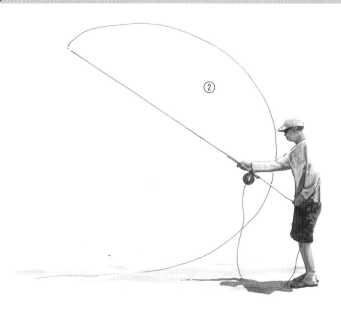

The resistance of the water (the haul) on both the forward cast and backcast will create enough friction and drag to project the fly line forward, acting as a double haul without any false casting.

The water haul is also a great way to master the double haul.

Flip cast

IF YOU LIKE TO SIGHT-CAST TO FISH CRUISING THE BEACH OR FLATS, IT'S CRITICAL TO LEARN the flip cast or "quick cast." This is a cast that may measure only a few feet, but it's good to know for those times when fish suddenly materialize at close range. Making a good flip cast, so you can quickly place the fly in the fish's hit zone, can make the difference between hooking your quarry or not.

Start by laying out thirty to fifty feet of line, then strip it in, leaving the last twenty-five feet of the fly line (and belly section) outside the rod tip. This will allow you to load the rod during the cast, thus minimizing false casting. Place the fly in the palm of your off hand (the hand not holding the rod) or between your thumb and index finger.

Hold the fly between your thumb and index finger.

When a fish swims within range—and remember, many fish will approach within twenty feet—make your back-cast while releasing the fly from your hand, then cast to the fish. If the fish is behind you, your backcast may actually be the cast you make to the fish. Don't make any false casts, if possible.

34

Casting into a crosswind

THROWING A FLY IN A CROSSWIND OR A FOLLOWING WIND OFF YOUR CASTING ARM'S shoulder is perhaps fly fishing's most troublesome cast. I have seen many casts blown and fish missed because of an angler's failure to properly execute this cast. No matter where you fish in the salt, you will, at some point, be tested by a crosswind or following wind.

When you're placed in this trying situation, the Belgian or helicopter cast is your most effective cast. This cast should be executed quickly, with a minimum of backcasts. When winds become erratic and disagreeable, as is their habit on salt water, this cast can be the great equalizer to a seemingly insoluble problem.

To do it, first make a high backcast; then, make your forward cast a high overhead cast (liken your casting arm to a helicopter's blade as you make the transition from side cast to forward overhead cast).

With practice, you can easily master this cast. Whether you are fishing on the flats, the beach, or the open ocean, it will give you confidence when you find yourself dealing with winds.

PART
4

Techniques

35

Blend into your environment

A stealthy approach starts with the correct clothes.

YOU'VE PROBABLY SEEN PICTURES OF A GUY WEARING A bright red shirt and yellow shorts, holding a good-size bonefish. This outfit might make for a pretty photo, and it may be okay for Mardi Gras, but it's terrible for fishing. When you're trying to be stealthy, a brightly colored fishing outfit will send fish darting for cover.

Blend into your environment. Match your clothes to your surroundings. If you are fishing the beach, wear neutral colors such as tan, light green, or even brown. For fishing the flats, a light blue shirt and stone-colored shorts or pants are your best choices. And don't overlook camouflage outfits when stalking spooky fish in shallow water. There are plenty of camouflage patterns on today's market that allow you to blend into the environment, giving you a decided advantage in fly fishing the marshes and backwaters.

36

The boat as a clock

IMAGINE A CLOCK LYING ON ITS BACK. ACCORDING TO MY FATHER, A WORLD WAR II veteran, the United States Army Air Force used it as a directional system to help gunners pick up the posi-

tions of attacking enemy fighter aircraft. Now imagine your boat as a flat clock, its numerals used by your guide to direct your attention to a fish's position and where to aim your cast. Think of the bow as twelve o'clock, starboard as three o'clock, the stern as six o'clock, and port as nine o'clock. Understanding this system will contribute to your success in taking more fish, making your fly fishing more productive and pleasurable.

My analogy may seem a bit farfetched, but as you progress as a saltwater fly angler, you will eventually hire a guide who will not only captain your boat but will also be a great source of information and suggestions. Almost all guides employ the clock system: When he says, "Tarpon at ten o'clock," you need to understand what he is saying and why, so you can act accordingly.

37

Learn how to clear your fly line

HOOKING A FISH ON FLY GEAR IS SOMETIMES THE EASIEST PART OF THE GAME; WHAT HAPPENS after the fish is hooked is probably more important. Nothing can demonstrate this more than clearing your fly line after a fish has been hooked. This is what I call the "hero to zero in three seconds."

Here is the scenario: You make a fifty-foot cast to a school of tuna, a tailing bonefish, or a string of tarpon. You begin stripping your fly back toward you, trying to snooker a fish into striking. A fish follows the fly to within a few feet of the boat, then strikes. You set the hook, and you're tight to the fish. The fish makes a lightning-fast run away from the boat. You look down and discover you've got a large pile of fly line at your feet. Now what?

First, transfer your thinking from the fish to the line—easier said than done. Let the fish run. He's hooked, and if you keep tension on him, he'll stay that way. Do not lift your rod tip; keep the rod angled at ninety degrees.

Do not hold the fly line. This will result in a broken tippet.

Now, focus on clearing the line at your feet while keeping a light grip on the line with your thumb and index finger. Allow line to run through your fingers until the line is tight to the reel. This may seem to take forever, but it will actually take only a few seconds.

If you notice a knot while clearing your line, do not attempt to undo it; instead, allow it to travel through the guides. In most cases the knot will not hinder the line-clearing process. You can deal with it later.

Once the fly line is on the reel, apply positive tension and begin fighting the fish.

Proper clearing of the line can make the difference between landing and losing a fish.

38

Coils in your fly line

COILS IN A FLY LINE ARE A BAD THING. THEY AFFECT YOUR casting; plus, they are more than likely to foul and hang up in a rod guide during a fight, often resulting in a lost fish, a broken tippet, or worse, a snapped rod tip. Regularly stretching your fly line can eliminate this problem.

Perhaps the simplest way to stretch a line is to strip out the length you'll need in a particular circumstance. Place the line beneath your foot, form a loop, and securely hold it about waist high. Then give the line a solid, steady pull, applying tension on the line between your hand and your foot. Repeat this process until the entire line has been stretched, and all the coils have been removed.

During the course of a day on the water, keep your line stretched by repeating this procedure every time you notice that coils are forming.

39

Don't take your eyes off the water

Focus!

ON MORE THAN ONE OCCASION, WHILE FISHING A SHALLOW flat for redfish or laying out a chum line for sharks, I have allowed my eyes to drift off the water for a split second, and in that brief period missed an opportunity to make a good fly presentation to the fish of a lifetime. Rushed, I made a sloppy cast and spooked my quarry.

When you're sight-casting, it's critical to keep your eyes riveted on the water, no matter how difficult it can be after hours spent squinty-eyed, looking for fish and finding none. Be visually disciplined! Be focused! For the minute you take your eyes off the water, that trophy fish will come finning into casting range.

If you are fly fishing at the beach, it's equally important to keep an eye on the surf. Waves may hit a lull, your focus drifts, and then a new set of waves sneaks up on you when you least expect it. You may not only lose your gear and end up soaking wet, but if you are precariously perched on some rocks, you could be swept into the water—a dangerous situation, to say the least.

How to hook fish that follow your fly all the way to the rod tip

IT'S VERY FRUSTRATING WHEN A GAMEFISH FOLLOWS YOUR fly practically to the rod tip, but refuses to strike. There is, however, an easy way to get a picky fish to take your offering. I call it "sweeping the fly."

When a fish has followed the fly to within a few feet of your rod tip (usually you'll have five to ten feet of line outside the tip), lower your rod tip and make a sweeping motion as if you were going to make a sidearm backcast. Don't pull the fly out of the water—just keep it moving. On the sweep, the fly will move smoothly through the water, doing a great impersonation of a fidgety baitfish attempting to escape a predator. This move enjoys a high percentage of success. The trick is to exercise control over your emotions and not to pull the fly from the fish's mouth if it strikes. The hook-set is always very close to you, so be prepared to let the fish run, which means managing the line as it shoots through the guides.

41

Fly fish from a kayak

THE KAYAK IS A STEALTHY AND effective vehicle to use for fly fishing, a means to access fishing areas where fish are normally easily spooked, such as flats, marshes, and kelp beds. In addition, a kayak is not only portable, but it requires a smaller investment than a flats skiff and is more environmentally friendly (no gasoline or motor oil required).

A properly equipped kayak can store a couple of fly rods, fly boxes, a Boga-Grip (for holding fish by the lip, for hook removal), and even a push pole.

Using a kayak, you can stand and sight-cast on shallow flats, or paddle offshore to the kelp beds. If you feel uncomfortable

The kayak is an affordable way to explore backcountry waters.

paddling with a double-bladed paddle, then a pedal kayak may be more to your taste and abilities. Yet another option is a kayak with a small, battery-operated trolling motor, which lets you cover more water and even work into the wind.

On a kayak, the fly line can be stripped right onto the deck without your having to worry about hanging up on boat cleats or other obstacles.

A sea anchor will help you stay in position if you're fishing structure or around kelp beds. On the flats, a small anchor can help keep you in one spot.

If you do opt for a kayak, consider using a longer fly rod, preferably a nine and a half-footer. A rod this long will help keep your line off the water on your backcast and enable you to make longer casts.

42

Stand-up paddleboard? Why not?

ONE OF THE HOTTEST NEW METHODS OF ANGLING FOR SALTWATER FISH ON THE FLY ROD IS from a stand-up paddleboard (SUP). Southern California fishermen have been fishing off their surfboards for years, but the recent SUP rage has created all sorts of venues for the more progressive saltwater fly fisher. Besides providing easier portability, the paddleboard gives you a better platform from which to spot, sneak up on, and cast to fish.

The SUP is an extremely versatile fishing platform, a craft you can launch anywhere, and all you need for transport is a cartop rack or a pickup truck. Much lighter than a kayak, the SUP is at home in shallow waters inaccessible by boat or in deepwater areas not frequented by the general public (simply toss it into a boat and take it where you want to go).

Outfit the SUP the same as you would a kayak, using a fishing box specifically designed for fly fishing, with a rod holder and places for your paddle, fly box, and other tackle. You can also build one to your own specifications.

If you use an SUP on a regular basis, you'll notice that your waistline will benefit. Paddling an SUP, whether kneeling or standing, is a great workout. Cancel that gym membership. Now you've got another excuse to go fishing . . . you're exercising!

As with kayak fishing, it takes some time to master the art of SUP fly fishing. You have to keep in mind, for example, that you will be pushed by the wind, so you need to be aware of your drift and compensate accordingly. Calm, glassy waters are best for the SUP, but offshore is not out of the question. In time, you'll really come to appreciate the benefits of an SUP.

The SUP allows for better sight casting than a sit-in kayak.

43

How to avoid cutting your fingers on the fly line: gaffer's tape

SALTWATER IS HARD ON FINGERS AND TENDS TO produce painful cuts, especially in your index finger, in just a few hours on the water. To counter this, buy gaffer's tape, available at any hardware store, and wrap your digits before you go fishing.

The tape has an adhesive that binds together after it is wrapped around your fingers and can be worn the entire day without replacement. Wrap your index, middle, and third fingers on your rod hand, as they take the brunt of stripping line. It's not a bad idea to protect all your fingers, for that matter.

Cut fingers can ruin your day. Protect them with gaffer's' tape. ▶

44

Know your birds

IN FISHING, THERE ARE MANY VISUAL INDICATIONS that fish are on the bite. One of the easiest and most reliable signs to identify is bird activity.

Some species of birds are better indicators than others, and you don't have to be an ornithologist to recognize the better ones; a basic knowledge of the bird kingdom will do. Let's look at the birds and how they rate in priority and importance to successful fish finding.

The best fish-locating birds of all, terns work diligently in searching for baitfish. If you spot them picking and fluttering in an area, that's a good sign that gamefish are working baitfish. Terns often fly ahead of a school of gamefish, picking up baitfish that have been pushed to the surface.

Keep an eye on bird activity. ▶

Pelicans: The big daddies of the seabird world. Though not as agile and swift as terns, pelicans will tell you where the main bodies of baitfish and gamefish are. Pelicans will dive with abandon into the center of a bait ball, filling their mouths with as many baitfish as possible. By habit, pelicans will not allow a bait ball to relocate too far from them. So if you spot a pelican positioned on the water, you can be sure that bait and gamefish are in the area.

Gulls are the scavengers of the sea. Seagulls are opportunistic feeders that will feed on anything, from popcorn to anchovies. Their presence is a good sign that baitfish are about, but they can hoodwink even the best fisherman by diving on anything they can eat, including everything from plastic bottle caps to sardines. Keep that in mind when turning to gulls to find fish.

45

Line management

Proper line management is essential for successful fishing.

ONE SURE WAY TO LOSE A FISH is through poor line management. The line, often coiled at the angler's feet during a hookup, will fly uncontrollably off the deck and through the guides as the fish makes its run for safety. This is the moment when line management is essential. If the fly line is brought tight once the fish has begun its run, the battle is half won. However, if loose fly line jumps off the deck and wraps around the angler's shoe, leg, boat bag, or whatever happens to be lying loose on the deck, it is quite possible that the line will come tight and the leader will break, resulting in a lost fish.

Losing fish in this manner happens to even the best saltwater fly anglers. The secret is to fish with a stripping basket or bucket. Not only will a stripping basket keep your fly line neatly coiled off the boat's deck, away from any obstructions; it will also keep it clean of sand, grit, mud, and grime.

How to retrieve a saltwater fly

Baitfish

IF YOU ARE USING A FLY THAT IMITATES THE MOVEMENTS OF A BAITFISH, TRY TO OBSERVE the behavior patterns of the actual baitfish. How fast are they swimming? Are they swimming in schools or small groups when being chased by gamefish? Are they stunned by gamefish before being eaten as they are sinking or, in fishing lingo, "on the fall"? Most injured baitfish swim in frenzied motions, so quick, short retrieves are generally the best. In conditions where the baitfish are lazily swimming about, try slower, longer strips to get your adversaries' attention.

Baitfish always swim into the current, so when fishing from a drifting boat, cast your fly upcurrent, then let it sink and drift in the current. At the end of the drift, as the fly swings behind the boat, allow it to gyrate, lifelike, in the current for a few seconds before beginning stripping. This technique often results in a strike, so hang on!

Crabs or Shrimp

If you're attempting to imitate a crab or shrimp, make short, small strips so the fly looks like it's scurrying along. This move usually gets a fish's attention. If you spot a gamefish eyeing the fly and beginning to approach it, stop stripping and allow the fly to sit motionless. Wait a few seconds, move it again in short spurts, and get ready!

Think like a baitfish.

The best rod angle for fighting fish on the flats or in shallow water

Use a low rod angle for maximum pressure when fighting fish in shallow water.

IN TROUT FISHING, WE ARE TAUGHT TO keep the rod high while fighting a fish. This accomplishes two things: First, it protects the light tippet, and second, it keeps the fish's head up, preventing it from moving into the current or deeper water. In saltwater fly fishing, however, we are using heavy, strong tippets that are virtually impossible to break, and enable you to exert maximum pressure when fighting a fish. To do this, employ a low rod angle and use the rod's butt section to do the fighting for you. When you're hooked up to a saltwater fish in shallow water, the higher the rod angle, the less pressure you put on the fish. Lowering the rod's angle will allow you to use the fly rod's butt section, allowing for more pressure on the fish.

48

Securing your fly to the stripping guide

MANY FLY FISHERMEN PAY LITTLE OR NO ATTENTION TO SECURING THE FLY TO THE ROD, A simple procedure that you should do automatically. When your fly is always secured in the same place, with no slack line, you can get to it quickly, without thinking, in case you have to make a split-second cast. This can prove the difference between a fish caught and a cast wasted.

Traditional hook keepers at the butt end of the fly rod, right above the handle, work well for securing your hook between casts or while the rod is in a holder. However, I find that if you pass the line around the reel seat and secure your fly to the first, second, or third stripping guide, you have a few more feet of fly line out of the rod tip, making it much easier to make a quick cast without having to strip any line off the fly reel. Remember, saltwater fly fishing can be a quick-fire, shoot-from-the-hip game; having a few extra feet of fly line extending outside the tip of your fly rod may mean the difference between success or failure.

One word of caution: Don't put the hook directly inside the guide. Instead, use the rod guide's leg bracing to hold the hook—a hook positioned inside a guide may damage the fragile ceramic ring.

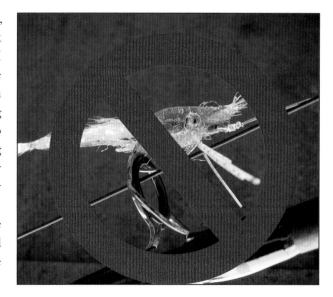

49

The short stroke

IF YOU HAVE SPENT ANY TIME FISHING ON CHARTER BOATS, YOU HAVE OBSERVED THAT the best anglers always bring their fish to gaff with as little fanfare as possible. These guys move fluidly, keeping constant pressure on the fish as it takes them around the boat, all with the intention of bringing in that fish quickly. You may also have noticed that they dig the rod tip deep in the water as they reel in line, each dig followed by a short lift of the rod tip, pulling the fish up from the depths. This technique is called the "short stroke," and fly fishermen can use it as well. There are four key elements to the technique.

1. Keep your shoulders square to the fish at all times. If your shoulders are not square, you lose leverage when lifting the fish from the depths.
2. Keep the rod tip pointed down at the fish, a move that will prevent you from bringing your rod up too high. Any rod angle higher than ninety degrees is of little help when fighting a bluewater gamefish with a fly rod. The fly rod is designed to fight fish from the butt end. Raising it above ninety degrees shifts the fighting energy from the butt to the weaker midsection and tip section, and that should never happen.
3. When you're bringing up a fish from deep water and the fish takes a break, put on the heat. Never let the fish rest. Always try to keep it moving up toward the surface. Break the fish as soon as you can.
4. Finally, when bringing a fish out of deep water, make short pumps of the rod while retrieving line as the rod tip drops.

Always apply maximum pressure when short-stroking fish.

Shuffle your feet while walking the flats or beach

THERE IS NOTHING MORE EXCRUCIATING THAN BEING STUNG BY A RAY WHILE YOU ARE walking the flats or beach. These injuries are not only painful, but if not treated quickly and properly, they can turn into serious health problems.

Even if you are wearing neoprene wading booties or flats boots, you are not totally protected from having a ray's barbed spike penetrate your foot or ankle. I've had that filth-encrusted spike poke through my boot and puncture my foot right to the bone! The sting was bad enough, but the painful throbbing that followed had me on the verge of tears.

The ray's stinger is sharp and pointed, and loaded with potentially infectious bacteria. Rays live on the shallow flats and surf zones, burying themselves in the sand for protection and camouflage, and if startled or stepped on, they swing their spiked tails in defense.

If you are fly fishing in the surf or the flats, shuffle your feet, pushing sand as you walk cautiously along the sandy bottom. If you have to pick up your feet, do it slowly and look down before placing them back on the sand. Shuffling also sends out warning signals to rays. They can feel the vibrations of your feet shuffling through the water and will swim away. Of course, you don't want to spook your prey with the same movements, so shuffle slowly and cautiously.

Beware the barbed tail!

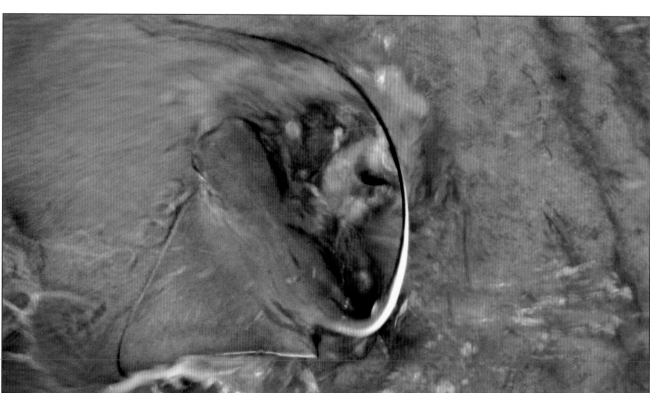

51

Adding depth to a sinking fly—the hit zone

WHEN FISHING IN DEEP WATER FOR SPECIES SUCH AS STRIPERS, TUNA, BONITO, YELLOWTAIL, or amberjacks, it is critical to get your fly to the correct depth in the water column. The hit zone can be just a few feet below the surface or as deep as thirty feet. A sinking line or shooting head is the accepted way of getting the fly into the zone, but there are other ways of adding more depth.

From a Drifting Boat

Position yourself in the bow or stern and cast upcurrent, or in the direction the boat is drifting. As the boat drifts, the fly will sink deeper. When the line is directly in front of you and comes taut, begin stripping in the fly.

From an Anchored Boat

The upcurrent cast works just as well from an anchored boat. This method has an advantage over the drifting boat in that the fly will sink deeper because the boat is not moving. This approach is especially effective if you're fishing around deepwater rocks, pilings, and offshore oil rigs.

From the Shore or Jetty

Thinking of swinging a fly for salmon or steelhead? The previously mentioned techniques are just as effective in sinking your fly from the beach or jetty. Determine the direction of the current or rip. Cast the fly up into the current and allow the fly and line to swing past you until the line tightens; now, begin your retrieve. Remember that many strikes occur as your fly is sinking or on the swing, so be alert for subtle and out-of-the-ordinary movements of your line.

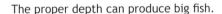

The proper depth can produce big fish.

52

Bow to a tarpon

Treat the tarpon like a king—BOW!

THE SIGHT OF A TARPON JUMPING AND TWISTING and gyrating in the air, in an attempt to dislodge a fly from its mouth, is an absolutely jaw-dropping experience. Few fish rival the strength and acrobatics that this great gamefish brings to saltwater fly fishing.

Once hooked, a tarpon's first reaction is to run for cover, then make numerous rod-jolting jumps as it attempts to rid its mouth of the annoying hook. Since tarpon are hooked at relatively close range, it's important that the angler point his fly rod directly at the fish the moment it makes its initial leap. This move, called "bowing," puts slack in the line, creating a shock absorber for the tippet. If the angler is unprepared and fails to bow, the tarpon will hightail it away from the boat, causing extreme pressure on the tippet, which often results in a broken leader and a lost fish.

To avoid this problem, the angler must anticipate when the tarpon will jump—not an easy task but one a successful tarpon angler must master. Another way to anticipate the jump is to listen to the sound of the reel's drag during the fish's run; when the sound reaches an ear-torturing howl, be ready, as the jump is about to happen.

53

How to tip and roll a fish

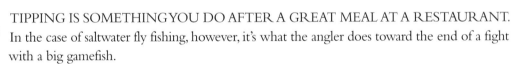

TIPPING IS SOMETHING YOU DO AFTER A GREAT MEAL AT A RESTAURANT. In the case of saltwater fly fishing, however, it's what the angler does toward the end of a fight with a big gamefish.

When a large gamefish makes a run directly in front of the angler and there is no good angle to let him apply pressure to move the fish's head and make him change direction, smart anglers do something called "tipping the fish." To do this, the angler tips his fly rod upside down, lowers the tip into the water, and applies pressure from under the surface. This pressure will in most cases stop the fish and roll him over.

Once the fish has rolled over, the angler can retrieve line while moving close to the fish (on foot or in a boat). Oftentimes the fish will concede for a short period, which will give the angler time to regain some line.

The "tip and roll" is always performed close to the end of a fight. It is a great way to get a fish to the boat quickly for a safe release.

The two-handed strip

SOME SALTWATER FISH REACT TO A FLY THAT IS STRIPPED AS FAST AS POSSIBLE. TUNA, barracudas, roosterfish, amberjacks, and yellowtail are good examples. These guys prefer a fly that moves like a racing car. If the fly isn't imitating a fleeting baitfish, and if it suddenly stops or even pauses, these fish will turn and swim away.

The two-handed strip is the perfect retrieve for these situations. This retrieve enables the fly to be stripped through the water without breaks or pauses, as happens with the conventional one-handed strip. The drawback to using this retrieve is that you have to place the rod under your arm, which makes it almost impossible to lift the rod tip for a strike. Instead, you have to use a strip-strike.

For a successful two-handed strip, do the following:

1. After the cast, place the rod under one of your arms.
2. Point the rod tip down, keeping the tip in the water at all times.
3. Begin the strip by pulling the fly line with your hand at the first stripping guide.
4. Repeat this with the other hand.
5. There should be a continual motion, changing hands with each strip. Vary the speed of the fly as you strip it through the water.
6. Strip the fly all the way to the boat and repeat; if you feel a hit, give your line a solid strip-strike.

This is a great technique for blue water as well as nearshore fly fishing.

Use a two-handed strip to imitate fast-moving bait.

55

Warm-up stretch

YOU MAY NOT CONSIDER SALTWATER FLY FISHING A PHYSICAL SPORT, BUT BE ADVISED THAT it's more physically demanding than fighting a rainbow or brown trout on the Henry's Fork. Saltwater gamefish are broad-shouldered fish that can have you crying "uncle" if you are out of shape. Just ask the guy who has spent a day on the ocean battling a yellowfin tuna on a twelve-weight fly rod, or the guy who has spent an afternoon walking five miles in ankle-deep beach sand searching for the elusive roosterfish.

Just as athletes warm up before practice and competition, it can really make a difference if you stretch your arms, legs, and back before making your first cast. This rule is especially important to the middle-aged fly fisherman whose only physical activity is changing TV channels. Be smart . . . warm up!

The long and sandy stroll . . .

PART 5

The Flies

Organize your fly box

AN ORGANIZED FLY BOX NOT ONLY reflects its owner's character, but also simplifies the process of selecting flies. The well-organized box will allow you to select the correct fly quickly in the heat of the moment, such as during a striper feeding frenzy, thus giving you more time casting and less time rummaging through piles of mixed feathers.

When stocking your fly box for bluewater fishing, make sure to include baitfish patterns, crab and shrimp patterns, and poppers. Most saltwater fish feed on some types of baitfish, so a selection of flies in various colors and sizes will be an asset when trying to match the baitfish in the place you are fishing. Divide your box into two sections. Place the bigger flies on one side of the box, the smaller crab and shrimp patterns on the other side. Coordinate and organize all flies according to sizes and colors.

Choosing the correct baitfish fly

PICKING THE CORRECT FLIES IS ONE OF THE KEYS TO CATCHING FISH. THIS CAN BE A DAUNTING task for the beginning angler, as most tackle shop fly bins are filled with huge numbers of flies in all shapes, sizes, and colors. Here are some basic guidelines.

Baitfish Patterns

I believe that a sparsely dressed baitfish pattern is preferable to a bulked-up, flashy fly because it looks more natural. I've also found that gamefish are far less selective when presented with a sparsely dressed fly. The fly is only a hint of what the fish is feeding on, and it often elicits a reflexive striking action. When gamefish do strike, they usually zero in on the fly's oversized eye, which closely resembles the large eyes of baitfish such as sardines, pilchards, and anchovies. For them, focusing on that eye results in fewer lost meals.

Color

Natural colors work best. Olive greens, browns, tans, and whites are all great color combos for baitfish patterns. Also, carry a selection of blue-and-white, red-and-white, and chartreuse-and-white flies, for those times when a bit more flash is called for.

Size

Fly size depends on what type of fish you're pursuing. In most saltwater fly-fishing situations, you'll need baitfish patterns that range from a small anchovy pattern in size 6 to a large sardine or pilchard pattern in size 2/0. Remember, it's all about matching the size of the baitfish that fish are feeding on.

Sometimes less is more.

58

Foolproof weed guard

THE HEAVY COVER FOUND IN MANgroves, estuaries, sloughs, and flats always poses problems for fly fishermen, as their flies constantly snag on eelgrass, turtle grass, and other vegetation. The key to catching fish in these areas is keeping your fly free of the salad and swimming naturally.

To make a foolproof weed guard, start with a piece of heavy, hard mono (forty- to sixty-pound) and make a U shape directly behind the eye of the hook. The piece should be long enough to touch the point of the hook when it is bent back. Tie the mono onto the shank, making certain that the U shape is at a ninety-degree angle from the top of the hook (pointing straight down). The mono will allow the fly to roll over the nasty stuff that flies without weed guards continually snag.

How to strip a Clouser Minnow

THE CLOUSER MINNOW IS ONE OF THE GREATEST FLIES EVER invented for the saltwater fly angler. Bob Clouser initially created this fly to target smallmouth bass on the Susquehanna River in Pennsylvania. Since then it has been used to catch everything from surf perch to tarpon. The Clouser Minnow is, quite simply, a must-have fly in everyone's saltwater fly box.

All saltwater gamefish are predators to some degree. Bonefish root around the bottom looking for shrimp and crabs. Bonito pursue wandering mackerel, while tuna chase down and buzz-saw through schools of bait. All of them pick off injured and helpless baitfish as they fall away from the main school.

Because of its unique look, the Clouser Minnow is able to imitate a baitfish in any of these situations. For rooting fish, it can be stripped like a fleeing crab with short jerks of the line, making it hop and skitter across the bottom. Cast into a feeding frenzy of tuna, it's deadly when stripped quickly, allowed to fall for a few seconds, then stripped again, thus imitating a hurt or scared baitfish.

When stripping a Clouser, keep the rod tip on the water at all times. This will ensure a positive hook-set when the fly is taken by a gamefish.

60

Night fishing for snook: Best fly

FLY FISHING AFTER DARK IS SOMETHING ALL FLY FISHERS should experience—it's a real trip! The sounds, smells, and feel are wonderfully exciting and exhilarating. Add some snook to this mix and you have the makings of a memorable evening.

Snook are night feeders, and are particularly aggressive when hiding in the shadows of illuminated piers, dock pilings, or mangrove-covered banks. When a baitfish swims into the well-lit area, it will become disoriented by the lights. This is when the snook will pounce, grab its meal, then quickly swim back to the darker waters, where it devours its prey.

Snook can be caught in these situations, but only if presented the proper fly. For my money, that fly would have to be a Black Marabou Toad, which has a long, flowing, rabbit fur tail. Cast it into the dark near a lighted pier, then retrieve it into the lighted area with quick, erratic strips. This motion, which resembles the darting and jumping of a confused baitfish, drives snook absolutely crazy.

PART
6

Catching Fish

61

Barbed or barbless?

MANY FLY ANGLERS ARE ADVOCATES OF CATCH-AND-RELEASE angling. To this end, a barbless hook is easier to remove from a fish's mouth, thus enabling the angler to release it quickly.

A side benefit of the barbless hook is that it is far more effective at penetrating the fish's mouth than the traditional barbed hook. This is especially true with species that have super hard mouths, such as tarpon.

Unlike barbed hooks, barbless hooks are also more easily ex-tracted from the backs of heads, ears, and other parts of the human anatomy.

◀ Give the fish a break; de-barb your hook!

62

Bite tippet for barracudas

WHEN FLY FISHING THE FLATS FOR BONEFISH, YOU'LL OFTEN SPOT BARRACUDAS SWIMMING into casting range. "Berries" should be cast to! But because a steel bite tippet is not a piece of the standard leader for bonefish, the chances of hooking and successfully bringing in the barracuda are slim, as their razor-sharp teeth will make fast work of any mono or fluorocarbon tippet. Here's a quick fix:

1. Take a six-inch piece of thirty-pound, single-strand, stainless steel wire, then make a very tight loop on one end with a Haywire Twist. Tie another Haywire Twist to the fly, leaving a loop in the fly end of the leader.
2. When fishing, keep this pre-rigged leader somewhere within reach (on your belt, or in a chest pack).
3. Once you spot a barracuda, take the prerigged leader with fly and slip it onto the hook of the fly you're using for bonefish.
4. Twist the stainless steel loop onto the bend of the bonefish fly hook, leaving just enough play in the loop so the barracuda fly and leader move freely but cannot detach while casting.

This method can save the day when the bonefish are tough to catch but the barracudas are willing to eat.

63

How to avoid bloody knuckles

AT SOME POINT IN YOUR SALTWATER FLY-fishing career, you're going to get bloody knuckles from your reel's handle. This will happen when a big gamefish boils away at top speed, causing the handle to spin violently and bash your knuckles in the process. And while some anglers may consider bloody knuckles to be a badge of honor, most of us consider it a painful reminder not to hold onto the reel handle while fighting a fish. So what do we do with the reel hand when we are engaged in a tough fish fight?

First, never, under any circumstances, wrap your fingers around the reel handle that spins as the fish runs; if your fingers happen to be in the way, the handle will pummel your knuckles.

Whatever you do, don't grab that handle!

A better option is to hold the reel handle between your thumb, index finger, and middle finger, so when the fish makes its run you can let go of the handle and allow the spool to spin freely.

64

The bonefish challenge

ONE OF THE MOST SOUGHT-AFTER SALTWATER GAMEFISH, the bonefish is elusive, spooky, and fast, a real challenge to the fly fisherman. Ranging in size from two to five pounds in the Caribbean, to eight to ten pounds in Florida and Hawaii, it lives in some of the most beautiful tropical settings in the world.

To find bonefish, look for areas where the fish are mudding or tailing in the crystal-clear shallow water of sand flats or coral reefs. Locating the fish, however, doesn't automatically mean hookups, as bonefish are always on the move, constantly changing directions, darting to all points of the compass.

For tackle, a six- to nine-weight rod matched with a large-arbor reel packed with 150 yards of backing and a floating line will work best in most situations. Use a ten- to twelve-foot leader, and practice casting with it before you actually go out on the water, as accurate presentations are critical.

Any size bonefish is a trophy. ▶

Striped bass

BORN AND RAISED ON THE WEST COAST, I HAVE HAD THE GOOD FORTUNE AND THE opportunity to fish striped bass on the Sacramento Delta. These expansive brackish-water wetlands, that resemble the Louisiana marshes, stretch from Sacramento west to San Francisco Bay and boast some of the best striper bass fly fishing in the nation. Differing from the East Coast striper experience where this prime game fish is fished from the shoreline or from a boat in open water, this California brethren is fished in brackish or fresh water in the late fall or early winter months. He's a great fly-rod fish, easily accessible from shore, boat, or kayak in the Sac's abundant and fertile waters.

The tackle is very similar to that used on the Eastern seaboard: seven- or nine-weight rods, slow-sinking, 200- or 300-grain sinking lines, and short leaders (six to seven feet).

The key to success on this fishery is finding the bait. There are huge populations of baitfish in the Sac Delta, and the stripers will begin shadowing bait fish into the Delta beginning in early fall and continuing through the early spring.

Be alert for any sign of birds, terns, or seagulls "pecking" the water, a good indication that stripers are pushing small bait fish just below the water's surface, against banks, sheltered coves, or dock pilings.

Once you have pinpointed surface disturbances, make a cast into the center of the commotion, allow your fly to sink, then quickly apply very aggressive, erratic strips that will give your fly the appearance of an injured baitfish. Once your line comes tight, hang on and prepare yourself for a very strong, fulfilling, and rewarding fight.

East-Coast Stripers

Though separated by 3,000 miles, the Eastern-Seaboard striper resembles his West Coast cousin in feistiness and willingness to hit a variety of flies including the Clouser Minnow and Lefty's Deceivers, two streamers flies favored off the Cape Cod Coast, where the Striper is found in the early fall during his migration south.

Not unlike the West Coaster, he is found in estuaries, flats, jetties, along the surf-line and offshore, and can be fished wading, or drifting in boat or skiff; One sure way of finding this primo-game fish in open water is to follow movement of gulls and terns circling and diving into balls of bait fish. This is the signal to break out the nine- to eleven-weight rod, a reel loaded with either a sinking-shooting head in 250 or 300 grams. Lengthy casts are not required, but accuracy is of the essence. Make your cast ahead of the fish, allow your fly to sink, then, with your rod tip pointed at the fish, retrieve your line in well-spaced strips. One caution: Do not lift your rod tip on the strike; with the rod tip still pointed in the fish's direction, pull straight back to set the hook, and hang on!

While we are at it, the Bluefish—a toothy critter not found on the West Coast—is also deserving of consideration when affording space to the striper. Although at times a very elusive fish, when a school is found working a school of baitfish, you will find this guy more than willing to wrap his choppers around streamer and popper patterns; snookering one on the water's surface is an awesome fly-fishing experience. Because of the fish's razor-sharp incisors, make certain that you employ not only a good nine-weight rod but also, for good-measure, a light, single-strand wire leader. It's true that wire can spook this fish, but this fish is able to chew through mono with the precision of a cross-cut saw ripping through a two-by-four.

Chumming for makos

FOUND ON BOTH THE ATLANTIC AND Pacific coasts, the mako shark is one of saltwater fly fishing's outstanding yet unappreciated gamefish. Hook one in the eighty- to 150-pound range, and you'll find yourself in a battle that will test all of your fish-fighting skills.

First things first. You're going to need a boat to get into this game. Ideally, you want a boat that's over eighteen feet, one that can handle fairly choppy seas. Most center consoles will do; however, a skiff with a beam of eight feet or wider and a not-too-deep V-hull will settle in the water better and reduce pitch and roll, making for a much more stable casting platform.

A chum line is the most effective way of attracting makos to within sight-casting distance of your boat. Chumming attracts larger makos, and will place you in the position of being able to pick and choose which fish you cast to.

To make a chum bag, first go to your local dock or fish market and try to find boats giving away belly sections or fresh carcasses of tuna, bluefish, or bonito. (Store-bought chum will suffice, if you can't find fresh.) Fill a burlap sack or store-bought chum bag, place it in a milk crate or five-gallon bucket and allow it to hang over the side. Once that chum slick begins to spread, it won't take long before any sharks in the area start to show up. One piece of advice: Less is more when chumming. You don't need much—no matter how small the slick, a shark can smell it from miles away.

Be patient when chumming. I will generally wait at least an hour and a half before moving to another spot. Once makos do find your slick and get into it, however, you can usually count on them sticking around for most of the fishing day. Drifting allows you to cover more water, and in the process attract more makos to your boat.

Use a stick to smash the carcasses and spread the fishy goodness.

California corbina from the beach

PERHAPS ONE OF THE MOST SKITTISH OF ALL THE WEST COAST GAMEFISH, THE CALIFORNIA corbina is a ghostly apparition that glides through the shallow waters of flats and estuaries, or off beaches, in the late spring and throughout the summer. This fish is extremely wary, and it's rare to find him within casting range.

There is, however, one well-founded method of approaching corbina without spooking them. During early morning hours, when the light is softer and before the masses have hit the beach, look for corbina in the shallow waters of the tidal flats. This is a time of day when the fish feels more secure cruising into the shallow water to feed on mole crabs, bean clams, and small baitfish inside the surf line.

Before casting your first fly of the morning, stand back and spend a few minutes scanning the surf's whitewater, sandbars, and tidal flats, looking for the telltale signs that spell corbina. In particular, look for the backs of corbina as they work these areas, searching for food.

Once you have located some corbina, quietly move yourself to a point that gives you sight advantage on the shoreline, making certain that you don't step into the water. Corbina are sensitive to even the slightest noise in the surf zone, so wading into the surf can send them scurrying into deeper water. Cast from the beach, perhaps even from dry sand.

When making your casts, keep your body and rod in low profile so as not to alarm the fish; too much exposed body or an overextended arm movement when casting will leave you staring into empty tidewater. Everything connected with corbina fishing demands stealth. If they are not disturbed and are focused on crab beds, corbina will often move so close that you can practically touch them with your rod tip.

Cast at least twenty feet in front of the fish, making sure that the fly doesn't hit the water too hard. Let it sink, then wait. Don't move the fly! If the corbina is interested, it will hit your offering without hesitation. Once hooked, it will scurry toward the safety of the surf zone at speeds that rival those of the bonefish and permit, so hang on!

A simple mole crab pattern will attract feeding corbina on the flats.

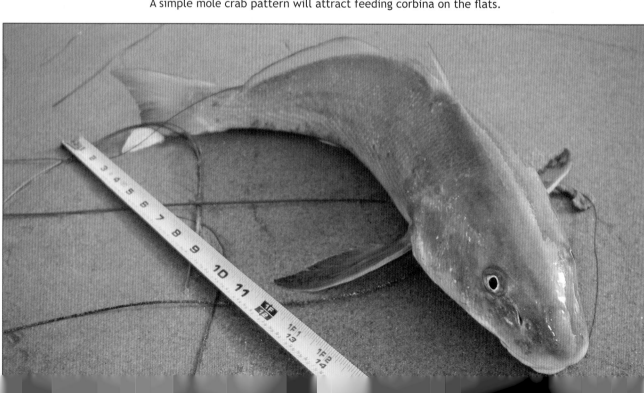

How to find fish in blue water

FINDING FISH IN BLUE WATER MAY SEEM TO BE A DAUNTING TASK. THE OCEAN IS HUGE, AND big gamefish such as tuna, dorado, sharks, and marlin can cover great distances in a matter of hours. But with good eyes and a little common sense, you can indeed find these fish in open blue water.

The first clue to locating fish in open blue water is bird activity: working terns, gulls, and pelicans. Locate the circling and diving birds, and you'll find fish nearby. If you see birds floating on the water, you should fish the area anyway, as a raft of birds may indicate that baitfish and gamefish are in the area, just not actively feeding at that moment.

Once the birds and bait are located, look for gamefish agitating the water's surface in pursuit of baitfish. The gamefish will push the baitfish up from the depths, forcing the prey to explode out of the water, an activity easily spotted at long distances. When this happens, the birds will also be going crazy, diving into the melee to pick off baitfish at the surface.

If you don't see any birds, look for structure such as floating kelp paddies or weed lines. Baitfish like to congregate underneath these structures for shelter, and where there are baitfish . . . there are gamefish! Pull up next to these floating structures and cast a fly out along the edge. Make a few strips and see if anyone is home. Sometimes you can even see the fish stacked up underneath the structure.

You may find other locals searching the kelp for fish.

69

How to fly-fish pier pilings

Pilings provide perfect cover for an ambush.

PIER PILINGS ATTRACT A VARIETY OF SALTwater gamefish, including snook, spotted bay bass, and croakers, as they provide perfect cover from which these predators can ambush baitfish attracted by all the currents and eddies. Fishing pilings requires some specialized tactics, however.

The first order of business is to determine which side of the piling is the leeward side (the side sheltered from the blowing wind). Position yourself upwind from the leeward side, preferably during high and low tides, so that you are casting down toward the pilings, allowing the current to take your fly as close as possible to the structure. Drift the fly through the pilings if possible. You may hang up and lose a few flies to the pilings at first, but once you get the hang of it, you'll catch more fish if you can get your flies right into the middle of the structure.

Once the fly is in the zone, make two or three strips, then allow it to drift back into the pilings. Fish will often strike the fly as it dead-drifts back toward the structure. If your first four or five casts produce zilch, move to the next piling. Once you've caught a fish, continue to fish that piling until the action slows or stops, then move on.

70

How to catch redfish

CATCHING A REDFISH ON THE FLY IS ONE OF SALTWATER FLY FISHING'S GREATEST EXPERIENCES. Not only are redfish willing to take a variety of flies and poppers, they also have a tendency to feed in very shallow water, making them the perfect saltwater fish for sight-casting. There is something special about casting to a redfish tailing along a grassy marsh bank, then watching the fly disappear into its mouth and the line come tight.

The redfish game is simple. All you need is a nine-foot, seven- or eight-weight rod matched with a floating line and a fly reel that can carry 150 yards of backing. Use a standard nine-foot leader with a fifteen- to twenty-pound test leader. If you're fishing for tailing reds, a crab pattern or spoon fly will do the job. A good bet when surface fishing along mangroves or grassy banks is a popper that creates surface noise and a highly visible wake.

In your search for areas where redfish are feeding, give special attention to oyster beds, mangrove shorelines, and shallow flats, where more often than not you'll spot redfish rooting around and kicking up bottom mud in their search for crustaceans and other food. When redfish are focused on feeding, it's possible to move in very close to them, making long casts unnecessary.

Once you've spotted the fish, cast your fly close to its head, make a one-handed steady strip of your line, and get ready for a strike.

Redfish weigh from four to forty pounds, but all feed the same way.

71

Taking the leopard shark

FROM EARLY SPRING THROUGH MIDSUMMER, LEOPARD SHARKS can be observed traveling in large schools along Southern California's beaches. The leopard, or "leo," is a fairly docile critter, spending its time feeding on crabs and baitfish in the shallow estuaries and bays. It's one of the strongest fighting species you can catch while fishing from the beach. It's also one of the largest, with some fish weighing fifty pounds and more.

The preferred fly tackle for the leopard is an eight-weight rod matched with a reel holding a 200-grain shooting head, and a five-foot, twenty- to twenty-five-pound monofilament leader, topped off with a Crease Fly.

When stripped and paused, the Crease Fly will suspend just off the bottom, making it a tempting target for any leopards in the area. Once a leopard decides to strike, it will do so without hesitation, making for an exciting hookup and fight. Be cautioned that what may appear to be a good strike may be only a reaction strike, so false hooking is not uncommon.

A leopard shark will run you up and down the beach for forty minutes. ▶

Bonito and False Alabacore (Little Tunny)

BONITO AND FALSE ALBACORE ARE FAVORITES WITH SALTWATER FLY FISHERMEN. WHAT bonito and false "albies" lack in size (a 12-pound fish is considered a trophy), these speedsters more than make up for by providing the fly angler fast-action, knuckle-bruising runs, whether fishing offshore in a kayak, in a skiff plying the bay and inlet waters, or fishing off the jetties.

The offshore bonito bite in spring can deliver some of the largest fish of the season.

Fly anglers can look forward to year-round action on bonito on bays and near shore waters. The West Coast has two runs of bonito each year, one in the spring and another in the fall, the spring-run generally producing schools of larger fish that tend to prowl in schools searching for anchovies and sardines. Though smaller than their spring-run relations, the fall-run fish provide fly fishermen plenty of action, especially in the bays and off the jetties.

False albacore are a wonderful fly rod fish and have, over the past several years, become a highly sought after game fish for the saltwater fly-rodder. Beginning in September and peaking in November, these "speeding bullets" can be caught from New England to the Florida Keys. The "albies" feed the same as bonito, cruising in schools and looking for schools of anchovies to feast on. Fly fishing for "little tunny," as they are called, is some of the most exciting fly fishing found on either coast.

A seven- to nine-weight rod, matched with a solid, large arbor reel that can store a 250-grain shooting head and 150 yards of backing, will cover any situation, offshore, bay, inlet, or jetty.

A good selection of baitfish patterns should include the "Clouser Minnow," "Lefty's Deceiver," and "poppers" in sizes six to 1/0. I have known fly fishermen who have taken the bonito on weighted "Woolly Buggers," a fly normally associated with freshwater fishing. When fly fishing never forget the adage, "Necessity is the mother of invention."

Both bonito and false albacore are often very selective in what they take; therefore, a smaller, more scantily-dressed fly can often produce more fish than does the larger, heavily-dressed fly. Toting a few smaller, scantily-dressed flies is a good idea.

When using a popper, especially when fishing from jetties or around breakwater rocks, I like to use a popper as a "splash-attractor" with the fly, usually a "deceiver," as a "trailer."

Poppers for calico bass

IF YOU HAVE EVER FISHED FOR largemouth bass, you know how exciting it is to watch a hungry bass explode on a properly placed popper cast along a weed line. Well, advance your excitement meter about one hundred clicks, and you have popper fishing for West Coast calico bass. These saltwater cousins of the largemouth bass live in the dense kelp forests along the Southern California coast, lurking in pockets and ambushing prey at every opportunity. They feed in small packs, and when one is hooked, four or five other calicos usually follow their kin to the boat.

These fish readily take to poppers plopped into a kelp paddy's pockets. There are other methods of catching these gamefish, but nothing matches the adrenaline rush of watching your brightly colored bucktail popper disappear into a swirl of salt water, then having this hard-fighting fish on the end of your fly line. It's something every fly fisher should experience.

This saltwater equivalent of a largemouth bass uses similar ambush techniques in the kelp.

During their March-through-June spawning period, calicos surface and congregate in large schools along the coastal kelp beds, a prime time to grab the fly rod and, using a kayak, stand-up paddleboard (SUP), or small skiff, venture offshore into the far reaches of the paddies and cast large poppers into the breaks in the kelp. Sometimes the strike is so violent that the calico, while trying to engulf the lure, will knock the popper completely out of the water. Once hooked, he will usually head deep into the kelp forest, winding your line around the stalks as he descends.

Keep your eyes peeled for gulls hovering over the kelp beds, a sure sign that something is about to happen. When the birds begin descending to the water in ever-tightening circles, get a move on it, as a feeding frenzy is about to begin.

A fast-action, nine-foot, nine- or ten-weight rod will work well for this fly fishing. Use an intermediate fly line and a straight, five- to six-foot length of fifteen- to twenty-pound monofilament leader. As for flies, the bigger and noisier, the better.

How to safely release a shark

SHARKS ARE WONDERFUL FLY ROD GAMEFISH THAT READILY TAKE flies and always provide outstanding sight-casting opportunities, be they on the flats or in the blue water.

Once you have hooked, played, and brought the shark to the boat, the biggest challenge is releasing it, no easy task in light of the fish's size and unpredictable nature. Make a wrong move and it can prove disastrous.

The safest method of releasing a shark is through the use of a long-handled release stick, an instrument with an open-ended steel attachment on its business end.

Once a shark is brought to the boat, place this release tool in the fish's mouth, keeping tension on the line with the leader hand. Slide the stick into the hook gap and, applying light pressure, push the fly. The shark will release itself without harm to itself or to you. The job will be even easier if you use barbless hooks.

A long-handled release stick keeps sharp teeth at a safe distance.

Use smaller flies for tuna and catch more fish

Presenting a smaller baitfish pattern often results in more frequent bites.

TUNA, INCLUDING BONITO, ALBACORE, AND LITTLE TUNNY (FALSE albacore) have exceptional eyesight, and can size up bait better than any other saltwater fish. If you are attempting to pass off any old pattern rather than matching the size of the bait being eaten, you are not going to enjoy much success.

The tuna will focus on one size of bait, and if your fly is even a tad larger than the bait, you will get refusal after refusal—which means it's time to switch to smaller flies.

If you're getting refusals even though you are stripping the fly fast enough, and you find the tuna following but not taking, scale down the size of the fly you are using, making certain it is smaller than the bait; if you are experiencing difficulty determining exactly what the fish are feeding on, tie on the smallest fly you have. I have on occasion used bonefish flies (sizes 4 to 6) for tuna, finding that the smaller flies work well when all else fails. Just make certain the hooks are extra strong. The last thing you want is hook failure once you've latched onto a monster.

How to find fish in the surf zone

THE SURF ZONE IS A GREAT PLACE TO START SALTWATER FLY FISHING, WHETHER YOU'RE targeting stripers on the East Coast or corbina on the West Coast. This bewildering area of crashing surf, rips, rock piles, and sandbars can be intimidating to the uninitiated. Don't let it get to you! These two simple clues about surf zone structure will help calm your doubts.

Rip Currents

Fish that live along beaches love structure, especially rip currents. These are small channels, usually twenty to thirty feet wide, created by waves washing on shore and then needing someplace to get back out to sea. These riverlike indentations run perpendicularly through the surf zone. Fish congregate on the edges or even within the rip to feed on baitfish, crabs, and shrimp. Rips can be very productive on both incoming and outgoing tides, and can be found along the edges of reef structures, alongside pier pilings, and randomly along sandy beaches.

Potholes

Where you find rip currents, you'll also find potholes, which are dark indentations located from a few feet to a few hundred feet from the shoreline. When you're observing a beach at low tide, try to remember the locations of potholes. Fish will stack up in them when the tide rises and covers them with water. They will, however, change location as the sand moves around.

Extreme low tide is a good time to check out structure that is normally underwater.

Feeding a fly to a tarpon

WATCHING A TARPON TAKE A FLY AND TAKE OFF, PLANING, JUMPING, AND TWISTING, IS AN exhilarating experience. To make it happen, you need to master the art of fly presentation.

First, no matter whether a tarpon approaches from left to right or right to left, never cast behind the fish, as this can spook him. Always place the fly ten to twenty feet beyond and above him at about a ninety-degree angle to his line of travel.

Allow the tarpon to swim to the fly, making certain not to move it until the fish has closed in; then, once the fish is positioned practically nose-to-nose with the fly, begin a slow, long, stripping retrieve. Think of it as teasing a cat with a toy mouse. Move the mouse too quickly and the cat loses interest; move it too slowly and it will not chase. Find the right speed and the cat will go for the mouse. In the same way, apply the right speed and tarpon will attack the fly. Strip it too fast, however, and you'll spook him.

Once a tarpon is focused on your fly, speed up the retrieve. Don't stop it! Keep it moving, and chances are he'll take it. When he does, give the fly a hard strip-strike. The tarpon's mouth is full of hard plates, and a timid strike won't allow the hook to penetrate. Drive that hook home, then hold on for the fight of your life!

There are few soft spots in the tarpon's mouth, so give a good hard strip-strike to set the hook.

Winter saltwater fly fishing

WINTER CAN BE THE BEST TIME OF YEAR TO CATCH SALTWATER FISH ON THE FLY. THE BEACHES, flats, and bays are practically deserted in wintertime, as most fair-weather fishermen have retreated to their firesides. It's time for the serious fly flinger to put on his thermals, grab his fly rod, and head for the water.

Two of my favorite wintertime fish are the speckled trout (or spotted seatrout) and the black drum, both species that thrive in cool water. The speckled trout is a coastal fish found on shallow mud and sand flats from North Carolina to Texas. A fish that generally travels in large schools, it's capable of providing fast action on the fly, whether you're wading or fishing from a skiff, a kayak, or a larger boat.

One proven way to locate specks is to look for depressions, channels, holes, and cuts on or along the flats. Once you have located a school, cast into the middle with a floating or intermediate line, a nine-foot leader, and a baitfish pattern such as a weedless Bend Back.

The key to catching speckled trout in cold water is to retrieve the fly *slowly*, using short, jerky strips. The strike is often as light as an aunt's peck on the cheek, so keep a close watch on your fly.

My other favorite winter fish, the black drum, is found on the same types of flats as the speckled trout. Also called common drum, this gamefish can weigh from five to fifty pounds. Look for them near breakwaters, pier pilings, channels, estuaries, and marshes.

I remember catching my first black drum, also known as a "swamp donkey." It was a bitter-cold January day. I was fishing for redfish (red drum) in Louisiana and spied a large fish tailing next to the shoreline. At first I thought it was a big redfish, but as I got a closer look, I realized it was an enormous black drum. My guide suggested I cast, and try to drop my crab fly right on the fish's nose. As soon as the fly hit the water, the fish turned, inhaled the fly, and took off, making a run that took me deep into my backing. Once I got the fish under control and finally played it back to the boat, I realized that I had found a new favorite gamefish.

The black drum is a finicky eater, and does not strike quickly or with vigor—but once hooked, he's a handful. If you decide to brave the winter elements and try for him, go with a nine- or ten-weight rod, a floating weight-forward line, a nine-foot leader, and a pocketful of crab patterns (black drum love crustaceans).

Speckled trout will keep you busy all winter.

PART

7

Mother Nature

How deep is a fathom?

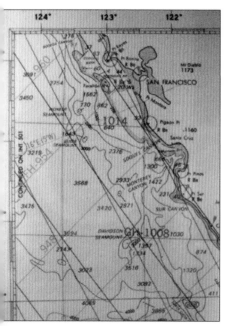

THIS MAY SOUND STRANGE, BUT THIS IS A QUESTION I HEAR MORE than any other question when guiding in salt water: How deep is a fathom?

The question may seem irrelevant; however, if you ever have to read a nautical chart, you'll notice that most charts record depths in fathoms, not feet.

Understanding how to read a chart can help you in navigating a channel, finding a secret hot spot, avoiding a sandbar, and, most important, getting back to the dock at the end of the day.

Here are some useful conversions for reading a nautical chart.

1 fathom = 6 feet
1 nautical mile = 1.2 miles
1 knot = 1.2 mph
1 meter = 3.3 feet

Most productive tides: Rising and falling tides

I REMEMBER FISHING OFF THE BEACH WHEN I WAS A BOY, AND NOTICING THAT ONCE THE water along the beach began to churn, I began catching fish. It was as if someone had turned on a switch, causing the water to come alive with baitfish, bird life, and hookups. A few years later I figured out that the ocean turbulence and activity were the result of a changing tide.

Tides are very important to fishing success in both offshore and inshore waters, dictating where the fish will feed, and when they will feed. Being familiar with the tide's ebb and flow will improve your chances for success, no matter where you fish.

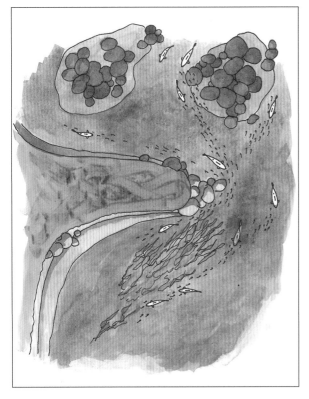

Rising tide brings in an abundance of baitfish and crustaceans.

Marshes, Flats, and Beaches—Tides Transport Bait

I find the rising tide to be the optimum time to fish. Flood tides bring in new water filled with baitfish, shrimp, and other forage for gamefish to feast on. The gamefish will herd the bait into tight groups. Like the bad guys in a Western flick lying in wait for the good guys, the gamefish lie in wait to ambush the bait as it moves into nearshore areas, using the shoreline as a trap.

Falling tides that flush out marshes, estuaries, and flats can prove beneficial to the saltwater fly fisherman, as gamefish predictably will wait in deep channels and holes, and on sandbars for a seafood buffet being swept toward them.

Offshore—Tide-creating Currents

Fishing offshore tides is different from fishing nearshore tides. Instead of the flooding and draining effect that tides have on inland flats and marshes, offshore tides are more about the movement of water, or current. This water movement is generated by both tide and wind. And the greater the current, the better the fishing. How does this occur? As water moves over offshore structure, drop-offs, rock piles, and even floating kelp rafts, the currents push the bait into tight groups, making them easier prey for predatory gamefish.

As the tide falls, the receding water pulls small, tasty creatures out of the rocks and marsh grass.

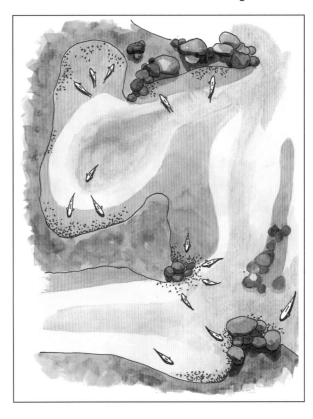

Tides and Moon Phase

Tidal movements correspond with the moon phase, with the most extreme tides occurring during new and full moons. Fishing during these times is usually most productive. Keep in mind, however, that a full moon allows fish to feed all night. When the moon is full, fishing at dusk and dawn is often most productive.

Remember: The more tidal movement or current (water moving in, out, or in a certain direction), the better the fishing!

Full and new moons produce strong tidal movements, which concentrate the bait.

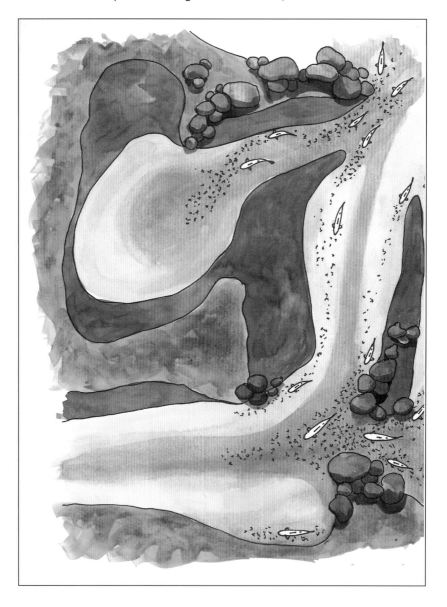

Stormy weather with dark clouds: Run for cover

CHANGING WEATHER CONDITIONS ARE PART OF FISHING. ONE MOMENT THE SKY WILL BE blue and the sun will be shining. The next moment, ominous black clouds with lightning, off-the-chart winds, and torrential rains will take over the day. Luckily, today's anglers are able to access any number of weather-predicting sites that provide up-to-the-minute data that will help them decide whether to stay home or get out on the water.

Common sense should also dictate what you decide to do, no matter how hot the fishing might be. If you are on the water and notice a potential storm on the horizon, run for shelter if you are fishing a beach or flats. If you are on the ocean, aim your boat's bow toward safe harbor. Once the storm has passed, return to your fly fishing. Be safe, not sorry.

If you see this . . . run for cover!

What to do about glassy water

IT HAPPENS ALL THE TIME. YOU'RE OUT FISHING, AND THE WATER IS AS SLICK AS GLASS. YOU can see the fish, but at the same time, they can also see you. Not only that, but they can also detect your vibrations when you wade, pole your skiff, or try to move in close by using your outboard. How can you get within range of them for a cast?

The fish will become skittish if you get too close. Just when you're about to give up, however, a breeze picks up, the water assumes some texture, and all of a sudden the fish are turned on and you've got a feeding frenzy on your hands.

Anglers have different theories on why fish feed more aggressively when the breeze picks up. My thought is that choppy water gives fish a feeling of security, and they're less vulnerable when feeding.

The point is that when you're faced with glassy water conditions, with fish not in a feeding mood, don't give up. Wait a bit, and the minute the water develops a small chop, begin laying out line.

A little texture on the water gives fish a sense of security and allows you to throw a fly without spooking them.

PART

8

The Traveling Saltwater Fly Fisherman

Fourteen essential items to pack for a saltwater fly-fishing trip

1. Pliers

Pliers have a number of functions. They make it easier to release fish, aid in pinching down hook barbs, cut wire or heavy monofilament, and open bottled beverages to quench your thirst on a hot day.

2. Tippet Material

Always carry enough monofilament or fluorocarbon to create leaders to meet your needs. Three spools of tippet material should suffice for most situations: twenty-, thirty-, and forty-pound test.

3. Towel

Once fish slime is on your hands, this sticky and smelly gunk will foul everything within reach: your gear, your clothes, the ham-and-cheese sandwich that you brought for lunch. Always carry a good, absorbent towel, one that can get the gunk off your hands and that can be rinsed after every use.

4. Sunblock

Besides ruining a fly-fishing trip, sunburn can ruin your life. Today's market is glutted with every sort of sun-protection ointment, and many provide excellent protection from the sun's rays. Once you have applied sunblock (do it more than once a day), rinse you hands thoroughly, as many fish can smell the chemicals on your fly or line. To be extra safe, wear it in conjunction with sun-protective clothing . . . and a hat.

The essentials

5. Raingear

Even if it's sunny and hot when you head out fishing, it might get cloudy and cold, or windy and rainy, before the day is over. Always take raingear whenever you go, just in case. It also pays to take along a large garbage bag to protect your gear.

6. Super Glue

Nothing is more annoying (and painful) than a cut or cracked finger while saltwater fishing. Whether you're on a flat in Belize or sixty miles offshore, Super Glue will close the cut and stop the bleeding, letting you keep fishing until you are able to deal with the condition back at the dock. Super Glue can also come in handy when you need to repair broken rod tips.

7. Duct Tape

As one of my fishing buddies once stated, "Duct tape is like The Force . . . it has a light side and a dark side and it holds the universe together." Like Super Glue, duct tape can take care of your many needs, be it securing a fly reel onto a broken reel seat, taping rod cases together for the flight home from a far-off location, or applying around your stripping finger for protection from the line.

8. Antibacterial Gel

When you're catching and releasing fish, there are going to be times when your hands suffer small nicks and cuts from razor-sharp teeth and spiny fins. An easy way to avoid nasty infections is to carry a pocket-size container of antibacterial hand wash and apply it generously throughout the day.

9. Gloves

Don't try to release or handle any fish bare-handed. Many fish have teeth, spines, stingers, and gills that can pierce your skin and cause infections. Wear good fishing gloves for any fish-handling chores.

10. Handheld Scale

The BogaGrip (with built-in scale) or another type of handheld scale will provide an accurate weight on that saltwater fish of a lifetime. Such scales pack easily and are worth every penny.

11. Hook Sharpener

Dull hooks are responsible for many lost fish. Even though many hooks are laser- or machine-sharpened, most saltwater fly hooks are made of stainless steel. When fished in rough areas such as jetties, rocks, coral, and even sandy bottoms, hooks will dull over time, and require constant sharpening. A good sharpener should always be a part of your kit.

12. Handheld GPS

One of the worst fishing nightmares is becoming lost or dis-oriented on the ocean, on the flats, or in a marsh's maze. A global positioning system (GPS) unit can prevent such situations. Using a GPS unit, you can also mark areas where the fishing is red hot, letting you return to the exact spot whenever you choose. Most GPS units contain moon phase and tidal information, both keys to successful fishing.

13. Headwear

A wide-brimmed hat can protect your nose, ears, and the back of your neck from sunburn. Don't wear a baseball hat unless you don't have a choice, as they afford only minimal protection from the sun's rays.

14. Tackle Bag

When shopping for a traveling tackle bag, choose one that will hold all the gear needed on your trip. Ideally, the bag should be made of a tough material and have many heavy-duty interior and exterior pockets. If you're going to fill it up, or if you're going to spend a lot of time going through airports, get a duffel bag with wheels.

84

No black-soled shoes!

IF YOU EVER GET A CHANCE TO FISH WITH a buddy whose skiff has a light-colored deck, don't wear black-soled sneakers, sandals, or loafers. If you do, don't be surprised if he never invites you to go on another fishing trip. There is nothing more annoying to a boat owner than black skid marks ornamenting his pride and joy from bow to stern, and being left to scrub them all off by himself. Leave the black-soled footwear at home.

85

Pack light

MANY FLY FISHERMEN FESTOON THEIR VESTS WITH useless stuff: dull-bladed scissors, wool fly patches, and rust-encrusted hemostats. In addition, they cram their vest pockets full with fly boxes of every size, each pocket on the verge of popping its stitching. And I would be remiss if I neglected to add the gigantic stripping baskets to my list of gear that serves no purpose other than to get in the angler's way. When fly fishing in salt water, go light.

Many places, such as beaches or flats, will force you to travel light—toting nonessential gear will wear you out over the course of a day. If you're going to be fishing in a skiff with a guide, ask him ahead of time what you need. In most cases, he'll have most of the gear anyway. Just bring your rods (two rods and reels will cover most situations) and a deck bag with necessities only. Leave the other stuff in your garage or tackle locker.

◀ A waist pack is all you need when fishing the beach or flats.

Learn from your guide

A GOOD GUIDE CAN PROVIDE YOU WITH A wealth of the information you need when fly fishing unfamiliar waters. His time spent on the water, logging hundreds of hours, studying the characteristics of different gamefish, and honing fly-fishing skills are almost guaranteed to make you a better angler. When you go to a different location and want to fish, hiring a guide is a worthwhile investment. Once you have enlisted his assistance, pay attention: Listen and learn! You might be a fly-fishing whiz on Montana's Beaverhead River, but you will find that saltwater fly fishing is entirely different from fly fishing in fresh water. Don't bend his ear with stories about your skills as a freshwater angler. You are there to learn from him, not vice versa.

Find a good guide and you may make a lifelong friend in the process.

87

Preserve your memories: Take quality photographs

THERE IS NOTHING BETTER THAN SEEING A BEAUTIFULLY COMPOSED PHOTOGRAPH OF AN angler with his saltwater trophy. Choosing the correct lighting, background, and angle can enhance any photo, and can make the difference between an average snapshot and something worth framing.

The memories a photograph can hold are priceless and something to be admired for years. Who doesn't want a photo of his hefty tarpon, caught on a fly in the Florida Keys?

There are now many affordable, easy-to-use, waterproof digital cameras on the market. Buy a good one; it will return your investment many times over. And learn how to use it *before* you take that one-week bonefishing trip to the Abacos.

When shooting, remember that good lighting is critical. Early mornings and late afternoons are the best times for taking photographs, as the light during these times of the day tends to accentuate the best colors. Bright sunlight in the middle of the day, on the other hand, is not ideal. It casts harsh shadows on the faces of anglers and on the fish. If you catch a good fish in the middle of the day and have to take photos in bright sunlight, shoot with the sun at your back and consider using a fill flash to illuminate your subject's face.

Be creative. Share the shot with your fish. Don't, for instance, just lift the fish out of the water and hold it up to the camera and smile. Perhaps a better shot would be to hold the fish halfway out of the water and shoot the photos from an angle, thus getting a well-composed picture of you and your trophy.

Always make the fish the focus of the photo. Whether your fish is the catch of a lifetime or your first catch of a given species, remember that the fish is the most important part of the photo.

Finally, taking a picture rather than turning your trophy over to a taxidermist allows you to release your fish unharmed to fight another day. Try fishing CPR . . . **C**atch, **P**hotograph, and **R**elease. Smile!

88

Preparation: The key to a successful fly-fishing trip

THERE IS NO SUBSTITUTE FOR WELL-THOUGHT-OUT PREPARATION WHEN IT COMES TO taking a saltwater fly-fishing trip. But for one reason or another, many anglers don't take the time to plan things out ahead of time, an error that can result in not having the right gear or clothing, ineffective casting (from not practicing before the trip), poor fly selection (from not studying an area's gamefish ahead of time), not to mention all the extra cash you'll have to shell out to buy the right equipment once you get to your destination. Here are a few things to consider when planning for your first saltwater fly-fishing trip:

1. A week or so prior to your trip, spend a half hour each day, or as time allows, casting into the wind, practice that will prepare you for those unforgiving, blustery winds you will encounter when fishing the flats and offshore. Work on distance. Casts of forty to fifty feet with no more than two false casts are a must.
2. Research which flies you'll need for the waters you're going to fish. If you are going to fish with a guide, ask him what flies are appropriate, and whether your guide will be providing them for you. Too many anglers show up at their destination with flies that are better suited for catching bluegills or trout, not saltwater species. Do your homework!

3. Be in shape: Hit the gym. Get a physical. Many saltwater fishing destinations place extreme physical demands upon the angler, especially locations in the tropics, where sun and wind can sap your strength in a hurry. Get off the couch and go for a walk. Your body will thank you.

4. Pack your bags, then repack them to eliminate unnecessary items. Pack only those things that you will absolutely need: tackle, clothes, toilet articles, medications if necessary. Above all, do not duplicate if it's not necessary.

5. If your trip is to a foreign country, study the culture, customs, and perhaps the language spoken by the natives. Having some background information on your destination can only help in the long run. Don't forget your passport—make sure it hasn't expired, and take a copy just in case.

Remember, if you are well prepared, you will have a much more enjoyable trip than if you were unprepared.

Don't bring too much extra gear, but make sure you don't forget any of the essentials.

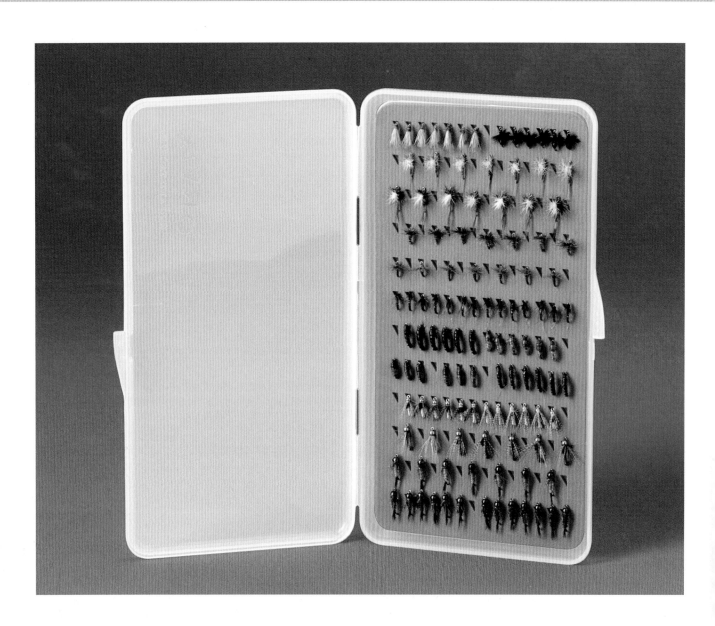

PART

9

Safety

Be prepared for a medical emergency

Bug repellent is a must in most saltwater destinations.

MANY SALTWATER FLY-FISHING destinations are in beautiful but remote locations that have few or no medical services. If you get sick or hurt, you could be in trouble.

Before you leave for a trip, research the medical services that are available at your destination, and plan accordingly. Also make sure to pack a comprehensive first-aid kit, complete with antibiotics, pain relievers, bandages (and tape), diarrhea medicine, and insect repellent.

To ensure your safe return home in case of serious sickness or injury, by all means purchase evacuation travel insurance.

90

How to remove a hook painlessly

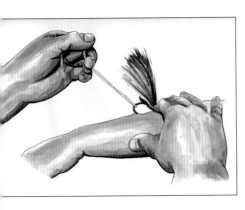

WITH WINDY CONDITIONS AND EVER-CHANGING CASTING directions, sooner or later you, your fishing partner, or your guide is going to get hooked by a fly. When it happens, hopefully it will be with a barbless hook, which is much easier to extricate from your arm, leg, back, or worse, your ear, than a barbed hook. Here's how to remove a hook painlessly and quickly:

1. Make a loop on the end of a piece of heavy monofilament, and place the loop around the embedded hook's gap.
2. Holding the tag ends of the mono loop, press down on the hook's eye.
3. A quick pull will free the hook from the victim's flesh.

After the hook is removed, thoroughly cleanse the wound. See a doctor if needed.

How to prevent seasickness

THERE IS NO WORSE FEELING than being on the ocean and having your innards suddenly go into nauseous convulsions. You're the victim of a scourge that has plagued humankind since we first hoisted a sail on the ocean. Its common name is seasickness, though those who have suffered from it may also call it "sea death," as many folks would rather be thrown to the sharks to put them out of their misery. It isn't fun.

Without getting into the medical reasons behind seasickness, there are a couple of things you can do to help avert having it happen to you.

First, watch what you eat the night before you go fishing. Eat light. A double helping of lasagna with some garlic bread and red wine on the side is going to sit in your stomach all night, and still be there the next morning.

Check the conditions before you head out.

If you eat light, yet still suspect that you're going to feel ill on the water, consider taking an over-the-counter medicine such as Dramamine or Bonine before you go out. Ear patches, wrist bands, and other medications can also be obtained, though in most cases you'll need a prescription from your doctor.

What has worked for many of my clients over the years is a teaspoon of pickled ginger, the kind you can get at your local sushi restaurant or Asian market. For some reason, this remedy works almost all the time. If you're on the water and start to get an upset stomach, eat a teaspoon of ginger—you'll be amazed at the results.

One old-timer's method for curing seasickness is to look at the horizon or a landmark and avoid looking down, a move that usually triggers the nausea.

Another trick, used by one of my older fishing buddies, is to never go out on the ocean without a box of Saltine crackers. Eating a few crackers always worked for him.

If all else fails, start the boat and motor into the wind. A breeze on your face will help you feel better.

Learn how to run a skiff

Knowing how to operate a skiff can be useful in an emergency situation.

WE TALK SO MUCH ABOUT how to pick the right flies, cast into the wind, and fight fish, but we rarely cover the importance of being able to operate a skiff if called upon to do so.

It's simple. If you're on the water in a boat or skiff, miles offshore or somewhere on the flats, and your guide, captain, or fishing buddy is for some reason unable to run the skiff—perhaps due to illness or injury—it's critical that you know how to run the craft back to shore and safety. The chances are slim that this will actually happen, but you never know. It happened to me once, and I'll forever be thankful that I knew how to operate a boat.

One painless way to learn the basics of running a boat is to enroll in a boating and water safety class.

When heading out for a day on the water, make a point of familiarizing yourself with the skiff's or boat's power unit. How does the motor start—with a key-controlled electric starter, or with a manual pull cord?

Does the boat or skiff have a center console with steering wheel, or is the motor moved by a tiller? Is there a kill switch that will deactivate the motor if the switch is detached from the key?

Where is the boat's GPS and navigation unit? Is it set to track back to the boat's launching point? Does the craft have a VHF radio? How is it operated and, in an emergency, how do you contact the Coast Guard?

And last, but hardly least: Where are the personal flotation devices and first-aid kit?

Familiarize yourself with all these aspects of boat operation, and you'll be able to return the boat and its passengers to safety if something happens to the boat's operator.

Sun protection

I KNOW IT LOOKS GREAT TO HAVE A TAN, BUT IN TRUTH, THAT TAN CAN EVENTUALLY TURN into skin cancer—and if you get melanoma, it can kill you. Here are some ways to keep those rays off your skin.

Sunblock

The recommended strength for sunblock varies. Some doctors say SPF 15 is adequate; many dermatologists say you should use nothing less then SPF 30. Whatever strength you decide to use, be smart and, during your day on the water and in the sun, take the time to reapply sunblock frequently, especially to your nose, ears, hands, and face—the parts of the body that take the brunt of the sun's rays. After application, be sure to clean your hands thoroughly so you don't get any sunblock on your fly or line. Gamefish can detect the odor and may spook.

Clothing

The best way to protect your skin is to completely cover your body with proven protective clothing. Most new outdoor wear is not only comfortable and functional, but has an SPF rating of 30-plus, which provides you with extra protection. These outfits come in an assortment of colors and styles for even the most fashion-conscious salt-water fly rodder.

Headgear

A hat is one of the most basic elements of sun protection. There is such a huge variety of hats available that it's largely a matter of preference. Some folks prefer the standard baseball cap, which provides moderate protection. Watch out for mesh trucker's caps, however, as the sun will penetrate right through the mesh. A wide-brimmed hat that covers your ears as well as your head and neck is better for overall protection. Then there's the balaclava, which is currently very popular and can be worn completely over the face, on the neck, or merely on the head. Several versions are available, and can be adapted to hot, warm, or cold conditions.

Stay covered up to avoid the sun's harmful rays.

PART
10

Tackle Care

The best way to clean fly line

KEEPING YOUR FLY LINE CLEAN IS AS IMPORTANT AS KEEPING RUST OFF YOUR HOOKS. FLY lines are exposed to all sorts of harmful things over the course of a fishing day or season. Heat, dirty salt water, sunscreen, and bug repellent can all harm your fly line. All will shorten your line's life if not gotten rid of.

To clean a fly line, basic dish soap and warm water work about as well as anything. Take the line and strip it off into a bucket containing dish soap and warm water. Allow the line to soak in the bucket for two or three minutes, then rinse it with fresh water. Next, take a clean cloth or sponge and wipe off the entire line before winding it back onto your reel. Your cleaning cloth will show you how much dirt was on the line.

To add a little extra slickness to your line, wipe it with a coating of silicone or fly line dressing after cleansing—this can add distance to your casts.

To get the most out of your fly line, give it a good bath after every couple of trips in salt water.

Regularly cleaning your fly line will help increase the distance of your casts and extend the life of your line.

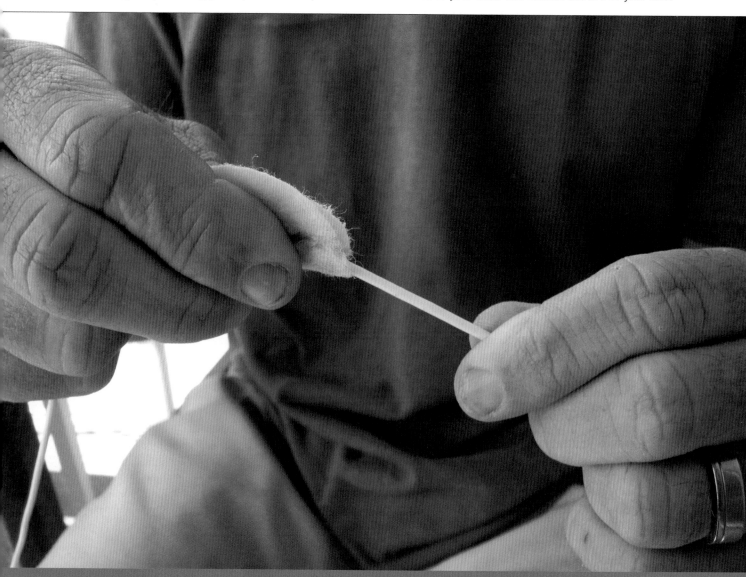

95

Keep your grip dry

WHEN RINSING OFF YOUR FLY ROD after fishing, be careful not to soak the cork grip. If the cork handle becomes waterlogged, the glue securing it to the rod will be compromised, and the grip could separate from the rod. When this happens, your casting will suffer, as the rod won't react the way it should. You'll be unable to properly tighten your reel to the reel seat, and sooner or later you're going to have a repair job on your hands.

Once you return from a trip, thoroughly rinse off all your gear, but don't put the rod the back in its case right away. Let it air dry completely before storing.

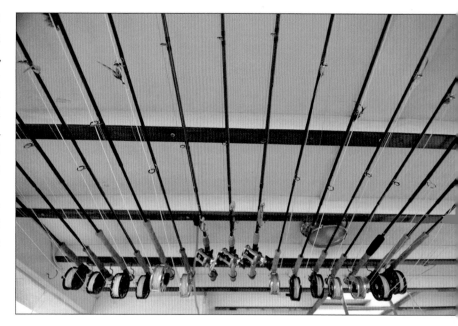

After a freshwater rinse, dry and store your gear.

96

Care of polarized lenses

POLARIZED EYEWEAR SHOULD BE AN INTEGRAL PART OF YOUR FISHING ARSENAL. FINDING a pair of polarized glasses that you like will take time and money, but the investment will be well worth it, as high-quality eyewear will save your eyes from the blistering sun. It will also cut the glare on the water, allowing you to spy fish that you wouldn't otherwise be able to see.

To get the most out of your polarized sunglasses, it's important to clean them correctly. Fresh water and either a chamois or camera lens cloth will do the job quite well. Make sure that the cloth you use is clean and stays that way by storing it in a dry, secure container, such as a locking plastic bag. Whatever you do, don't wipe your eyewear with toilet

paper, paper towels, or your shirt. Toilet paper and paper towels are made from wood products and will scratch your glasses. Your shirt will pick up salt particles, dirt, and grime, which can also scratch and ruin your lenses.

I would also advise to stay away from commercially produced glass and lens cleaners. Although they work well for some glasses, such cleaners contain chemicals that will eventually remove your glass's polarizing film. The same can also be said for sunscreens.

Finally, consider lightly oiling the metal hinges on your glasses to prevent saltwater corrosion.

Protect your eyewear investment by giving it the same attention and care you give to your rods, reels, and other equipment.

◀ Use fresh water when cleaning polarized lenses.

97

Rinsing your fly reel

SALT WATER IS CORROSIVE AND A REAL THREAT TO YOUR EQUIPMENT, ESPECIALLY YOUR FLY reel, which is perhaps the most vulnerable of all your gear. Your reel not only takes a beating from fighting fish, but it also gets tossed around on boats and on sandy beaches, and suffers the occasional dunk in salt water or roll in the sand. In light of these threats, it pays to pamper your reel. Wash it after every trip to the salt.

The correct way to remove saltwater residue from your reel is to take a hose with a spray nozzle and adjust it to the fine-mist setting. Spray your reel lightly without forcing water into its working parts. When finished, dry the reel with a clean rag or car chamois. It's that simple. At the end of the season, give it a thorough washing by taking it apart, rinsing and drying every part, then applying oil or grease to all moving parts. I also advocate returning your reel to the manufacturer for periodic tune-ups. Treat your reel as well as you treat your car (or better). You've got a lot riding on that one piece of equipment.

Salt water will ruin even the best reel. A quick rinse makes a big difference.

98

How to keep hooks from rusting

THERE IS NOTHING MORE ANNOYING THAN REACHING INTO YOUR FLY BOX AND PULLING out a fly with a rusty hook. Salt water will rust and corrode a hook overnight, and if you think that stainless steel hooks are not affected by salt water, guess again.

There are a couple of ways to keep rust from ruining your favorite patterns. One way is to spray your flies with a light mist of fresh water at the end of each day, then let them air dry thoroughly. Whatever you do, don't use a hair dryer, unless you want to end up with a gooey ball of feathers.

Mild dish soap also works well. Put a drop in a container with fresh water, drop your flies in, replace the lid, and give it a good shake. Next, pour out the water and rinse the flies with more fresh water. Finally, set them out to air dry.

You may also want to hit your flies with a little WD-40 at the end of your trip. This will add a protective coating to your hooks, one that will keep rust at bay. Just be careful not to saturate them, or your flies will become gummy with oil.

Don't waste a good box of flies. Give them a rinse!

PART

11

On the Water

Don't crowd your neighbor

Fishing shoulder to shoulder is annoying and can be dangerous.

ENCROACHING ON SOMEONE'S SPACE can make people uncomfortable and can get downright ugly. Have you ever had another fisherman cast over your line? Or perhaps you're running a chum line and another boat cuts right through the middle of it? How about having another boat crowd you while you're trying to cast to surface-feeding fish? Or, what if another angler crowds you when you're fishing a quiet stretch of beach?

These are all prime examples of one angler invading another angler's space. Ultimately, they're cases of bad manners. And sadly, this type of behavior happens all too often.

Unless you wish to be branded a lowlife (or worse), avoid confrontations with fellow anglers by observing good on-the-water manners. When sharing a stretch of beach, it is always a good practice to allow at least one hundred yards between you and other shore anglers. If someone is fishing a particular area, stay clear—if you must pass him, walk quietly around him, allowing enough room for him to continue making his backcasts. And never walk up to him and break his concentration by blurting, "How's the fishing?"

Treat other anglers the way you'd like them to treat you, and we'll all be better off.

Maximize your time on the water

OVER THE YEARS, I'VE RUN INTO ANGLERS WHO THINK THAT HAVING HIGH-END RODS, REELS, huge fly selections, and the latest waders will ensure them a high degree of success. What they did not take into account was how much work, practice, and dedication it takes to be a successful saltwater fly angler. They assumed that a few weeks of practicing the double haul was enough to make them skilled enough to catch lots of fish.

Practice is fine, but the truth of the matter is that nothing can match spending time on the water. It doesn't matter whether you're casting flies to surf perch on a local beach or fishing offshore for tuna—time spent fishing will help you hone your skills. Catching fish is of secondary importance.

The key is to try to learn something each time you hit the water. If the bonefishing is tough on the flats, practice casting into the wind. If no makos are showing up in your chum slick, practice tying the Bimini Twist. If there are no stripers along the beach, try to figure out the best tides and areas to fish.

Sight casting to a rolling tarpon in Belize

PART

12

Good Reads

101

Read a good book

This book would not be complete without giving you a reading list to get you through the slow days. Here are some of my favorites.

Adams, Aaron J. *Fisherman's Coast: An Angler's Guide to Marine Warm-Water Gamefish and Their Habitats* (Stackpole Books, 2003)

Adams, Aaron J. *Fly Fisherman's Guide to Saltwater Prey* (Stackpole Books, 2008)

Blanton, Dan. *Fly-Fishing California's Great Waters* (Frank Amato Publications, 2003)

Combs, Trey. *Bluewater Fly Fishing* (Lyons and Burford, 1995)

Curcione, Nick. *Baja on the Fly* (Frank Amato Publications, 1997)

Curcione, Nick. *The Orvis Guide to Saltwater Fly Fishing* (The Lyons Press, 1993)

Curcione, Nick. *Tug-O-War: A Fly-Fisher's Game* (Frank Amato Publications, 2001)

Hanley, Ken. *Fly Fishing the Pacific Inshore* (The Lyons Press, 2003)

Kreh, Lefty. *Fly Fishing in Salt Water* (The Lyons Press, 1997)

Kreh, Lefty. *Presenting the Fly* (The Lyons Press, 1999)

Kreh, Lefty, and Mark Sosin. *Practical Fishing Knots* (The Lyons Press, 1991)

THE
ORVIS®
— GUIDE TO —
BEGINNING FLY TYING

101 TIPS for the Absolute Beginner

Preface by
TOM ROSENBAUER

David Klausmeyer

Skyhorse Publishing

Contents

Preface

WHEN WE DECIDED THERE WAS A NEED FOR A 101 TIPS BOOK ON FLY TYING, THE LIST OF possible authors was very short, and Dave Klausmeyer was at the top. I've known Dave for about twenty years, and have watched him grow from a fly-fishing historian and bamboo rod maker to a superb editor, teacher, and photographer. And having Dave slaving by himself on some arcane bit of history or planning strips of cane in his basement is a waste of his greatest talent, which is his gregarious, open, and sympathetic manner whenever he meets a fellow fly tier. He's always happy, typically hilarious, and constantly has his ear open to what's new.

All of those talents come through in this book. From the very first entry about washing your hands and its reference to what your mother always told you, Dave endears himself to us with his openness and easy-to-read style. He has also never forgotten what it's like to be a novice fly tier with burning questions that have to be answered *right now* because you have thread hanging from a size 16 half-finished Parachute Adams and you don't know how to make a parachute post. Yeah, you could sort through all the videos on YouTube and then get sidetracked on watching a talking dog video or a clip on fly fishing for Dorado—meanwhile your Parachute Adams hangs unfinished. Wouldn't it be easier to just open a tightly organized book and find just what you are looking for, from a guy who has been at it for more years than you've been alive, as opposed to some bozo on YouTube who may have begun tying last week?

I've written a couple of fly tying books myself, and looking through these chapters I can't believe I have never mentioned stuff like thinking ahead to the next step, how to store your flies, how to read a pattern description, or whether natural fly tying materials are safe to handle. Dave has listened to novice fly tiers, carefully, and has really answered questions that both novices and experienced hands ask all the time.

I know he has answered these questions because I do a weekly podcast on fly fishing, and all of the topics I cover are suggestions from listeners. I have kept track of all the questions about fly tying I've been asked in more than 120 podcasts, and I was truly floored to find out that Dave has answered every one.

I know this book will be a treasured guide, but I also know it will make you chuckle. Who else would do a chapter called "The Craziest Fly Ever?" and then proceed to tell us about a fly tied out of a condom? Only Dave, who knows full well that fly fishing and fly tying are supposed to be fun, not deadly serious, and that fun should extend to the way we learn new stuff.

—Tom Rosenbauer
March 2012

Introduction: Enjoy the Odyssey

CHANCES ARE YOU FLY FISH. HOW DO I KNOW THIS? BECAUSE YOU PURCHASED OR HAVE been given a book about how to tie flies. Sure, there are a few folks who tie but have no keen interest in fishing; they tie simply for the joy of crafting beautiful flies. These fly tiers, however, are in the minority. For the vast majority of us, learning to make flies is the next step in our odyssey to become more complete anglers.

For novice tiers, making flies that catch fish seems like alchemy. We lash bits of feathers and fur to pieces of bent wire to trick wild, scaly creatures into thinking we are giving them something good to eat. If that doesn't sound like turning lead into gold, then I don't know what does. But fly tying is not alchemy: if you have the interest, you can learn how to make your own flies that catch fish.

My goal is to take some of the mystery out of fly tying—to make it seem less like alchemy and more like a craft that you can enjoy and perhaps even master. We will deal with the most elemental basics of fly tying: how to read a pattern recipe, the three attributes of a good fly, and even how to store the flies you tie. We will discuss how to select a quality yet affordable fly-tying vise, and how to set up your fly-tying station to reduce back, neck, and eye strain. We will study the basic types of materials you will need to get started, and I will show you how to save money tying your own flies. Next, we will see how to craft the basic types of flies you will want to add to your fishing kit, and I will even challenge you to develop some of your own unique patterns. You might just create the next "hot" fly!

There's an expression in fly fishing called "time on the water." It means that your knowledge and ability to fish grows in direct proportion to how much time you spend on the river, lake, or shore with a fly rod in hand. You are the pupil, the water is the classroom, and the fish are the teachers. You'll never graduate if you don't spend sufficient time in school.

This same principle is true for learning to tie flies. Nothing replaces "time at the vise" for developing your fly-tying skills: learning to master thread control, selecting and manipulating materials, and crafting durable flies that do not easily fall apart. Any expert can demonstrate the finer points of fly tying, but how quickly you develop your skills is directly related to how much time you spend at the vise. How much time? This depends upon your schedule and how much free time you can devote to the craft, but there is a similarity between learning to tie flies and learning to play the piano: you will get more out of practicing one hour per day for five days than playing five hours before going to your next music lesson. Tie flies when time permits—even if it's only 30 or 45 minutes per session—but tie regularly, and you will develop the skills to make the patterns necessary to catch fish on your local waters.

You're already a fly fisher. Now you're ready to take the next step and become a fly tier. In short order, you will be catching fish with the very flies you tie. Enjoy the odyssey!

David Klausmeyer
First day of Spring, 2012

First Things First: What You Need to Know to Start Tying Flies

1

Wash your hands

YOUR MOTHER TOLD YOU TO WASH YOUR HANDS BEFORE EATING, AND YOU SHOULD WASH them before tying flies, too. Having hands free of dirt and natural oils is especially important when using light-colored materials. Grime and oil are easily transferred to tying materials, and nothing spoils the appearance of a nice fly more than soiled ingredients. It is especially easy to discolor light-colored flosses and threads.

When you're finished tying, wash your hands once again. Use plenty of soap and hot water to remove any dyes, preservatives, and other chemical agents that get transferred from the materials to your hands while tying.

Don't crowd the hook eye

RUNNING OUT OF SPACE ON THE HOOK SHANK SO YOU CAN'T MAKE A NICE THREAD HEAD and tie off the fly is one of the most common fly-tying mistakes. All beginners experience this problem, and even advanced tiers occasionally run out of room before they're able to complete the fly. Here's a simple way to avoid crowding the eye of the hook.

The size of the thread head is typically equal to the width of the hook eye—maybe a little larger. When beginning the fly, start the thread down the shank a distance equal to the width of the eye. This first thread wrap is a marker; don't tie any materials on the hook between this spot and the hook eye. When you're ready to complete the fly, wrap the thread head on the bare length of shank behind the hook eye.

Tie the head of the fly on the bare piece of shank behind the hook eye.

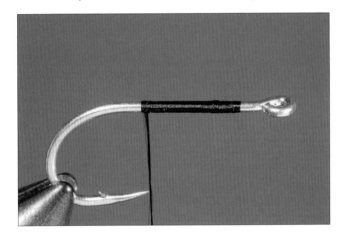

Think ahead to the next step

FLY TIERS AND CHESS PLAYERS HAVE SOMETHING IN COMMON: A CHESS MASTER THINKS several moves ahead when playing a game, and a good tier thinks several steps ahead when dressing a fly.

When tying a material to the hook, think about the next ingredient you will apply and how you will use it. Leave the thread hanging at the best position to add the next material. Be sure to leave ample room to add each material required to tie the pattern. And don't make a lot of needless and extra wraps of thread when tying on each ingredient; excess thread wraps create bulk and do not add to the strength of the fly.

As you gain skill and begin tying more complex flies, you will have to plan further ahead. Mentally divide the hook into the sections that will hold the tail, the body, and the front of the fly. Do not allow one section of the fly to encroach on the space required to make another part of the pattern.

The legendary Warren Duncan tied this Blue Charm salmon fly. Warren planned ahead and carefully allowed ample room to make the various parts of the body.

Dick Talleur made these outstanding classic wet flies. he carefully planned each step when tying them.

4

Start with flies you know will catch fish

"WHAT FLIES SHOULD I LEARN TO TIE FIRST?"

All beginning tiers ask this question. It is important to learn to make flies you know will maximize your odds at catching fish to increase your confidence both as an angler and a tier.

Inquire at your local fly shop or fishing club about the three to five best patterns that catch fish in your local waters. Tell the shop owner or club members that you are a beginning tier, and that you do not want overly complicated patterns—just solid, easy-to-tie flies that catch fish. Buy only the materials you will need to tie those flies; you'll probably discover that you can use the same thread, hooks, and other ingredients to make more than one of the patterns. It's also likely that the fly shop attendant or a club member will offer some valuable pointers or even a fly-tying lesson.

Gain confidence tying and catching fish with those basic flies, and gradually add new patterns to your fly-tying repertoire as you gain experience.

The classic March Brown is just the sort of fly that catches trout in May and June.

The Bi-visible is an example of a dry fly that catches trout almost everywhere.

5

Develop consistency in the appearance of your flies

YOU CAN ALWAYS TELL FLIES DRESSED by an accomplished tier: They have the same proportions and style. And you can always spot the patterns of a neophyte: They're a hodge-podge of sizes, shapes, and proportions. It's easy to understand how an experienced tier can make ten of the same pattern all look pretty much alike, but even when he changes patterns—say, from tying a Royal Coachman to a Quill Gordon—he uses the same sense of proportions in the tails, wings, and hackle. When the novice makes ten of the same fly, however, they often look as though they came from ten completely different tiers; the tails, bodies, wings, and hackles are all different sizes and tied with very different proportions.

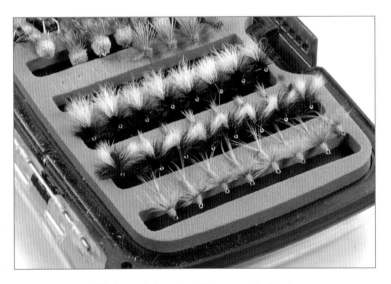

All these dainty dry flies were obviously made by the same fly dresser.

Pay close attention to the proportions you use when tying a fly. And be mindful of the height of the wings, the length of the tails, the width of the hackle collars, and so on. Don't hop around tying different patterns; tie ten of the same fly to develop a sense of size and proportion. Before you know it, the contents of your fly box will look like a polished army ready for inspection and to do battle with the fish.

The author tied these imitations of a golden stonefly nymph. They all look very similar.

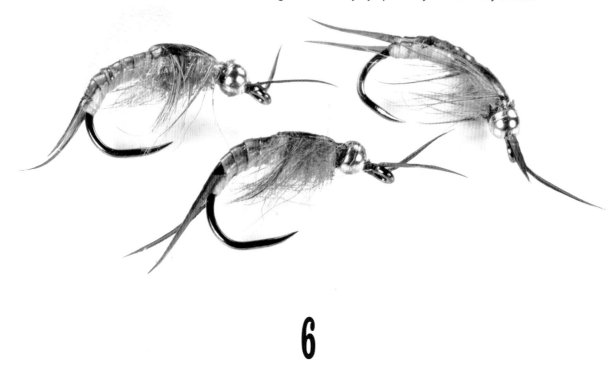

6

The three attributes
of a good fly

WHAT MAKES A GOOD FISH-CATCHING FLY? THIS IS ONE OF THE MOST DEBATED QUESTIONS in the sport of fly fishing. And as a fly tier, this question will always be on your mind: Will the fly I am tying really catch a fish?

Scientists have determined that fish have a poor ability to detect details in the objects around them, so adding lots of extra features to our flies to precisely match the appearance of real food probably makes little difference. Fish react—feed, flee, mate, and more—out of instinct and impulse; they do not have the brainpower to make thoughtful, reasoned decisions. This is why they ignore the hooks and tippets hanging off our flies.

The best flies match three basic characteristics that fish are looking for in the food they eat: size, shape, and natural-looking movement. A good fly matches the general size of a real food item: an insect, baitfish, or perhaps some form of crustacean. A quality fly should also match the general shape of real food. And finally, the fly should imitate the movement—or lack of motion—of real food.

The color of the fly is less important than the size, shape, and action of the pattern. An olive or black Woolly Bugger, for example, is a known fish-catcher; the soft, marabou tail has a natural swimming action that few fish can resist.

The Crystal Bugger is a great trout and bass pattern. The bright body attracts the attention of the fish, and the wavy marabou tail makes the fly look alive in the water.

7

How to read a fly pattern recipe

TYING A FLY IS A LOT LIKE BAKING A CAKE: YOU MAKE BOTH USING A VARIETY OF ingredients. A fly recipe is very similar to a cake recipe in that it lists everything you need to make the pattern: the hook, thread, feathers, furs, and all of the other materials. Check out the following recipe for the classic Fan-wing Royal Coachman dry fly; it lists everything you will need to tie it.

The first ingredient is the hook; place this in the vise when you start the fly. Next comes the thread; the first tying procedure is to wrap some thread on the hook shank. The remainder of the materials are listed in the order in which you will tie them to the hook.

Hook: Light-wire, dry-fly hook, size 16 to 12.
Thread: Brown 8/0 (70 denier).
Tail: Golden-pheasant, tippet fibers.
Body: Peacock herl and red floss.
Wing: White-hen, chicken hackle tips.
Hackle: Brown.

8

Will I save money tying my own flies?

WHETHER OR NOT YOU SAVE MONEY TYING YOUR OWN FLIES DEPENDS UPON HOW MANY you make. First, if you tie a lot of different patterns, and are always adding more to your repertoire, you probably will not save money; tying a great variety of flies requires buying many more materials, which increases the expense of tying. On the other hand, if you specialize in making a few choice patterns that catch fish on your local waters, and you fish and tie a lot, you might break even and perhaps even save a little money making your own flies.

Tying flies in order to save money is probably a mistake. Instead, think of fly tying as a wonderful extension of your fishing; it gives you an opportunity to enjoy the sport when you are not on the water, and you will discover the added thrill of catching fish with your very own flies. In fact, many tiers in northern climates consider winter as "fly-tying season."

Should I buy a fly-tying kit or individual materials?

A FLY-TYING KIT IS A WONDERFUL CHRISTMAS OR BIRTHDAY PRESENT FOR A FLEDGLING fly fisher; it will open that person's eyes to the possibilities of making his or her own flies. If you already own a fly-tying kit, congratulations: You're about to embark on a wonderful new hobby!

A fly-tying kit might not be the best choice for someone who has decided to take up tying and plans to make a lot of his own patterns. It's hard for a manufacturer to assemble a kit that contains only the tools and materials every tier will use, so it might contain some things that will be of no use to you. A kit offered by a leading company in the fly-fishing industry, however, will contain a more useful variety of tools and materials.

Selecting a fly-tying kit or purchasing tools and materials a la carte depends upon your level of interest and goals. If you just want to dabble and test your interest in the craft, a quality kit is a fine starting point; If you are determined to tie a lot of flies and are willing to do the research about what you will need to get started, then buy individual tools and materials.

Another example of a fine fly-tying kit offered by the Orvis Company.

The Orvis Clearwater Fly-Tying Kit is a fine starting pointing for new tiers.

Where can I learn more about fly tying?

WHILE IT USED TO BE DIFFICULT TO FIND INFORMATION ON TYING FLIES, SUCH IS NO longer the case. Today we have a variety of great sources for learning how to tie.

Almost all fly shops and fly-fishing clubs offer fly-tying classes; some conduct classes on an on-going basis, and most of these sessions are free or cost very little. Many adult education programs also offer fine fly-tying classes; If your local adult-ed program does not offer a class, call and request that they start one. Your local bookstore or library will probably have a shelf or two featuring fly-tying books, and there are instructional DVDs and videos that teach everything from beginning to the more advanced forms of fly tying. There are also dozens of websites containing homemade fly-tying videos; Some of this content is of low quality, but a great deal of it is actually very good and useful. And last but not least, *Fly Tyer* magazine, which is the world's largest magazine devoted to art of tying flies, contains articles that appeal to both novice and experienced tiers.

Fly fishing and tying have a great literary tradition. These two classic volumes offer much wisdom to modern fly tiers.

How should I store my flies?

YOU'VE WORKED HARD TO TIE YOUR FLIES; NOW YOU MUST ASSURE THAT THEY'LL REMAIN in good condition for when you go fishing. Properly stored, a fly will last many years.

Always select a fly box designed to accommodate the type of flies you tie. A box made to store saltwater patterns is larger and can hold bigger flies, and a box designed for freshwater streamers is longer so the flies can lay flat and not become permanently bent during storage. Larger boxes also contain ample space to allow air to circulate between the flies to keep them dry.

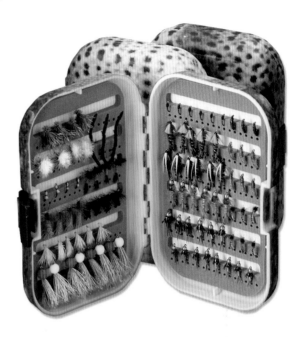

Dry-fly, wet-fly, and nymph boxes are generally smaller and easily fit in a vest pocket. Many boxes have small individual compartments; These are particularly good for housing dry flies so the fine hackle collars do not become bent. Many fly boxes have foam ridges to hold nymphs and larvae patterns; simply stick the hooks into the foam to secure the flies in place. The best fly boxes have watertight seals to keep their insides dry if they fall into the water.

Always open your fly box after fishing to allow the contents to dry. Just a couple of moist flies can raise the humidity inside a closed fly box and cause hooks to rust. Place a desiccant pack inside the box to absorb moisture and keep your flies dry.

Basic terminology: What is a nymph, larva, emerger, and dry fly?

BEFORE WE CAN TALK ABOUT TROUT FLIES, WE MUST ESTABLISH A COMMON LANGUAGE describing the different patterns we will tie. Although some tiers split hairs and quibble about these definitions—what's a hobby without a bit of good-natured quibbling—any experienced angler will understand these terms.

A *nymph* is generally an immature stonefly, mayfly, damselfly, dragonfly, or other insect living along a streambed or lakebed. Almost all of these insects spend the majority of their lives under the water and emerge to reproduce. We tie a nymph to imitate one of these forms of trout food.

A *larva* is generally an immature caddisfly living along the streambed or lakebed.

(Important note: Nymphs and larvae constitute the bulk of a trout's diet.)

An *emerger* is the stage of an insect swimming or crawling to the surface to turn into a winged adult.

A *dry fly* is an imitation of an adult insect. A dry fly is designed to float on the surface of the water. Use a dry fly when the trout are visibly eating adult insects from the surface.

Here we see (*clockwise starting at the top*) a dry fly, a larva, an emerger, and a nymph.

13

What is the best-selling fly in the world?

DO YOU WANT TO KNOW WHAT CATCHES FISH? HOW ABOUT WHAT TO TIE? PERHAPS WE CAN answer these questions by seeing what flies anglers are buying.

According to Umpqua Feather Merchants, which is the leading commercial fly-tying outfit, the Copper John is the best-selling fly in the world.

Colorado's John Barr created the Copper John. His pattern displays many of the most modern features used to tie small nymphs: a bead head, a copper wire body, and a dab of epoxy on the wing case. The success of the Copper John led other fly designers to include these components in many of their patterns.

With the introduction of Ultra Wire, which is copper wire anodized in a wide variety of colors, the Copper John is now dressed in yellow, olive, green, blue, and many other colors. While he does not know the reason, Barr says that a red Copper John catches more fish than any other variety of his famous fly.

There are many variations of the common Copper John. Here we see a rubber-legged version.

14

Commemorative flies are fun to tie

AS YOUR FLY-TYING SKILLS DEVELOP, YOU MAY WISH TO CREATE FLIES FOR FAMILY AND friends. You can tie a new fly to commemorate an important event, or you can name a fly for a cherished person in your life. Tying these sorts of flies is fun, and the people who receive them are thrilled.

Charlie Mann, of Maine, is a lifelong outdoorsman and supporter of the Maine Warden Service. Charlie has named many of his classically inspired streamers for game wardens and others who make Maine an important destination for anglers and hunters. Here we see his commemorative fly called the Maine Guide. Charlie designed this lovely streamer using the colors found in the shoulder patch awarded to the skilled outdoorsmen and women who earn the rank of Registered Maine Guide.

Have fun and create your own original patterns. Give them to friends and family, and watch their faces light up!

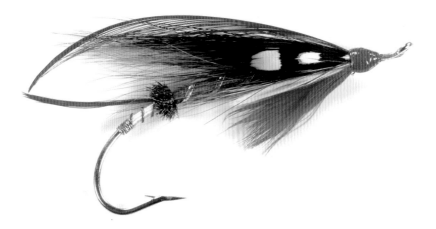

CHAPTER

2

Choosing and Using the Right Tools

15

What is a fly-tying vise?

THE VISE IS THE TOOL THAT HOLDS THE HOOK AND ALLOWS YOU TIE ON THE FURS, FEATHERS, and other materials. The head of the vise holds the jaws and the jaws' locking mechanism. The head, in turn, is attached to a stem and some sort of clamp or heavy pedestal base. This is the original style of fly-tying vise, and many excellent examples are still manufactured. Select one of these vises only if you have no interest in learning rotary fly-tying techniques.

The head on a rotary vise easily turns the hook so you can apply materials while spinning the hook. Even if you do not use rotary fly-tying techniques, a rotary vise lets you easily turn the hook so that you can inspect all sides of a fly.

Go to a quality fly shop and ask the proprietor to show you the features and benefits of the different vises he carries. Ask him to demonstrate using the vises in your price range.

The Dyna-King Kingfisher is a high-quality entry-level vise that will last a lifetime.

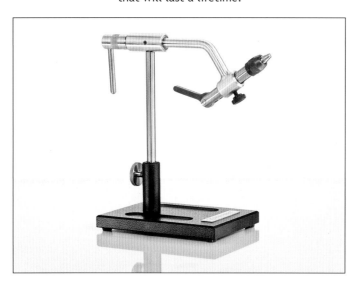

16

How to select a vise

THE VISE WILL PROBABLY BE YOUR LARGEST SINGLE EXPENSE WHEN GETTING INTO FLY tying, but a quality vise will offer a lifetime of service and enjoyment. You will use your vise to tie all of your flies. As a result, you will want to carefully consider which vise you purchase. Consider these questions when choosing a vise.

- Will the vise accommodate all of the sizes of hooks I plan to use? Clamp the smallest and largest hook in the vise to see if they fit.
- Will this vise hold a hook securely without applying a great deal of force to close the jaws?
- Do I have to spend a lot of time adjusting the vise to get the jaws to hold the hook properly? (You want to spend your time tying flies, not fidgeting with your tools.)
- Does the vise offer sufficient working room between the hook and bench top? Can I adjust the vise to get more working room?
- Does the vise come with accessories such as a bobbin rest and materials clip (used to conveniently hold tinsel and similar materials out of the way while tying other parts of a fly)?
- Does the vise come with a good warranty?

The HMH Spartan accommodates other jaws and a variety of accessories.

If you plan to tie midges and other tiny flies, make sure your new vise can accommodate the small hooks.

17

Do you need a vise with a C-clamp or a pedestal vise?

WHEN SELECTING A VISE, ONE OF THE FIRST DECISIONS YOU WILL HAVE TO MAKE IS WHETHER to buy one with a c-clamp or heavy pedestal base. A c-clamp locks the vise to the table or tying bench, and is therefore the most secure type of vise. You can place a vise mounted on a pedestal on any table, bench, or even a lapboard, so it is very portable. When choosing between a c-clamp or pedestal vise, consider the type of flies you plan to make and where you plan to tie.

Tying a deer-hair bass bug requires placing a lot of tension on the thread and hook. Most tiers who specialize in making bass bugs prefer using vises with c-clamps so the fly remains stationary when tension is applied to the thread. With a c-clamp, however, you are limited to using only tables and benches that will accept the size of the clamp you are using. As a result, these vises are not very portable; I have taught many fly-tying classes where students arrived with c-clamp vises that did not fit the tables that were provided.

Pedestal vises are portable and perfectly acceptable for tying the majority of flies; thread used to tie the average trout fly, for example, will snap before the vise moves on the table. And, of course, you can move the vise out of the way when preparing or counting out materials, and move it back into position when you're ready to tie. Just be sure to select a pedestal vise with a heavy base; Avoid any pedestal made of aluminum or some other lightweight material.

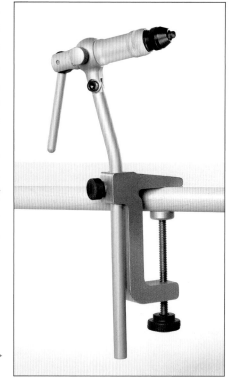

The Renzetti Apprentice
is an example of a vise
with a c-clamp base. ▶

18

What is rotary fly tying?

MOST PEOPLE THINK THAT YOU TIE A FLY BY PLACING A HOOK IN A FIXED VISE, AND YOUR right hand (assuming you are right-handed) wraps the thread and other materials onto the hook shank. This is the traditional way of tying a fly. With rotary fly tying, however, the opposite occurs: The head of the vise and hook rotate while your hands remain stationary, holding the materials. As if by magic, the ingredients wrap onto the shank as the hook spins.

Check out the example of wrapping a tinsel rib in the accompanying photographs. I placed the hook in the vise so it will spin, with the shank acting as the axis of the turning hook. The rib neatly wraps on the hook as I turn the vise. This method works for applying most ingredients that are wrapped on the hook shank: thread, floss, tinsel, wire, dubbing, and many braided materials.

Rotary fly tying is a favorite technique of commercial fly tiers interested in increasing their production.

1. Start tying the fly: tie on a piece of tinsel and wrap the floss body. Hang the thread on the bobbin rest.

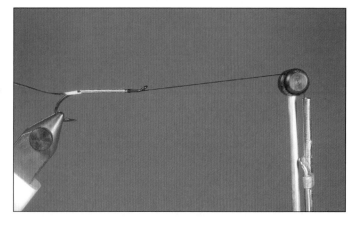

2. Turn the head and jaws on the rotary vise;
The tinsel neatly wraps up the body.

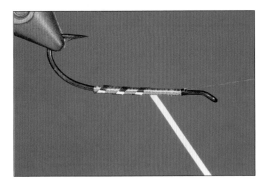

3. Tie off and clip the excess
piece of tinsel.

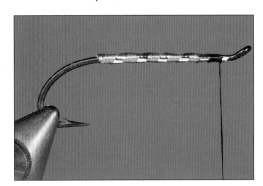

19

The proper way to place a hook in the vise

MANY BEGINNING FLY TIERS ARE SURPRISED TO LEARN THAT THERE IS A CORRECT—AND AN incorrect—way to mount a hook in the vise.

Some manufacturers report receiving returned vises that have tiny chips in the tips of the jaws. Fly tiers see photographs of flies perched in the very ends of the jaws, and believe this is the proper way to clamp a hook in a vise. In truth, very little clamping pressure is needed when you're taking a photograph; When tying a fly, however, you have to apply more pressure to tightly clamp the hook in place. As a result of this increased force, the tips of even the best vises might chip.

When clamping a hook in the vise, place the hook deep into the jaws to maximize the amount of surface contact between the inside of the jaws and the hook; this will reduce the amount of pressure you will have to apply to get the hook to hold still while tying the fly. Position the hook shank level or cocked slightly upright; do not place the shank angling downward or the thread will slip off the front when completing the fly.

This fly is perched in the tip of the jaws.
This is the wrong way to mount a hook
in the vise.

This is the correct way to place a hook in a vise;
The jaws can clamp the hook without applying
excessive pressure on the locking mechanism.

20

How to maintain a vise

A QUALITY VISE REQUIRES VERY LITTLE MAINTENANCE. BUT, EVEN THE BEST VISES—MADE of the finest materials—will eventually show small amounts of fine rust, especially on the jaws.

Remove the last hook when you're done tying. Release the tension on the jaws and locking mechanism.

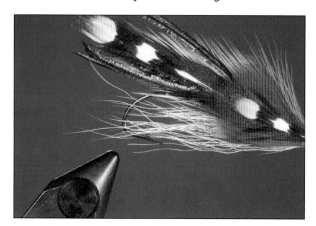

If you detect rust on your vise's jaws, remove it using grade 0000 steel wool. Lightly buff the metal to remove the rust. NEVER use a coarser grade of steel wool or apply too much pressure, as this can scratch the surface of your vise. Every few months, lightly spray the metal surfaces of the vise with fine oil. Use a clean cloth to wipe away any excess oil.

Apply one tiny drop of fine oil to every pivot point and joint on the head and stem of the vise. Wipe away any excess with a clean cloth.

Always remove the last hook from the vise jaws when you complete your tying session. Never leave a hook clamped in the vise with the idea that you will return later to complete the fly; Relieve the tension on the vise to avoid fatiguing the jaws or locking mechanism.

21

What other fly-tying tools do I need?

GOING TO A SPECIALTY STORE AND ASKING "WHAT do I need" is a dangerous question: An unscrupulous or unknowledgeable proprietor might load you down will all sorts of gadgets that will not meet your needs. This short list of small tools is all you will need to start tying flies.

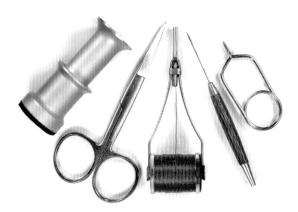

- A quality bobbin holds spooled materials such as thread and floss while you tie a fly.
- A bodkin, which is a heavy needle with a handle, is excellent for picking hairs and other fibers off of a fly, applying cement to the thread head of a finished pattern, and numerous other uses.

- A hair stacker evens the tips of a bunch of hair when tying the wing on an Elk-hair Caddis and similar flies.
- High-quality scissors. You can skimp on expenses in some areas, but purchase the best scissors you can afford.
- Hackle pliers grasp the tip of a hackle while you wrap the feather on the fly.

22

A backing plate reduces eye strain

A BACKING PLATE IS A DEVICE THAT SETS behind the vise and contrasts with the color of the pattern you are tying, making it easier to see the fly and reducing eyestrain. For example, tying a brown fly against a dark wooden tabletop is difficult; a background of a different color makes it much easier to see your work.

Commercial backing plates are available for most vises, but anything that contrasts with the color of the fly you are tying will work; even a sheet of paper will make it easier to see the fly.

You can purchase a backing plate to fit the stems of most vises, but you can also use a sheet of paper or anything that provides contrast to the color of the fly you are tying. ▶

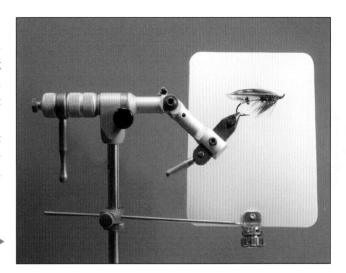

23

Select the correct scissors for the job

QUALITY SCISSORS WILL CUT ALMOST ANY FLY-TYING MATERIAL, BUT MANY ARE DESIGNED for specific applications. For example, use scissors with fine tips, lightweight handles, and small serrations to trim natural materials such as hair, fur, and feathers. If you plan to tie deer-hair bass bugs, select scissors with thicker serrations in one blade: The serrations hold the hair fibers while the sharp, non-serrated blade does the actual cutting.

Synthetic materials are especially tough on fine scissors and will quickly dull the blades. If you plan to use a lot of synthetic hair and flash materials, buy scissors specified for use with these types of ingredients. The blades will be a little heavier and probably made of carbon steel so they can hold an edge longer.

Never use fine-tipped or lightweight fly-tying scissors to cut wire or other metals. These materials will quickly dull the blades and loosen the screw or rivet holding the blades together. Either use scissors marketed for use with these materials, or purchase an inexpensive pair of scissors that you replace when the blades become dull and unusable.

Bass-bug guru Chris Helm crafted this great mouse using deer hair. Scissors designed to clip deer hair make the job much easier.

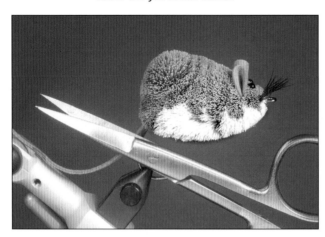

Fly-tying expert Pat Cohen crafted this amazing fish using spun deer hair.

24

Proper bobbin technique for improved thread wrapping

YOU'VE MOUNTED A SPOOL OF THREAD IN YOUR BOBBIN, AND STARTED THE THREAD ON the hook: Great, you're ready to tie a fly! But, did you know that there are simple techniques that will make it much easier to use and control your bobbin?

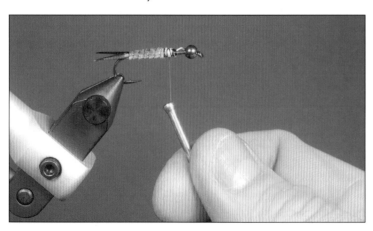

First, grasp the narrow bobbin tube between your thumb and forefinger, and place the spool of thread and body of the bobbin in the palm of your hand. The ends of your fingers should be near the tip of the tube. This will give you the best grip on the bobbin and increase your control over the tool.

Second, only a short piece of thread should extend between the tip of the bobbin and the hook. Using the smallest amount of thread will increase your ability to control the tension and accurately place thread wraps on the hook.

25

Off-hand tying techniques

HOW YOU HOLD THE BOBBIN AND USE YOUR DOMINANT TYING HAND IS IMPORTANT TO your ability to efficiently tie nice flies. How you use your non-dominant off hand is equally important to developing correct fly-tying skills.

You'll typically hold materials on the hook using your off hand while wrapping the thread and tying them to the fly using your dominant hand. Carefully and accurately position the materials on the hook. Grasp the materials as close as possible to the hook so they remain in place and do not roll around the shank when applying thread pressure; Avoid holding your fingers far from the hook when applying new materials to the shank.

1. Grasp the end of the material near the tips of your fingers. Place the material in position on the hook. Tie the material in place.

2. Always avoid holding your fingers far from the hook when applying new materials to the shank.

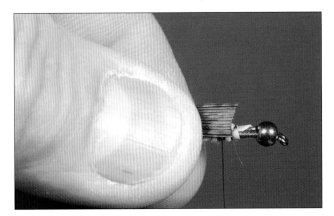

26

The half-hitch is a very important knot

THE HALF-HITCH IS AN ESSENTIAL KNOT FOR TYING NEAT FLIES: IT IS A SNAP TO MAKE, IT does a fine job of holding things in place between steps, and it adds no bulk. In fact, rather than making a complicated whip-finish to complete the head of a fly before snipping the thread, just make three or four half-hitches and add a drop of cement. I've used this method of finishing flies for more than thirty years, and my patterns never fall apart.

Stop struggling to learn how to use a whip-finishing tool. Instead, learn how to make a simple half-hitch. With practice, you can place a half-hitch exactly where you wish on the hook.

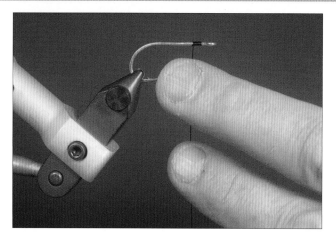

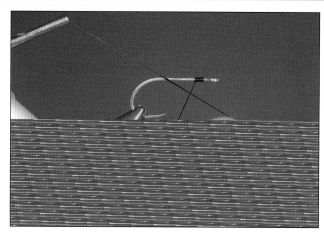

1. Extend about four inches of thread from the tip of the bobbin. Hold the bobbin in your off hand. Place the tips of your forefinger and index finger against the thread.

2. Raise the bobbin to the left and turn your fingers so the thread crosses.

3. Place the loop of thread on the hook.

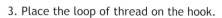

4. Pinch the loop of thread between your index and forefinger. Start drawing the bobbin and thread to the left to close the loop.

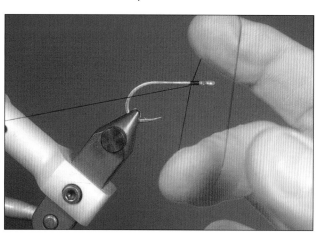

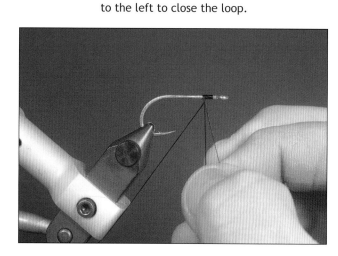

5. Continue drawing the thread to the left to completely close the loop of thread on the hook. Continue grasping the loop until the knot tightens.

6. Our half-hitch knot is done. With a little practice, you can place a half-hitch anywhere you wish on the hook.

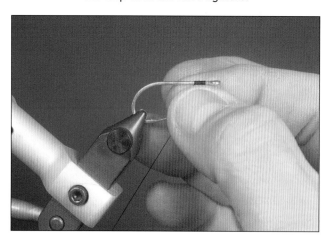

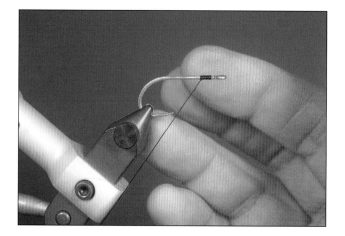

Which bobbin should I use?

OUR GOAL IS TO DEMYSTIFY FLY TYING AND MAKE IT EASY AND ACCESSIBLE. HOWEVER, JUST like with selecting the correct scissors to do a job, it helps to understand the different types of bobbins and choose the one that best meets your needs.

A bobbin is a simple tool that holds spooled materials, typically thread or floss. The bobbin makes it easy to grasp the spool while tying a fly, and it allows you to let the spool hang from the fly without unraveling. You'll find a selection of bobbins in the fly-tying section of any fly shop.

First, you'll need a bobbin to hold spools of thread. This sort of bobbin will have a narrow metal tube made of metal or hard plastic. Sometimes the tip of a metal tube has a ceramic insert to prevent the thread from contacting the edge of the metal tube and fraying; this tool is called a "ceramic bobbin." A ceramic bobbin costs a couple of dollars more than a plain metal-tubed bobbin, but it is typically worth the slight extra expense.

If you plan to tie flies requiring floss bodies, such as classic wet flies, streamers, and salmon or steelhead flies, you will want a floss bobbin. A floss bobbin has a wider tube to accommodate this thicker material. While you can simply clip a length of floss off the spool, tie it to the hook, and then wrap the body of the fly, placing the spool in a bobbin keeps the floss cleaner and you will waste less material.

In addition to the bobbin, a bobbin threader is a convenient tool for getting the thread or floss through the narrow tube. You can purchase an actual bobbin threader at your neighborhood fly shop, but a looped piece of monofilament will also serve as a simple and inexpensive threader.

Here we see the tips (*left to right*) of a plain metal-tubed bobbin, a ceramic bobbin, and a floss bobbin.

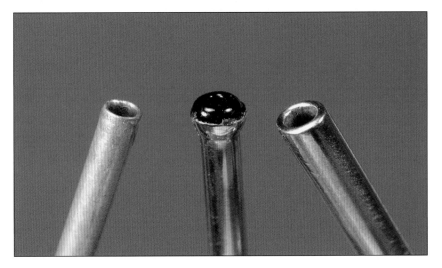

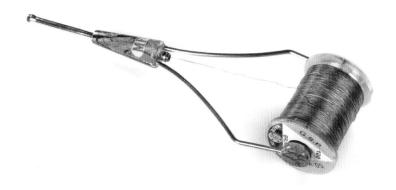

Set your chair and vise
at the proper height

SELECT YOUR CHAIR AND TYING WORKBENCH OR TABLE CAREFULLY. YOUR CHAIR SHOULD
be comfortable and offer ample back support. Tie at a table, desk, or bench that allows you to set the vise jaws about
even with your lower chest. If your arms or shoulders become fatigued, try lowering your vise; If the back of your
neck becomes strained because you are humped over while you tie, raise your vise so you're looking straight at the fly.

    Too many tiers complain of shoulder and neck pain. You can largely eliminate these common problems by choos-
ing the proper chair and placing the vise in the correct position.

Select a workbench that lets you set the vise jaws
about even with your lower chest. Now
add a comfortable chair with good back support,
and you're ready to tie. (*Courtesy of Orvis*)

Feathers, Furs, and More: Selecting the Right Materials for Tying Flies

Is it okay to substitute materials when tying a fly?

MANY FLY TIERS BELIEVE THEY MUST USE THE EXACT INGREDIENTS LISTED IN A PATtern recipe when tying a fly; they would never dream of using other brands or colors of materials. But what happens if your local fly shop doesn't have one or more of the ingredients specified in the recipe? Does this mean you can't tie the fly? Of course not.

Feel free to substitute with other materials when tying a fly. It is often possible to select a different but similar color or brand and create a close copy of the pattern. So what if your finished fly looks a bit different? It just might catch more fish.

Look at this basic Bead-Head Hare's-Ear Nymph; this is one of the first patterns you'll learn to make in fly-tying class. The original recipe calls for hare's-ear dubbing for the body, but you can substitute with standard rabbit dubbing or a wide variety of packaged natural, synthetic, and blended natural/synthetic dubbings. You can make the tail using pheasant tail fibers, hackle fibers, or almost any mottled duck flank fibers. In fact, you can tie this pattern using a regular nymph hook, a long-shank nymph hook, or even a curved-shank nymph hook. You can use an almost unlimited combination of materials to create a very similar fish-catching pattern.

Count out the materials before you tie

ONE OF THE SIMPLEST WAYS TO INCREASE YOUR FLY-TYING speed is to count and lay out the materials you will use before making a group of flies. Let's say you want to tie a half-dozen Light Hendrickson dry flies. Lay out six size 14 dry-fly hooks, six light ginger hackles, a small bunch of Hendrickson pink dubbing for making the bodies, and several wood duck feathers for fashioning the wings. Place a spool of pink or tan thread in your bobbin. Now you're ready to tie the flies. This simple method will keep your workspace cleaner, you'll tie more efficiently, and you'll make more flies in less time.

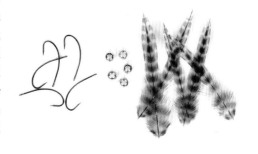

Simple ideas for storing materials

HOW ARE YOU GOING TO STORE YOUR GROWING COLLECTION OF FLY-TYING MATERIALS? AN efficient storage system should serve three goals: keep your fly-tying area clean, organize your materials so you can quickly find what you need, and protect natural ingredients—hair and feathers—from pests. There are many wonderful fly-tying stations that are also great-looking pieces of furniture and fit well into most homes.

A tackle box is another option. A big tackle box conveniently holds large amounts of materials and is portable. Select a tackle box that has trays for arranging small tools and spools of thread and wire, and a long, flat bottom for accommodating dry-fly hackle capes and similar bulky objects. Plastic freezer bags are ideal for organizing groups of materials; you could have separate bags containing packs of hooks, floss, dubbing, and so on. Store the bags in the tackle box, and toss in a few mothballs to ward off pests that might attack your precious materials.

This storage system is particularly ideal if you do not have space in your home or apartment to set up a permanent fly-tying station, or if you'd like to take your tying materials with you on your next fishing trip.

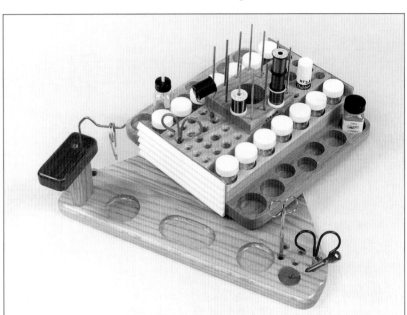

This fly-tying station, manufactured by the Oasis Company, is both efficient and looks great.

Deciphering thread sizes

THERE ARE A WIDE VARIETY OF THREAD SIZES, BUT YOU'LL ONLY NEED TWO OR THREE TO make the majority of flies; the other sizes of thread—at the very large and extra small ends of the range—are for specialized applications. Typically, use size 3/0 for tying saltwater flies and bass bugs, size 6/0 for freshwater streamers and nymphs, and size 8/0 for trout dry flies. Note, however, that there is no industry standard for determining the diameter ratings of thread, and one manufacturer's size 6/0 might be comparable to another company's size 8/0.

Recently, some fly-tying materials suppliers adopted the "denier" thread rating system from the garment and cloth industries. This method rates the actual weight, rather than the diameter, of the thread, so you can make exact comparisons between different brands of thread.

Size 3/0 = 210 denier
Size 6/0 = 160 denier
Size 8/0 = 80 denier

33

Soft materials give flies realistic movement

WHICH IS THE MOST IMPORTANT: TO FISH WITH A FLY THAT LOOKS REALISTIC, OR TO USE one that has a realistic swimming action? As you gain more fly-fishing experience, you'll probably come to the conclusion that flies that pulsate, swim, and breathe in the water catch more fish. While it's hard to give small flies realistic swimming action, it's relatively easy to make larger patterns such as streamers appear to be alive. Using soft, flowing materials is the key.

Marabou and soft hackles pump and flow in the water. Soft hairs also make flies look alive. Some synthetic materials are a little too stiff and make flies look like swimming paint brushes, which is no surprise because some of these ingredients are used in real brushes. Soft, synthetic hairs, as well as flowing flash materials, are great for tying baitfish imitations that look alive.

Always remember to consider how a fly looks *and* behaves in the water, and that how a fly moves is often more important.

The White Marabou Muddler, featuring a white marabou wing, is one of the author's favorite trout and bass flies. ▶

Protect the environment: Use non-toxic wire, beads, and cone heads

AT SOME POINT YOU WILL TIE FLIES REQUIRING LEAD WIRE WRAPPED ON THE HOOK SHANK, and perhaps dumbbell eyes or bead heads. These materials add weight to the flies so they sink. They are most commonly used on freshwater nymphs and streamers, and on many saltwater baitfish imitations.

Here's the rub: You will occasionally lose a fly, and you do not want to add lead to the environment. In fact, there have been proposals to eliminate the use of lead sinkers for baitfishing, much like lead shot was prohibited for hunting waterfowl many years ago.

Rather than using lead wire, beads, and dumbbells, select non-lead substitutes such as tungsten, which is heavier than lead and will quickly sink your subsurface flies to the desired depth. Brass beads are also commonly available.

Tungsten beads, dumbbell eyes, and cove heads add weight to flies and are lead-free.

This crab pattern was tied using a lead-free dumbbell.

35

What glues do I need?

New Jersey's Bob Popovics is famous for his Surf Candy series of saltwater baitfish imitations. The epoxy head on this Surf Candy is very durable.

ALL FLY SHOPS CARRY HEAD CEMENT. DAVE'S Flexament is a popular cement that remains slightly flexible when dry; it is ideal when you want a durable yet slightly soft and flexible finish. For most other fly-tying applications, ordinary clear fingernail polish is an ideal and commonly used cement.

Epoxy is also widely used to tie flies. Hundreds of saltwater patterns specify using epoxy to form the heads and backs of these flies; a few tiers have even developed reputations for creating patterns featuring epoxy. Avoid using five-minute epoxy; this material hardens too quickly and you'll waste more glue that you will use. Select a variety of epoxy with a longer curing time, and apply the glue to a batch of flies at one time.

Be sure to follow all the warning labels on the glues you select, and be sure to use these products with adequate ventilation.

36

What is the difference between dry-fly and hen hackle?

HACKLES ARE THE FEATHERS THAT COME FROM THE NECKS OF CHICKENS. THEY ARE ONE OF the most important ingredients for tying trout flies.

As the name implies, use dry-fly hackle to make flies that float. The best feathers contain lots of stiff fibers that keep flies perched on the surface film. The quills are also narrow to reduce bulk, and they do not twist when you wrap the feathers around hooks.

Use hen hackle to tie wet flies and nymphs. The softer fibers give these flies realistic swimming action that mimics insects struggling to the surface.

Fly shops sell both dry-fly and hen capes, which are the complete pelts of feathers. A quality cape contains hundreds of feathers in a wide range of sizes. You can also buy packages of hackles to tie smaller batches of flies; these offer a great way to save money and still tie with high-quality materials.

Purchase the best hackles you can afford. Nothing leads to frustration faster than tying with poor-quality hackle.

This adult drake imitation (*left*) was tied using a dry-fly hackle; the bead-head wet fly was made using a wet-fly hackle. ▶

37

What are the different ways to wrap a hackle on a hook?

THERE ARE TWO BASIC WAYS TO WRAP A HACKLE ON A HOOK. WRAPPING THE FEATHER around the hook behind the eye is the first common method. This creates what is called a "hackle collar," and is used to tie high-floating dry flies. A hackle collar typically consists of four or five turns of hackle around the hook, but some patterns, such as a bushy Royal Wulff, will have many more wraps.

Spiral-wrapping the hackle up the hook is the second most common method. If you take a beginner's fly-tying class, this might be the first technique you'll learn when the teacher shows you how to make a Woolly Bugger; this is often the first fly covered in tying classes.

Use fine dry-fly hackles for making floating flies. Select saddle hackle when tying Woolly Buggers and some large nymphs.

This classic dry fly, tied by Mike Valla, has a typical hackle collar wrapped at the base of the wings.

A saddle hackle spiral-wrapped up the body of this large stonefly nymph imitates the legs of the natural insect.

How to start the thread on the hook

1. Place the thread against the hook. Hold the tag up and to the left at a 45-degree angle. (The spool of the thread and the bobbin are down and out of the photo.) Begin wrapping the spooled thread onto the tag.

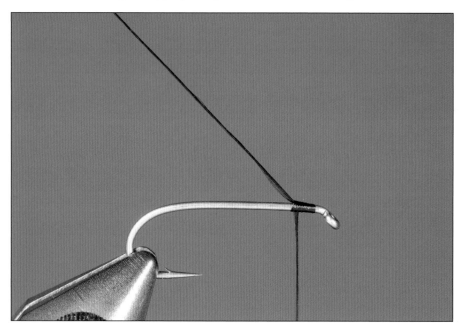

2. Continue holding the tag end of the thread at a 45-degree angle. Wrap the spooled thread toward the end of the hook. Each new thread wrap slips down the tag and neatly into place on the hook.

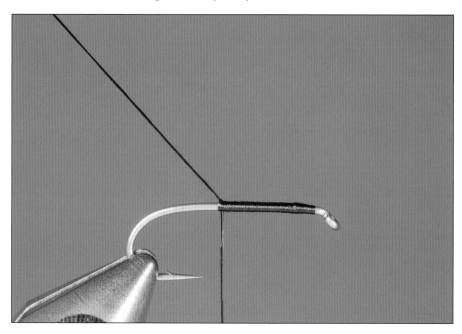

YOU'RE AT YOUR FLY-tying station and a hook is in the vise. All the materials are laid out in front of you, and the thread is your bobbin. You are ready to tie a fly! The first step is to start the thread on the hook shank. It sounds simple, yet this basic fly-tying procedure stymies many novice tiers. Here's how to start the thread on the hook.

First, grasp the bobbin in your dominant hand, and the tag end of the thread between the thumb and forefinger of your other hand; the entire length of thread should measure only about two inches. Next, place the thread against the near side of the hook; most tiers position the tag end of thread above the hook shank. Hold the tag end at a 45-degree angle, and make four or five wraps onto the base of the tag. Continue holding the tag end at a 45-degree angle and wrap toward the end of the hook; each new wrap of thread will neatly slip down the tag into position on the hook. Wrap the thread all the way to the end of the shank and tie the fly.

Measuring materials and leads to consistency

ONE OF THE HALLMARKS OF A GOOD FLY TIER IS THAT ALL OF HIS PATTERNS LOOK THE SAME; they appear as though they all popped out of the same vise. The key is maintaining similar proportions in the various parts of the flies. The length and number of fibers used to tie the tails are roughly the same. The diameter of the bodies is the same. The size and proportions of the wings are the same, and a careful tier uses the same number of wraps to make the hackle collar. Whether he is dressing dry flies, nymphs, streamers, saltwater patterns, or bass bugs, he plans ahead so each component looks the same.

The hook is a very convenient measuring device for judging the length and proportions of the parts of the flies you tie. The overall length of the shank, width of the gap, and the length from the hook point to the tip of the barb are just a few of the dimensions you can use for measuring materials. When you change hook sizes, the sizes of these dimensions will change accordingly; whether you are tying a size 22 or size 12 fly, the proportions remain consistent.

Use the hook to measure the dimensions of the different pats of a fly. For example, the length of the hook is a great way to gauge the length of a feather wing.

What is dubbing wax and why is it important?

DUBBING WAX IS AN ESSENTIAL INGREDIENT FOR TYING THE DUBBED BODIES on many important dry flies, nymphs, and wet flies. This extra-tacky wax comes in tubes. All fly shops stock it.

Dubbing wax is extremely easy to use. When you're ready to tie the body of the fly, swipe a small amount of wax on the thread. Next, spread a pinch of dubbing on the waxed section of thread; the wax makes the dubbing adhere to the fine thread. Spin the bobbin to tighten the dubbing around the thread like rope. Wrap the dubbed thread up the hook to make the body of the fly.

Here's an important tip: Keep the tube in your shirt pocket or close to your skin to keep the wax warm and soft. Softer wax is much easier to apply to the thread.

The importance of learning thread control

NOTHING IS MORE FRUSTRATING THAN HAVING THE THREAD SNAP AT A CRITICAL MOMENT when tying a fly: the thread unwraps, materials come loose, and the fly falls apart. Sometimes a small burr in the end of

a metal bobbin tube nicks the fine fibers and weakens the thread, but I think some tiers leap to blaming their tools rather than examining their tying skills.

Mastering proper thread control is a basic fly-tying skill that is easy to master. Here's how.

Place a spool of thread in the bobbin, and mount a stout hook in the vise. Start the thread on the hook. Next, tightly grasp the spool of thread so no more thread can come out of the bobbin. Pull the bobbin until the thread snaps. Repeat this procedure several times until you have a feel for how much tension you can apply to the thread until it breaks. Repeat this exercise whenever you change thread diameters. You will quickly master thread control and rarely break thread when tying.

Tying a small, dry fly requires using very narrow thread. Learn the breaking strength of the thread you are using before tying the fly.

42

Are natural fly-tying materials safe?

I NEVER THOUGHT I'D HEAR THIS QUESTION: "ARE MY FLY-TYING MATERIALS safe to use?" But, several suppliers of fly-tying materials, especially the farmers who grow chickens for hackle, report receiving calls from concerned tiers asking about the safety of their natural materials—feathers and furs. Most of the concern arose from reports of the spread of avian flu. Rest assured that your fly-tying materials are completely safe to use.

The packaged materials you purchase at your local fly shop have all been carefully washed and preserved. This processing kills any bacteria that might have been on these products. They are entirely safe and disease-free.

Remember, however, that many of these materials contain dyes, and they certainly contain residue from the tanning process. When using natural materials, keep your fingers away from your mouth and eyes, and wash your hands to remove any chemical residue when you are done tying flies.

43

A dash of flash can improve a fly

TIERS HAVE ADDED FLASH TO THEIR FLIES FOR CENTURIES. TRADITIONALLY, TINSEL AND WIRE were used to brighten patterns, but today we have many more options.

Almost all fly shops carry Krystal Flash and Flashabou, as well as many varieties of similar materials marketed under a host of different names. A few strands of one of these materials added to the wing of a streamer will brighten the fly and improve its ability to attract fish. And a small piece of Flashabou or similar material, pulled over the wing case of a nymph, will turn a decent fly into a real trout catcher. Some tiers use dubbing with flash to tie the bodies of dry flies; they swear that a bright floating pattern catches more fish than its dull-bodied cousin.

Flash materials are especially important to tying saltwater flies. A few strands of flash brighten a fly so a fish can see it from a greater distance, and the flash mimics the scales of a natural baitfish.

A few strands of flash material mimic the scales of a real baitfish.

Use ultra wire to make variations on established patterns

ULTRA WIRE, A PRODUCT OF WAPSI FLY, IS COPPER WIRE ANODIZED IN MANY COLORS. ULTRA Wire is a fine material for making variations of established patterns and creating your own original flies.

Ultra Wire comes in four sizes, so you can use it to tie a wide variety of flies. It is durable, easy to use, and has become a favorite material for making fish-catching nymphs, wet flies, and streamers. Use regular copper or silver Ultra Wire as called for in your favorite fly pattern recipe, or use another color of Ultra Wire to make a neat variation of that pattern. Simple products such as Ultra Wire open new and exciting possibilities in our tying.

Red Ultra Wire jazzed up this simple modern-looking nymph pattern.

45

What hairs and furs do I need to tie flies?

THERE ARE DOZENS OF HAIRS AND FURS USED TO TIE FLIES, BUT YOU ONLY NEED A FEW DIFferent varieties to start. You'll find everything you need at your local fly shop.

A patch of elk hair is essential for making the Elk-Hair Caddis, but fine deer hair is a perfectly acceptable substitute. Squirrel tail hair—gray and red fox squirrel—is ideal for making the wings on streamers. Bucktails, which come in natural and many dyed colors, are essential for making the wings and bellies on baitfish imitations.

You'll see a lot of patterns that call for hare's-ear dubbing for making the bodies on smaller nymphs and wet flies. Some tiers buy the masks (yes, the faces) of rabbits, and clip the fur from the skins. A better solution is to purchase packaged hare's-ear dubbing; it comes in natural and a rainbow of dyed colors.

Angora dubbing or a similar coarse hair is ideal if you wish to tie larger nymphs. Angora gives a fly a fuller body, and the thicker fibers create the impression of legs.

Remember that all of these hairs and furs come in a variety of dyed colors, increasing the possibilities for crafting great fish-catching flies.

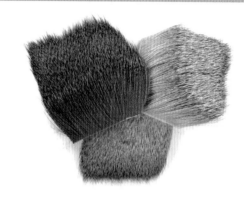

Even deer hair comes in a rainbow of colors.

46

Clean glue from the hook eye before removing the fly from the vise

IT'S UNAVOIDABLE: YOU WILL GET SOME GLUE IN THE HOOK EYE WHEN FINISHING A FLY. Even the most experienced tier occasionally gets a drop of cement in the hook eye. The seasoned fly dresser, however, knows to immediately remove the glue before popping the fly from the vise rather than trying to poke it out when fishing.

A bodkin needle is a handy tool for removing this glue. A better method, however, is to thread a small hackle or piece of peacock herl all the way through the hook eye. The soft, feather fibers neatly clean away the cement and leave the eye open for your tippet when fishing.

Spend your time on the water casting to the fish, not primping your flies!

Always clean the glue from the hook eye before placing ▶ a new pattern in your fly box.

Accurate thread wraps reduce bulk

A BIG, BULBOUS THREAD HEAD OR THICK BUMPS IN THE BODY RUIN THE APPEARANCE OF A finished fly. Typically, this common problem is due to using too many and needless wraps of thread. Further, making a few accurate and firm wraps creates a more durable fly than using a bunch of haphazard wraps.

Apply the material to the hook, and make one or two loose thread wraps. Check that the material is in the correct position. Next, slowly tighten the thread and simultaneously make a couple more firm wraps to lock the material in place. Follow this simple procedure every time you add a material.

With practice, you'll quickly use this simple technique when wrapping thread. Your flies will have a trimmer, more polished look, and they will be more durable and less apt to fall apart when fishing.

Learn how to make accurate thread wraps, and you'll soon be tying flies such as this classic salmon pattern.

48

Avoiding unsightly bumps in fly bodies

YOU WANT TO MAINTAIN THE SLENDER APPEARANCE IN FINE FLY BODIES MADE WITH FLOSS, thread, tinsel, and similar materials; small bumps will spoil the appearance of the finished flies.

The tag ends of the materials you tie to the hook should almost equal the length of the shank. The long tag ends will create a level underbody. And use size 8/0 (70 denier) or 6/0 (140 denier) flat-waxed thread. Spin the bobbin counterclockwise after every dozen wraps to remove any twist from the thread and keep the material lying flat and smooth on the hook.

1. Tie on the tinsel and red floss. Note that the tag ends of the material equal the length of the hook shank.

2. Wrap the thread up the hook. The tag ends under the thread create a level underbody.

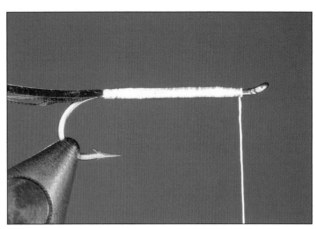

3. Here is the completed body of the fly. The body is level and smooth.

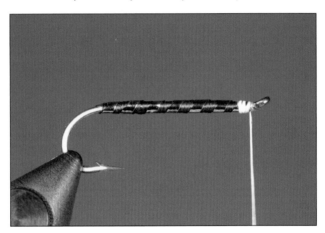

49

The parts of a hook

YOU PROBABLY ARE FAMILIAR WITH THE TERMS HOOK EYE AND POINT; EVEN IF YOU ARE NOT, you could probably figure them out just by looking at a hook. There are, however, terms that describe many of the other parts of a hook as well.

Barb: The small, sharp tab of metal pointing in the opposite direction from the hook point. The barb prevents the hook from becoming accidentally disengaged from the flesh in the fish's mouth.

Bend: The bend is part of the hook that bends down and curves to the sharp end of the hook.

Eye: The ring at the front of the hook where you tie the fly to the leader when fishing. The eye can be straight, turned up, or turned down.

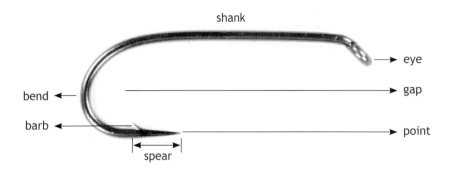

Gap: The distance between the hook point and the shank.

Point: This is the sharp business end of the hook.

Shank: The shank is the length of the hook from the eye to the beginning of the bend. The shank can be straight, but on some nymph hooks it is slightly curved.

Spear: The distance between the tip of the point and the tip of the barb.

50

De-barb the hook before tying the fly

The barb was mashed down on the hook before tying this fly.

MANY ANGLERS USE BARBLESS hooks to reduce damage to the mouths of the fish they catch, and to speed up releasing fish. While you can buy barbless hooks, most anglers simply crimp down the barbs on their flies. There is a chance, however, that smashing down the barb will weaken the hook and cause it to break; this problem is more common with fine dry-fly hooks than heavy-wire streamer or saltwater hooks. If you plan to fish barbless, bend down the barb before tying the fly. This way, if the hook does break, you've only wasted a hook, not your time and materials tying a fly.

Poppers are fun and easy to make

FLY FISHING FOR BASS AND PANFISH IS A HOOT, and so is making poppers. If you plan to spend any time fishing for these easy-to-catch species, then you should also schedule some time to make a few poppers.

Small corks, which you can buy at almost any hardware store, are ideal for making popper bodies. In addition to the corks, you'll need hooks, size 3/0 thread, superglue, feathers, rubber legs, and a couple of bottles of hobby enamel paint. Simply wrap a layer of thread on the hook shank, and cut a shallow, narrow channel in the side of a cork. Coat the thread with superglue, and press the hook into the channel in the cork. Paint the body in your favorite colors, and tie feathers, rubber legs, and perhaps a few strands of flash material behind the body.

Many fly shops sell small kits containing popper bodies, hooks, and construction instructions. Be sure to follow the instructions for selecting the correct type of paint for the materials used to make the bodies.

52

Craft store fun

WHILE WE ENCOURAGE YOU TO support your local fly shop whenever possible, it's impossible to talk about modern fly tying and not mention the great materials found in crafts stores.

Your local crafts store, as well as the crafts section of a large discount retailer, is a treasure trove of ideas for creating scads of new fish-catching flies. Look for closed-cell foam, felts, paints, epoxies and glues, doll eyes, sparkle and flash materials, and so much more, and imagine all of the original patterns you will be able to create.

Making flies requires developing the proper tying skills and having a good imagination. Visit your local crafts store, let your imagination run wild, and develop your own new flies using unusual fly-tying materials.

Tying Dry Flies That Ride Higher and Float Longer

What are the parts of a dry fly?

WHILE THERE ARE A WIDE VARIETY OF DRY FLIES, MANY CONTAIN COMMON PARTS. MOST dry flies, especially the popular patterns, contain the following ingredients: a tail, body, wing, and hackle collar.

Body: A body is commonly made with fine dubbing, a hackle quill stripped of its fibers, thread or floss. A body might have a rib tied of fine wire or thread. The rib strengthens the body and creates a segmented appearance.

Hackle collar: The hackle collar is one of the most outstanding features of a dry fly. Wrap a feather plucked from a hackle cape around the hook shank to form the collar.

Tail: A tail is typically tied using the fibers from a hackle or other feather, or some fine hair.

Wing: Dry-fly wings are tied using fine hair such as calf tail, feather fibers, sections clipped from feathers, and whole feathers.

54

Three common dry-fly wings

READ FLY-TYING BOOKS AND MAGAZINE ARTICLES, AND YOU'LL FIND A GREAT MANY STYLES of dry-fly wings. When learning to tie flies, however, concentrate on making the three most common forms of wings.

Hair wings are made using elk hair, deer hair, or some other fine hair. Tie this style of wing flat along the top of the hook to simulate caddisfly or stonefly wings.

Upright wings are made using feather fibers, sections of fibers clipped from whole teal, wood duck, or mallard flank feathers, and the entire rounded tips of hen hackles or English partridge feathers. Tie these wings to the top of the hook to simulate mayfly wings.

Wing posts are used to tie parachute dry flies. A wing post is typically fine hair or polypropylene yarn, and a hackle is wrapped around the base of the wing post to complete the parachute.

◄ Hair wing

Wing post

Upright wings using sections of feather

55

Prepare the hackle before tying the fly

TAKE A FEW MOMENTS TO PREPARE A HACKLE before tying it to the hook. It takes just seconds, it will make wrapping the feather around the hook much easier, and the finished fly will look much better.

Note the fibers brushed out perpendicular to the feather stem. Strip and discard these fibers, and use ► the remaining piece of hackle to tie the fly.

First, select the proper hackle to match the hook size. Typically, the length of the fibers should equal one and one-half to two times the width of the gap. This rule of thumb usually applies to both wet and dry flies.

Strip the excess fluffy fibers from the base of the hackle. Continue stripping fibers from the bottom one-quarter to one-third of the feather until you reach the thinnest part of the quill; this is called the "sweet spot" of the feather.

Next, strip a few more fibers from the side of the feather that will lay against the hook shank; this will allow the feather to wind neatly onto the hook.

56

How to wrap a regular dry-fly hackle

WRAPPING A HACKLE COLLAR FOR TYING A standard dry fly is one of the most important things you will learn. It is often best to practice wrapping hackle collars on a bare hook before attempting to tie a fly.

After preparing the hackle, start the thread on the hook. Tie the bare hackle stem to the hook with the dull, concave side of the feather facing you. (The concave side is the side of the feather that was against the skin of the hackle cape.)

Wrap the hackle after you have tied the wings. Grasp the tip of the feather with hackle pliers. Make one complete wrap of hackle behind the wings, then make one complete wrap

1. Tie the feather to the hook with the concave side facing you.

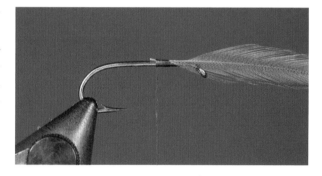

directly in front of the wing. Now make three or four more close wraps of hackle; the quills should actually touch. Tie off and clip the excess hackle tip. Make a neat thread head, whip-finish the thread, and clip.

2. Grasp the tip of the feather with your hackle pliers (outside of the photo). Raise the feather and make one complete wrap around the hook.

3. Continue wrapping the hackle up the hook.

4. Carefully catch and tie off the remaining piece of hackle. Cut off the excess hackle. Brush back the hackle fibers. Make three or four firm thread wraps to lock the hackle collar in place.

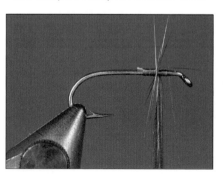

Judging hackle size

CHOOSING THE CORRECT SIZE OF HACKLE TO MAKE A DRY OR WET FLY IS ONE OF THE challenges you will face as a new tier. You can buy presorted hackles packaged to tie flies in a limited range of sizes—for example, a package might contain feathers to tie size 16 and 14 flies—but you will eventually want to own full capes that offer the complete range of feather sizes. This will require you to judge the length of the hackle fibers to match the size of fly you are making.

A hackle gauge, which you'll find in your local fly shop, is a handy tool for measuring the size of a hackle. Simply bend the feather around the post in the base of the gauge to fan out the hackle fibers; this is similar to wrapping a hackle around a hook shank. Read the length of the fibers on the gauge.

Another option is to place a hook in your vise and fold the feather around the bottom of the hook as if you were going to wrap the hackle collar. The fibers will fan out so you can judge the length. If the fibers are too long or short, select another feather and repeat. Typically, the fibers should equal about one and one-half times the width of the hook gap, but you can adjust this dimension as you gain more experience as a tier and angler.

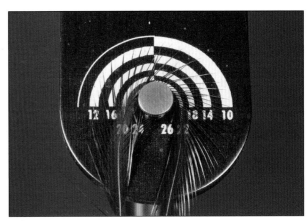

This hackle gauge, which fits onto the stem of a vise, is offered by Whiting Farms.

58

Dubbing for dry flies versus wet flies—What's the difference?

DUBBING IS USED TO TIE THE BODIES OF TROUT FLIES. WHEN MAKING IMITATIONS OF THE most important adult insects—mayflies, caddisflies, and stoneflies—use dubbing that has fine fibers and twists easily on the thread. This material makes compact, slender bodies that best match the profiles of real insects.

Most modern dry-fly dubbing is some variety of synthetic material. Antron dubbing, which comes in a dizzying array of colors, is one of the most popular. Add a package of olive, tan, brown, and golden yellow dry-fly dubbing to your fly-tying kit, and you'll be set to make imitations of dozens of important adult insects.

Use coarser dubbing for making nymphs and wet flies. Once again, think of the real insects: a nymph or emerging insect usually has a broader body and dangling, kicking legs. A material containing thick, coarse fibers yields a thicker body and imitates the legs of the natural insect.

Rabbit dubbing is ideal for making the bodies on small nymphs and wet flies. The soft fur helps create a narrow body, and the guard hairs mimic the legs of the insect. Coarse, Angora goat dubbing remains a favorite material for tying larger stonefly and dragonfly nymph imitations. A small selection of colors—black, brown, dark olive, tan, and golden yellow—is all you'll need to tie most nymphs and wet flies.

Use fine dubbing when tying flies such as this Sulfur Compara-dun.

59

What is cul de canard?

The tier used gray cul de canard to make the wing on this emerger imitation.

CUL DE CANARD FEATHERS, WHICH COME from the rump of a duck near the preen gland, have become one the most important ingredients for tying high-floating dry flies. You'll want to add cul de canard to your collection of fly-tying materials as soon as possible.

Some tiers believe that cul de canard, which comes in many natural and dyed colors, contains oils that keep these feathers afloat, but this is not so: One of the first steps in the dyeing process is to remove most of the natural oils so the dyes will adhere to the material. Yet, dyed cul de canard still floats like a cork. How can this be? Because the fibers on a cul de canard feather have microscopic hooks that trap air bubbles and keep the feather (and the duck) afloat; one cul de canard feather contains thousands of these tiny hooks.

Use cul de canard to make the wings on dry flies. Develop your own unsinkable flies, or add cul de canard to established patterns: a single cul de canard plume, placed under the wing of an Elk-Hair Caddis, increases the buoyancy of this time-tested fly.

60

How to make a parachute wing post

TO TIE PARACHUTE-HACKLED DRY FLIES, YOU'LL FIRST NEED TO KNOW HOW TO TIE THE proper wing post.

You may make the wing post using several common materials, including closed-cell foam and fine hair. Polypropylene yarn, which comes in a variety of realistic and bright colors, is one of the easiest ingredients to use. Many tiers select white, fluorescent pink, or fluorescent orange because these wings are easy to spot on the water; use one of these colors if you plan to fish in poor light or if you're having difficulty seeing your flies on the water.

In addition to the wide selection of colors, polypropylene yarn adds little bulk to a fly and requires only a few well-placed thread wraps to lock in place. Polypropylene wing posts are particularly useful when dressing small flies.

1. Fold a small section of yarn under the hook. Lock the yarn in place using three of four figure-eight wraps crossing on the bottom of the hook.

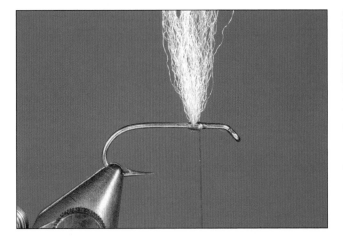

2. Wrap the thread up the base of the wing post. We'll complete tying the fly in the next tip.

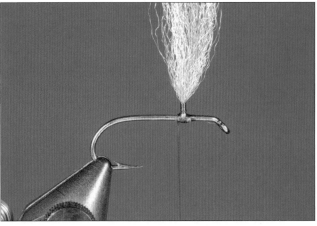

61

How to wrap a parachute hackle

TYING A PARACHUTE HACKLE MAY SEEM LIKE AN ADVANCED FLY-TYING TECHNIQUE, BUT IT really isn't complicated. The key is to break the task down into several steps.

First, wrap a small thread base around the base of the wing (see Tip No. 60.) Next tie the hackle to the base of the wing. Before wrapping the feather, tie the body of the fly. Finally, wrap the parachute hackle.

Think of these tasks as small individual steps, and you will quickly learn how to make fine parachute hackle dry flies.

1. Tie the hackle to the base of the wing post. Wrap the thread to the end of the hook shank.

2. Tie on several hackle fibers to form the tail of the fly.

3. Spin a pinch of fine dubbing on the thread and wrap the body of the fly.

4. Wrap the hackle down the wing post to form the parachute hackle collar. Carefully tie off the hackle behind the hook eye, and clip the surplus. Wrap a neat thread and tie off the thread; It's okay to brush back the hackle fibers and wing if you need room to work. Snip the thread.

How to tie split upright wings

MANY OF OUR MOST FAMOUS DRY FLIES ARE TIED WITH TWO SPLIT, UPRIGHT WINGS: THE Royal Wulff, the Quill Gordon, the Light and Dark Hendricksons, and many others. Some of these wings are tied using fine hair such as calf tail (select the straightest you can find—nothing with a lot of curl), mallard flank feathers, lemon wood duck flank feathers, and mallard flank feathers dyed to imitate wood duck.

The trick is not to tie on two separate wings, but to tie on a single clump of material—hair or feather fibers—and then divide the wings into two. If necessary, place careful thread wraps around the base of each wing to hold it in place. When learning to make this style of wings, it helps to start tying a slightly larger fly to get a feel for working with the material and crafting the wings. For example, if you wish to tie a batch of size 14 Light Hendricksons for the early May hatch on a local trout stream, start by making a size 10 or 12 fly, then tackle the smaller pattern.

Let's see how to tie a pair of classic upright and divided wings using a wood duck flank feather.

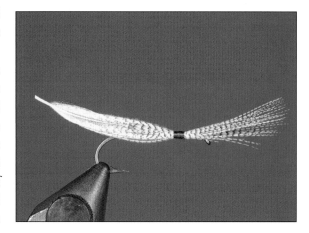

1. Tie the feather to the top of the hook; the tips of the fibers, which will form the wings, are about equal to the length of the hook shank.

2. Hold the clump of fibers upright. Fold and pinch the base of the fibers back. Wrap a tiny dam of thread in front of the clump to hold the fibers up.

3. Split the clump in two. Make a series of figure-eight wraps between the fibers to create the two wings.

63

How to tie a wulff hackle collar

This unusual looking Royal Wulff has a very specific purpose; this heavily hackled and bushy fly is used to catch Atlantic salmon and steelhead. The fly makes a wake across the surface of the water and generates angry strikes from the fish.

TO TIE THE ROYAL WULFF AND SIMILAR HIGH-floating dry flies, you'll need to learn one of two primary ways to create the trademark bushy hackle collars.

First, you can use an extra-long, dry-fly saddle hackle. One of these feathers, which sometimes measure up to ten inches long, is sufficient to tie collars on either three or four regular dry flies or one or two Wulff patterns.

You may also use two or three normal cock hackles to make a single Wulff hackle collar. Wrap one hackle on the hook, then tie off and clip the surplus hackle tip. Wrap the second and then the third feathers to create a bushy Wulff hackle collar.

The key to both of these methods is to allow ample space on the hook shank to fashion the collar. Also, rocking the feathers back and forth while wrapping prevents each new wrap of hackle from binding down the fibers of previous wraps.

64

Quills make great dry-fly bodies

STRIPPED HACKLE QUILLS ARE A TRADITIONAL ingredient for tying slender, tapered, segmented bodies on many dry and wet flies. The material is easy to use, and the finished bodies are very realistic looking.

The long feathers from the base of hackle capes are ideal for making stripped quills; they are rarely used for tying flies and are otherwise wasted. Pluck enough feathers for the flies you wish to tie. Strip the fibers from the hackles to reveal the bare quills. Place the quills in a dish of water to soften for tying; dry quills might crack and split when

◀ Mike Valla, a master at tying the classic Catskill dry flies, dressed this timeless Quill Gordon.

wrapping fly bodies. Next, tie the slender tip end of the quill to the end of the hook. Grasp the fatter base of the quill with your hackle pliers, and wrap the body. Tie off and clip the excess quill, and complete the fly. You can leave the body in the natural color of the quill, or allow it to dry and then color it with a permanent marker. I also strengthen the quill body with a drop of cement.

Stripped peacock quills, which are pieces of peacock herl with the turquoise green fibers removed, are also used to tie the dainty bodies on classic dry flies. Sometimes you can find packages of stripped peacock quills in a fly shop, but you'll probably have to make your own. Simply draw a piece of herl between your forefinger and thumbnail; the nail will strip the fibers from the quill. You can also remove the fibers using a pencil eraser.

Mike Valla tied this perfect Cahill Quill dry fly.

65

Big ideas for tying tiny flies

SOMETIMES TROUT ARE FEEDING ON SMALL INSECTS; YOU'LL SEE THEM SIPPING THE BUGS from the surface of the water. You'll have to match the hatch with an imitation of the same size; without a diminutive dry fly or emerger, you will not catch fish. Tying small flies—sizes 20 and smaller—is consequently another fly-tying skill you will want to learn.

Use a vise that has jaws that can accommodate small hooks and leave ample room for you to tie the fly; If you are in the market for a vise, buy one that will allow you to tie flies of all sizes. Fine-tipped scissors are also essential for tying small flies; with them, you will be able to slip the scissor tips in and carefully snip excess materials from the hook. Thin-diameter thread such as size 8/0 (70 denier) is another mandatory item for tying tiny flies. There is also gossamer gel-spun thread, size 50 denier, which is very narrow yet extremely strong. And, you might wish to use some sort of magnifying device—a gooseneck magnifier or even low-power reading glasses—to better see your work.

Spinners are critical to consistent fishing success

MANY NEW ANGLERS AND FLY TIERS OVERLOOK THE IMPORTANCE OF SPINNERS TO consistent fly-fishing success. A spinner is an adult mayfly that has returned to the river or lake to mate, with the females laying their eggs. After mating, the exhausted insects lie on the surface of the water with their wings outstretched.

Sometimes using a spinner imitation, such as this Rusty Spinner, is the key to fishing success. Be sure to make a few spinners whenever you tie dry flies.

Looking like small crosses, the spinners are easy targets for trout that want to gorge themselves. When the trout exhibit this feeding behavior, no fly other than a spinner imitation will catch a fish. I have experienced this on Vermont's Battenkill River, Colorado's North Platte, and even in remote waters in Labrador.

There are many spinner patterns, but the easiest solution to creating a good imitation is to tie a regular dry-fly tail and body. Next, tie a few strands of white or light-gray polypropylene yarn across the top of the hook to form the wings of a spent spinner. Spin a tiny pinch of dubbing on the thread and wrap the thorax of the fly.

Whenever you tie a few dry flies to match the mayfly hatches on your local waters, be sure to twist up a few spinners. On your next fishing trip, you'll be prepared to match the beginning as well as the end of the hatch, and you'll continue catching fish throughout the day.

Foam flies float forever

CLOSED-CELL FOAM HAS BECOME A FAVORITE MATERIAL for tying dry flies. It is tough, comes in many colors, and is unsinkable. You can buy sheets of foam in several useful thicknesses for making the bodies of flies, and narrow cords of foam for making wing posts. Some tiers use foam to create outlandish-looking grasshoppers, crickets, and similar patterns, and others incorporate foam into more realistic looking flies.

 This foam-bodied salmonfly imitation is unsinkable!

Foam flies are especially useful as part of a dry fly-dropper rig. Use the foam fly as a high-floating strike indicator. Attach a short piece of tippet material to the bend in the fly's hook, and tie a small nymph or emerger to the other end of the tippet.

When tying with foam, take care not to cut into the material with the thread. Hold the material in position, and make two or three gentle thread wraps. Gradually tighten the thread and make two or thread more wraps. If necessary, add a small drop of superglue to the thread wraps to lock the foam to the hook.

68

Tie off—don't clip—the excess hackle tip

FLY-TYING GURU AL BEATTY SAYS IT IS BETTER TO tie off—not clip—the excess hackle tip after wrapping the collar of the fly. He uses this simple method to create good-looking, fish-catching patterns.

Tie the fly and wrap the hackle following the regular methods. Carefully tie off the excess hackle tip using three wraps of thread. Next, lift the hackle tip, and wrap the thread between the hook eye and the surplus tip. Fold the tip up into the hackle collar. Wrap the thread back over the base of the tip; the tip becomes hidden in the full hackle collar. Wrap a neat thread head, and tie off and clip the thread.

This method of tying off the excess hackle tip is quick and easy, and prevents small fibers from clogging the hook eye and making it difficult to tie the fly to the leader while fishing.

1. First, wrap the hackle collar of the fly. Wrap the collar almost to the hook eye. Do not tie off and clip the excess hackle tip yet.

2. Tie off the hackle tip on top of the hook. Brush back the hackle fibers and surplus piece of feather. Wrap the thread toward the end of the hook; wrap over the hackle tip and the base of the first few fibers.

3. Clip the excess hackle near the thread head; any remaining piece of feather blends into the collar.

Tie visible dry flies

POOR EYESIGHT, FOAM AND FROTH IN THE WATER, AND LOW-LIGHT CONDITIONS CAN MAKE it difficult to see your fly on the surface of the water. But it is easy to tie flies that you'll be able to spot on the water a country mile away.

Tie the wings of the fly using brightly-colored, feather fibers or polypropylene yarn. Fluorescent orange, yellow, and chartreuse are favorite colors for making flies more visible. Use the identical tying techniques you would use when tying a regular pattern. And don't worry: There is no evidence to suggest that these brightly colored wings spook even the wariest fish.

Keep an eye on your fly: give it a colorful wing so you can see it on the water under all fishing conditions.

A bright yarn wing post makes it easy to spot this fly on the water.

What is a terrestrial, and why should I care?

MANY OF THE FLIES WE TIE ARE DESIGNED TO IMITATE AQUATIC INSECTS: STONEFLIES, mayflies, caddisflies, damselflies, dragonflies, and more. Aquatic insects live their immature lives in the water, and eventually emerge to mate. The females then drop their eggs into the water to repeat the lifecycle.

Terrestrial insects are born and live exclusively on dry land: grasshoppers, ants, crickets, beetles, inchworms, and anything else that can fall into the water and become a meal for the fish. During mid to late summer, terrestrial patterns can spell the difference between having a good or a great day on the stream.

If you live in grasshopper country, be sure to tie a few 'hopper' imitations for mid-summer fishing.

Wherever you fly fish for trout, terrestrials will catch fish. In fact, many anglers travel to Montana in August to cast grasshopper imitations into that state's rivers, and cricket patterns have an important place on Pennsylvania's storied limestone streams. As a tier, you will want to learn to make some patterns to match these important insects.

CHAPTER

5

Tying Nymphs and Emergers That Catch More Trout

What are the parts of a nymph?

NYMPHS ARE CRITICAL TO TROUT-FISHING SUCCESS, AND YOU'LL WANT TO LEARN HOW TO make a variety of these important patterns. First, we need to review the basic parts of a common nymph imitation. A basic nymph contains a tail, abdomen, thorax, wing case, and legs.

Abdomen: This is the first section of the body. Although the entire body is sometimes fashioned with the same material, the abdomen is usually quite distinct from the front of the body. Natural and synthetic dubbings are the most common materials for tying the abdomen. An abdomen often has a rib made of wire to increase the strength of the fly and create a segmented appearance.

Legs: Almost all nymph imitations have some sort of legs. On smaller patterns, such as the Hare's-Ear Nymph, the coarse guard hairs in the rabbit dubbing used to tie the thorax are sufficient to suggest legs. You can also use feather fibers or strands of rubber to make legs on nymphs.

Tail: The tail and antennae are commonly tied with feather fibers, fur, or rubber legs. A tail made using a small tuft of soft rabbit fur flows in the water and makes a nymph look as if it is swimming and struggling in the current. Only larger stonefly nymph imitations typically have antennae.

Thorax: The thorax is the front half on the body. The thorax is typically thicker than the abdomen to create the proper silhouette. A slightly coarse variety of dubbing is ideal for making a nymph thorax. A thorax usually does not have a rib.

Wing case: This is the back of the thorax. The wing case is sometimes referred to as the *wing pads*.

Rubber legs, tails, and antennae for nymphs

YOU CAN USE MANY NATURAL MATERIALS to tie the tails, legs, and antennae on nymphs; hackle fibers, biots, and some stiff hairs are popular ingredients. Rubber legs, however, make some of the best appendages. This inexpensive material comes in several thicknesses and colors, and it is extremely easy to use. All you have to do is fold a piece of rubber legs around the thread and tie it to the end of the fly to make the tails. Repeat this to tie a set of legs to each side of the fly, and repeat this again to tie antennae on the front of the fly.

My first choice is to use rubber legs when tying nymphs. The material is indestructible when tying and fishing.

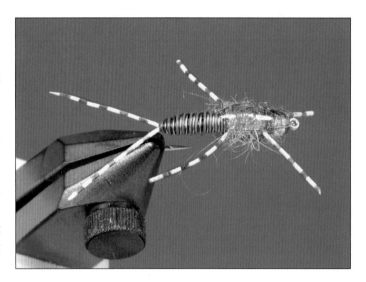

Do you need to tie realistic-looking flies?

EVERYONE WANTS TO LEARN HOW TO TIE FLIES that look like real insects, but simpler generic patterns probably catch more fish. The competitors in the World Fly-Fishing Championships have learned that it is better to use flies that suggest the appearance of a variety of insects than it is to mimic specific species of bugs. These expert anglers argue that the general size, shape, and color of a pattern is far more important than if it bristles with realistic-looking tails, legs, and whiskers. Now we know why the time-honored Hare's-Ear and Pheasant-Tail Nymphs—which can imitate a large number of insects anywhere in the world—remain so popular.

The realistic looking nymph on the left is great, but the two simpler flies on the right will probably catch more fish.

It's easy to get overwhelmed with the huge number of patterns found in books, magazines, and online. To avoid confusion, learn to tie a handful of flies that match a cross section of the most common nymphs you find clinging to the rocks in your home waters.

74

Pheasant-tail fibers make realistic-looking nymph bodies

WITH TIME, YOU WILL LEARN HOW TO USE DUBBING TO MAKE THE BODIES ON NYMPHS AND wet flies. If you're still fumbling with this technique, however, spend an evening making flies using pheasant-tail fibers.

All fly shops sell pheasant-tail feathers. When wrapped on a hook shank, the fibers make wonderfully segmented and mottled bodies. The famous Pheasant-Tail Nymph is made almost entirely from the fibers of a pheasant-tail feather; this pattern, which was first created more than 100 years ago, is still used around the world to catch trout.

You can also use pheasant-tail fibers to make a realistic looking caddisfly case. This easy-to-tie pattern, which is an excellent imitation of the common *Hydrosphyce* larva found in many rivers, is simply pheasant fibers for the body and chartreuse tying thread for the head. How simple is that?

So, if you're still struggling to use dubbing, make some flies using pheasant-tail fibers, go to your local stream, and catch some fish!

Pheasant-tail fibers were used to tie the tail and abdomen on this nymph imitation.

Tricks for stronger wing cases

MANY NYMPH PATTERNS CALL FOR WING CASES MADE OF SLIPS CLIPPED FROM TURKEY OR pheasant-tail feathers. These flies are great for catching trout, but the wing cases are a little fragile and the teeth of fish quickly tear them up.

A drop of cement on top of the wing case toughens this part of the fly; a drop of epoxy makes it indestructible. If you prefer the duller appearance of the natural material, place the drop of glue on the inside of the piece of feather before folding it over the top of the fly to create the wing case.

Another option is to replace the piece of feather with a narrow strip of mottled-colored Thin Skin. This vinyl material comes in a wide variety of colors, including imitations of turkey and pheasant feathers. It's a great substitute for real turkey and pheasant.

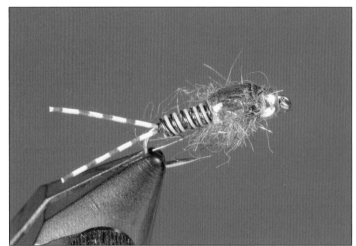

A drop of epoxy on the wing case made this pattern almost bulletproof. ▶

Flashy dubbing improves nymphs and wet flies

ONCE UPON A TIME, ALL WE HAD WERE PLAIN DUBBINGS: RABBIT, BEAVER, ANGORA, AND A host of other natural furs. You'll still find all of these materials in the fly-tying section of any well-stocked fly shop; they are required ingredients for making many of our most important patterns.

Today, however, we can also select from a host of new flashy dubbing materials. Some of these dubbings are blends of natural furs containing pinches of fine-fibered synthetic flash materials; a dash of flash can transform an ordinary fly into a real fish-catcher. Other products are 100 percent synthetic dubbing.

While some manufacturers add flash fibers to brighten plain, old-fashioned dubbing, there is also a practical reason for creating blended dubbing: Most synthetic dubbing is hard to apply to thread to wrap a neat body. With blended dubbing, the natural fur acts as a binder; it readily adheres to the tacky wax applied to the thread before adding the dubbing.

Unless you have a specific reason for using pure synthetic dubbing, blended dubbing is actually easier to use.

The body on this simple larva imitation was made using a blended flash dubbing.

77

Do the twist with peacock herl

MANY FAVORITE PATTERNS REQUIRE PEACOCK HERL FOR PARTS OF THE BODIES. THESE metallic-green feather fibers, which come from the tail feathers of a peacock, make lovely flies, but the material is fragile and can quickly break when fishing. Twisting the herl around a piece of thread, like twisting the strands in a piece of string, strengthens the material and makes for a more durable fly. Let's see how to tie a strong peacock herl body on a simple wet fly.

1. Start the thread and leave the tag end of the thread hanging off the rear of the hook. Tie on the hackle. Tie on the peacock herl and a piece of wire.

2. Twist together the herl and thread tag.

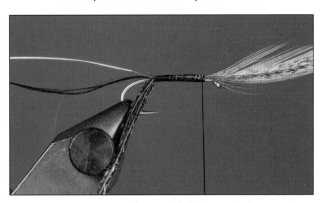

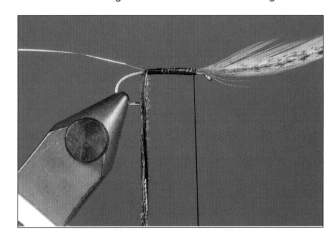

When starting the thread on the hook, do not clip the tag end; leave it hanging off the back of the fly. Next, tie on the hackle. Wrap the thread to the end of the hook and tie on two pieces of peacock herl and a piece of wire; we'll eventually use the wire to make the rib of the fly. Twist the herl around the thread tag, and wrap the body of the fly.

We'll complete this wet fly in the next tip.

3. Wrap the body of the fly. Tie off and clip the excess herl and thread tag. We'll finish the fly in the next tip. ▶

78

A counter-wrapped rib strengthens a fly body

A RIB OF WIRE OR NARROW TINSEL GIVES A FLY A REALISTIC SEGMENTED APPEARANCE and a dash of fish-attracting flash. When applied properly, the rib will also strengthen a body made of floss, thread, or peacock herl.

The trick is to counter-wrap the rib over the body; in other words, wrap the rib in the opposite direction from which you wrapped the body. Although the teeth of a fish might nick the body, the counter-wrapped rib prevents it from falling apart. This simple precaution will save your favorite flies—nymphs, wet flies, dry flies, and streamers—from hard use.

Let's complete the fly we started tying in the previous tip.

1. Counter-wrap the wire rib over the body. Tie off and cut the surplus wire.

2. Carefully wrap the hackle to form a sparse collar; the fibers suggest the legs of an emerging nymph. Tie off and clip the excess hackle.

Glass beads brighten flies and catch more trout

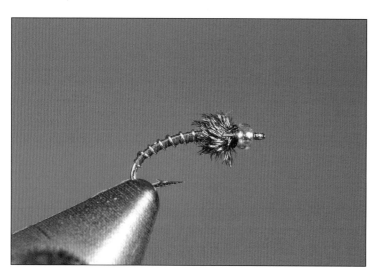

PAT DORSEY IS ONE OF COLORADO'S best guides. After many seasons fishing his local rivers, he has unique insights into what catches trout. As a guide, Pat has to get his clients into fly fishing; he carries flies that he knows will help them succeed.

Pat created what he calls his Mercury series of flies. These subsurface patterns feature small silver-lined, fly-tying glass beads that look like mercury in tiny thermometers. The beads brighten the heads of the flies and attract the attention of the fish. You can add these beads to medium-sized nymphs and even your smallest midge imitations. As a bonus, silver-lined beads comes in a variety of colors, not only clear.

Try this experiment: tie a few of your favorite wet flies and nymphs with and without these bright beads. Take them to your local river and see which flies catch more trout.

80

The craziest fly ever?

FLY FISHING IS CONSTANTLY EVOLVING. SOMETIMES new flies are developed to match changing fishing tactics, and sometimes fishing methods develop to take advantage of new patterns. Wladyslaw Niebies's unique fly is sometimes called Vladi's Worm—other times it is called the Condom Worm. Yes, Wladyslaw, who is one of the world's leading competitive fly fishermen, makes this fly using a real latex condom.

First, Wladyslaw bends a streamer hook to shape. He then wraps lead wire to make an exaggerated hump at the end of the hook shank. Next, he ties on and wraps a condom up the hook to form the worm. (You can easily substitute with a fly-tying material called Scud Back.)

How ingenious is that? The wire and hook shape force the fly to turn over in the water and not snag the streambed, and the finished pattern imitates an aquatic worm. Vladi's Condom Worm spawned the revolutionary methods called European nymph fishing.

What's the moral of this story? Never be afraid to experiment with your fishing or fly tying. Try developing new patterns and angling methods. Who knows: perhaps you'll come up with the next fly that will revolutionize fly fishing?

81

Different styles of nymph hooks

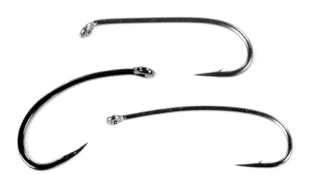

WHEN I STARTED TYING FLIES, ALL TROUT-FLY hooks had straight shanks. There's nothing wrong with straight-shanked hooks, except that most insects have slightly curved bodies. When nymphs are dislodged from the streambed and float with the current—which is when they are most vulnerable to fish—they generally assume a tucked or curved posture. A fly tied on a curved-shank, heavy-wire hook imitates the appearance of a real insect.

There are many brands and varieties of curved-shank nymph hooks. Some shanks have gentle curves; these hooks come in the widest range of sizes. Other hooks, often called scud or emerger hooks, have sharper bends and come in smaller sizes; these hooks are great for making a wide variety of small mayfly and stonefly nymphs, as well as scuds and emergers.

82

Simple tips for making better floss bodies

SOME OF OUR MOST FAMOUS WET FLIES ARE TIED WITH FLOSS BODIES. MANY YEARS AGO, tiers used real silk floss, but today you'll find spools of Rayon and other modern flosses in fly shops. Here are a couple of tricks to making perfect floss bodies.

There are two types of common floss: single strand and four strand. Four-strand floss is more difficult to use because you will have to separate and clip out an individual strand to tie each fly. Single-strand floss is a snap to use: just place the spool in a fly-tying bobbin, and tie the fly.

You'll place a clockwise twist in the floss as you wrap the material up the hook. Spin the bobbin counterclockwise after every ten wraps to remove this twist and keep the floss laying flat on the hook.

Finally, fold and tie down the tag end of the floss over the top of the fly. This will prevent the fine floss strands in the body or tag from slipping down the back of the hook when fishing the fly.

83

What is a soft-hackle wet fly?

SOFT-HACKLE WET FLIES ARE SOME OF THE OLDEST PATTERNS. PRIMARILY OF ENGLISH origins, they date back to at least the late fifteenth century. These patterns are sometimes referred to as soft hackles, and sometimes as wet flies; together—soft-hackle wet fly—the term is a perfect description of how they are tied, and how they are fished.

The key feature is a sparse, soft-fibered hackle that readily moves in the water and gives the fly the appearance of swimming as a real insect. The tail—if the fly has one—is generally tied very sparse, with feather fibers. The body is typically thread or floss, sometimes ribbed with tinsel. Other popular body materials are peacock herl and dubbing. Fish a wet fly under the surface to imitate a struggling nymph or emerging insect.

This classically inspired wet fly sports a modern bead head.

Many sparse soft-hackle wet flies are tied in dingy colors—brown, tan, and gray—similar to real insects; others are made with vibrant colors, especially bright floss bodies, tinsel ribs, and colorful feather wings.

Some classic wet flies have some of the most fanciful names: Greenwell's Glory, Parmacheene Belle, Bradshaw's Fancy, and Tup's Indispensable. And, before there was the Hare's-Ear Nymph, there was a simple wet fly called the Hare's Ear.

Make no mistake: These patterns have stood the test of time because they catch lots of fish!

84

What are the best hackles for tying wet flies?

FLY TIERS HAVE USED THE FEATHERS FROM MANY DIFFERENT SPECIES OF BIRDS TO MAKE the hackles on wet flies: snipe, woodcock, grouse, English partridge, plover, starling, chicken, and more. Tiers simply used whatever birds—and feathers—were handy when creating their flies.

Today, due to regulations prohibiting the hunting of some species of birds, we have a more limited selection of feathers. But, we still have an ample variety of feathers from which to choose and can tie terrific soft-hackle wet flies.

Small hen hackles, in natural and dyed colors, are fine for tying wet flies. English partridge, which has always been an important ingredient for these patterns, is still widely available. And Coq de Leon, which is a Spanish variety of chicken now bred in the United States for its feathers, offers hackles that are a dead ringer for partridge. You'll find all of these feathers, and many others, at a well-stocked fly shop.

This buggy-looking wet fly was tied using a ginger-colored hen hackle.

Wrapping the hackle on a wet fly

A WELL-TIED, SOFT-HACKLE WET FLY HAS A VERY SPARSE HACKLE COLLAR. TYPICALLY, THE collar requires only one or two wraps of hackle. The goal is to add a few feather fibers to suggest the legs of a struggling nymph or emerger; an overly dressed fly will look unnatural.

There are two ways to wrap the collar. The first is simple: Tie the feather to the hook, make one or two wraps of hackle, and then tie off and clip the excess. This direct method produces a fine fly that will catch fish.

Some tiers prefer to make wet flies with hackle fibers that sweep more toward the rear of the fly. This requires folding the fibers in the same direction before wrapping the hackle. First, tie the hackle to the hook in the normal manner. Rub your thumbnail or the dull side of your scissors on the side of the feather you wish to fold. Lightly pinch the fibers together, and wrap the hackle once around the hook. Tie off and clip the surplus piece of feather. Folding the hackle is a slightly more advanced technique that yields a fine-looking wet fly.

1. We've tied on the hackle, the hackle-fiber tail, and a body using floss and peacock herl. Note that we tied on the hackle with the concave side facing us.

2. Make no more than two wraps of hackle; the fibers are supposed to suggest the legs of a nymph, so you don't want to overdress them. Tie off and clip the surplus piece of feather. Wrap a neat thread head, tie off, and snip.

How to make a dubbing loop

MAKING A DUBBING LOOP IS A BASIC FLY-TYING TECHNIQUE; IT IS ESPECIALLY IMPORTANT for making nymphs and wet flies.

A dubbing loop is a simple way to apply dubbing—natural or synthetic fur—to a hook to create the body of the fly. First make a four- to five-inch-long loop of thread. Lightly smear dubbing wax onto the thread; this soft wax helps the dubbing adhere to the thread. Next, spread a pinch of dubbing in the loop. Spin the loop closed to form a miniature rope. Wrap the twisted loop up the hook to create the body of the fly.

Pay close attention to the proportions of dubbing you use when making a dubbing loop. Many tiers use too much dubbing, which results in a fat body. It requires only a pinch of dubbing to tie most flies. When in doubt about the amount of dubbing you are using, cut it in half; a slender fly typically looks better than an obese one.

We'll tie a complete wet fly in this tip. The thorax, which is rabbit dubbing, gives the fly a buggy appearance and prevents the soft-hackle fibers from collapsing against the hook when fishing.

1. Tie on the hackle, the tail, and a tinsel abdomen. Make a four-inch-long loop of thread. Wrap the working thread (coming out of the bobbin) at the base of the loop; these wraps lock the loop in place. Next, wrap the thread to the base of the hackle.

2. Lightly smear dubbing wax on the thread loop. Insert and spread a pinch of dubbing in the loop. Twist the loop closed.

3. Wrap the loop and dubbing on the hook to create the thorax of the fly. Tie off and clip the excess dubbing loop.

4. Wrap a sparse hackle collar. Tie off the surplus feather tip and complete the thread head.

The pinch wrap for making wet-fly wings

MANY WET FLIES HAVE WINGS. THE WINGS ARE OFTEN SLIPS CLIPPED FROM MATCHING TURkey or goose wing quills. You'll find matched sets of feathers in almost any fly shop.

Clip a narrow slip from each feather. Place the slips together with the tip edges even. Grasp the slips between the thumb and forefinger of your non-tying hand, with the butt ends showing. Next, place the slips on top of the hook exactly where you wish to tie the wings. Pinch the wings and hook shank between your fingers, and make one loose wrap of thread on the base of the wings. Slowly tighten the thread and make two or three more wraps. Remove your fingers to check the position of the wings. If necessary, lightly adjust the slips until the wings are in the correct position. If you're still not pleased with the appearance of the fly, unwrap the thread and try again.

1. Clip slips from a matching set of duck quills.

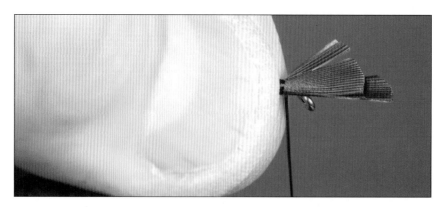

2. Place the wings back to back with the tips even. Slip the wings onto the top of the hook. Pinch the wings to the hook and make two light wraps of thread. Continue pinching the wings in place, and slowly tighten the thread by pulling down on the bobbin.

3. Remove your fingers and examine the wings. If you are not entirely pleased with the results, you can rock the wings into position, and sometimes you will have to completely remove the wings and try again.

4. Carefully clip the butt ends of the wings; two or three small cuts typically work better than one complete cut.

88

Hotspots catch more fish

ADDING HOTSPOTS TO NYMPHS AND LARVAE PATTERNS IS ONE OF THE NEWEST INNOVATIONS in fly fishing. This is another lesson we are learning from the competitors to the World Fly-Fishing Championships.

Experienced anglers are discovering that a bright pinch of dubbing in the body, a band of bright thread or floss, or even a bright red or orange bead, can increase the ability of a fly to catch fish. This speck of color, which we call a hotspot, seems to attract the attention of the fish. The shape of the fly, as well as the proper presentation, then get the fish to strike.

The pinch of pink dubbing in the body adds to the fish attracting appeal of this simple caddis larva imitation.

Making Meaty Streamers for Catching Trophy Fish

What is a streamer?

A STREAMER IS USUALLY A FLY DESIGNED TO imitate a baitfish. If it is true that big fish eat little fish, you'll typically catch larger fish using streamers. Streamers are important when fishing for large trout, and if you fish for bass, plan to tie a wide variety of streamers. Streamers are also important to success when fishing for saltwater species, especially striped bass, bluefish, false albacore, bonito, snook, and tarpon. Streamers were some of the first flies ever tied, and they remain a staple of most fly-fishing kits.

Streamers are also the most commonly used flies to catch Atlantic salmon and steelhead. Salmon and steelhead flies, like the one in the accompanying photograph, are some of the most beautiful and complex ever created. Tiers spend many years perfecting their craft, and often use a dozen or more materials to tie a single fly.

What is an attractor pattern?

SURE, ALL THE FLIES WE TIE ARE SUPPOSED TO ATTRACT AND CATCH FISH—NO ONE WANTS to tie flies that scare fish away. But, did you know that there are actually two different classes of flies: imitations and attractors?

Some patterns are tied to imitate specific forms of fish food; these are called *imitations*. Other flies match no specific form of fish forage, yet under the right circumstances they do an admirable job of attracting and catching fish; these patterns are called *attractors*. Although there are all sorts of attractor flies—dry flies, nymphs, and wet flies—streamers have always been used for catching most species of gamefish. And, when salmon and steelhead enter rivers to spawn and are no longer actively feeding, brightly-colored-attractor streamers are popular for catching these gamefish.

A fish attacks an attractor pattern out a sense of curiosity, territoriality, or anger.

Do you need special tools to tie saltwater flies?

GENERALLY SPEAKING, YOU WILL NEED NO SPECIAL TOOLS FOR TYING THE MAJORITY OF saltwater patterns. The vise, bobbin, and scissors you use for making trout flies and bass bugs will suffice for tying saltwater flies. If, however, you plan to specialize in dressing saltwater flies, you might wish to consider selecting tools better designed for holding larger hooks and cutting hard synthetic hairs.

It seems counterintuitive, but it's actually harder to get a vise to grasp a large saltwater hook; some vises must apply considerable force in order to hold the hook stationary. Some vises have small grooves machined in the jaws to grasp and hold larger hooks securely; these vises are ideal for tying everything from the tiniest trout to the largest saltwater flies.

Many saltwater flies require synthetic materials. These plastic and Mylar ingredients quickly dull ordinary scissors, so plan to include a set of scissors designed for cutting synthetic materials to your fly-tying kit.

And finally, if you make flies featuring epoxy, you'll want to add some sort of device that slowly turns the flies while the epoxy hardens.

The Apte Tarpon fly is one of our most famous patterns; it was even depicted on a United States postage stamp.

Should I use more synthetic materials to tie saltwater flies?

MANY SALTWATER FLIES ARE MADE WITH SYNTHETIC MATERIALS. PLASTIC HAIRS, SYNTHETIC yarns, and large dumbbell eyes are common features on contemporary saltwater patterns. However, almost all of the classic saltwater flies are tied using common natural ingredients such as hackles and animal hair.

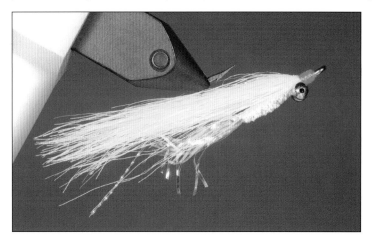

This saltwater fly was tied using only synthetic ingredients.

Make Lefty's Deceivers, Clouser Minnows, Bend Backs, and Whistlers using ordinary feathers, bucktail, tinsel, and thread. You can add a few strands of Flashabou or Krystal Flash to these flies if you like, but all of the other ingredients come from natural sources. And these flies still catch fish!

Study the latest fly-tying books and magazine articles, however, and you will see many patterns tied using only synthetic ingredients. These flies also catch their share of fish.

Synthetic or natural materials? The choice is yours.

Translucent streamers imitate real baitfish

SMALL BAITFISH SUCH AS MINNOWS AND DACE, AS WELL AS IMMATURE TROUT, BASS, OR other gamefish species, are all somewhat translucent, making that a key feature to include when tying their imitations. The best streamers, which often mimic baitfish, have a natural, translucent quality. Streamer wings tied with bucktail are also translucent. In fact, bucktail and marabou (which consists of soft, billowy feathers, usually from domestic turkeys) are both great natural materials for tying translucent wings that look alive in the water. If you prefer using synthetic fly-tying materials, use only small bunches of hair—Fishair, craft fur, or whatever—to create translucent wings that mimic the profiles of baitfish.

A good baitfish pattern matches the streamlined shape and translucence of a real fish.

Bucktail and hackles create streamers that appear slightly translucent in the water. ▶

94

Superglue welds, dumbbells, and bead-chain to flies

WHETHER YOU WISH TO TIE FLIES TO CATCH TROUT, BASS, OR SALTWATER FISH, YOU WILL want to add a few Clouser Minnows to your fly box. Many other subsurface patterns also feature bead-chain eyes. The trick to these patterns is securing the dumbbell and bead-chain eyes so they do not roll around the hooks. A drop of superglue will weld these parts in place and reduce the chance that they will move.

First, wrap a layer of thread on the hook where you plan to tie on the dumbbell or bead-chain eyes. Tie on the eyes using a series of firm figure-eight wraps. Make three firm wraps between the eyes and the hook shank; these wraps should tighten the figure-eight wraps and cinch the eyes to the hook. Place a small drop of superglue on the thread wraps in the middle of the dumbbell or bead-chain, and make another series of firm figure-eight wraps. The fresh glue will penetrate all the thread wraps and lock the eyes in place.

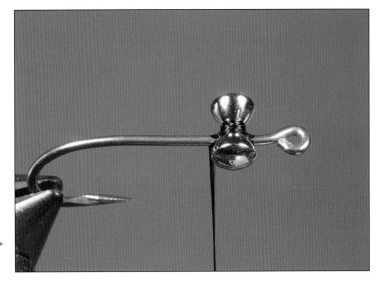

A drop of super glue applied to the tight figure-eight wraps prevents the dumbbell from turning on the hook. Tying on the dumbbell is usually the first step in tying the fly. ▶

Selecting bucktail for streamers

ALL FLY SHOPS CARRY BUCKTAILS. A BUCKTAIL IS JUST WHAT IT SOUNDS LIKE: THE TAIL OF a deer. This universal fly-tying material comes in natural and a wide variety of dyed colors. Bucktail hair is one of the most commonly used materials for tying freshwater streamers and many saltwater patterns; a streamer that has wings tied using only bucktail hair is simply called a "bucktail."

It's temping to buy the largest bucktail hanging on the pegboard wall in your local fly shop, but that might be a mistake; although it contains the most hair and seems the more economical choice, the hairs might be poor for tying good flies. Many bucktails have crinkled hair, but a good one for tying streamers has straight hair. The flies tied using this material will have a sleeker, more streamlined appearance that simulates the profiles of a real baitfish. In addition to having fairly straight hair, a prime bucktail will have few broken strands.

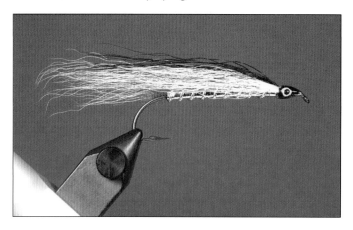

A. K. Best is a fly-tying legend who lives in Colorado. This is his version of a Blacknose Dace sporting a bucktail wing.

Selecting saddle hackle for tying streamers

SADDLE HACKLE IS COMMONLY USED TO tie the wings and tails on streamers and saltwater flies. Saddle hackles are the long feathers that hang down the sides of the back of a chicken, similar to a saddle draped over the back of a horse. Saddle hackle comes in natural as well as a wide assortment of dyed colors.

There are two ways to purchase hackle. Your local fly shop will carry entire pelts of saddle hackle, as well

◀ The author did the honors in tying this classic Gray Ghost. He selected feathers with full, rounded ends for the wings.

as individual packages of feathers. Avoid extremely long and skinny saddle hackle; these feathers come from chickens bred for dry-fly hackle and yield flies that look like swimming pencils. When tying streamers, select saddle hackles that have a fuller appearance and slightly rounded tip ends; these create flies that better match the silhouette of a baitfish.

97

What threads should I use to tie streamers and saltwater flies?

WHITE, BLACK, GRAY, AND RED ARE THE MOST POPULAR COLORS OF THREAD FOR TYING freshwater streamers and saltwater flies. And be sure to use white thread under any light-colored body materials such as floss; when the fly is wet, a darker color under the body will bleed through and spoil the appearance of the fly.

Select size 3/0 (210 denier) thread for tying most saltwater baitfish imitations and large streamers. Size 6/0 (140 denier) is fine for making small saltwater flies and most freshwater streamers.

Fine, clear monofilament thread is also popular for tying many saltwater flies and some streamers. This thread is very strong, and the transparent thread head you tie to complete a fly will allow the underlying materials to show through and match the color of a baitfish from the tip of its nose to the end of its tail.

98

Choosing marabou for streamers

MARABOU COMES FROM THE FEATHERS FOUND UNDER THE WINGS OF BIRDS. THESE SOFT, billowy feathers give flies great swimming action when wet. Many knowledgeable fly tiers say marabou is one of their favorite materials for making streamers.

Marabou originally came from the marabou stork. Today, due to sound conservation regulations, taking a stork for any reason is no longer permitted. Nowadays, all fly shops sell marabou that comes primarily from domestic turkeys and chickens. Packages of marabou are widely available in white and many dyed colors. But all marabou is not created equal for tying. Chicken marabou is fine for tying tails and other parts on nymphs and small flies, but you'll need something larger to tie the tails on Woolly Buggers and the wings on Marabou Muddler Minnows.

Use a sharp eye when selecting a package of marabou for tying streamers. Avoid marabou with thick stems that reach far up the feather. Instead, select a package with full, fluffy feathers and thin stems.

Although a popular fly-tying ingredient, marabou is not easy to tie to the hook; the soft fibers have a tendency to twist around the shank when tightening the thread. Lightly moisten the feather when tying the marabou to the fly. And measure the length of the wing or tail before tying on the feather. Adjust the feather until you are pleased with the appearance of the fly, and then tighten the thread. Clip away the excess butt end of the feathers; never cut the tip end.

Select marabou with thin stems and long, fluffy fibers.

99

What hooks should I use to tie streamers and saltwater flies?

FOR TYING FRESHWATER STREAMERS DESIGNED TO IMITATE REAL BAITFISH, SELECT HEAVY-wire, long-shank hooks. Many of these hooks are designated as 4X and 6X long, but there are also 8X-long hooks that can easily measure three inches long. Most tiers prefer using 4X- and 6X- long hooks because it takes less time to make the bodies of the flies, and some anglers complain that 8X-long hooks do not hold fish as well as slightly shorter hooks.

There are various types of hooks designed for tying saltwater flies. These hooks are designed not to corrode in salt water. Stainless-steel hooks are the most common variety; these come in a wide variety of sizes and lengths to make all styles of saltwater patterns. You'll also find hooks with various finishes that are designed not to corrode. Almost all of these hooks are excellent for tying flies, but you cannot sharpen the points if they become damaged. Sharpening a hook will require removing the finish and makes the point susceptible to rusting.

And finally, salmon and many steelhead flies are tied on hooks blackened with a procedure called *japanned*.

Here we see three styles of streamer hooks (*from the top going clockwise*): freshwater streamer hooks, stainless-steel saltwater hooks, and salmon/steelhead hooks.

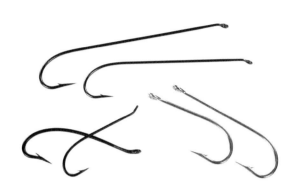

100

Making shallow-water saltwater flies weedless

IF YOU PLAN TO TIE FLIES TO FISH THE FLATS FOR BONEFISH, REDFISH, AND PERMIT, YOU'LL want to create patterns that do not catch grass and other vegetation. Sometimes, you'll even want the fly to rest on the bottom until a fish approaches, and then bring it alive with a stripping action; this also requires a pattern that will not snag.

Many of these flies, called flats patterns because they are commonly fished on sand and coral flats, have small dumbbells tied on the tops of the hooks. The dumbbells add weight to the top of the flies and cause them to flip over in the water so that the points are on top and cannot catch on the bottom. A small loop of heavy monofilament, tied on in front of the hook point, prevents the fly from catching grass and other debris.

This fine crab imitation sports both a small dumbbell and monofilament weed guard. ▶

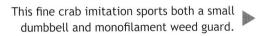

Adding a monofilament weed guard to a large fly is easy

BRUSH, LOGS, MANGROVES, PILINGS, BOAT DOCKS, AND SIMILAR STRUCTURES WHERE FISH hang out can claim flies—and lots of them! If you plan to fish such places, you'll want to add weed guards to your streamers and saltwater flies.

A monofilament weed guard is easy to tie. First, start the thread at the end of the hook shank. Wrap the thread halfway down the bend of the hook. Tie on the end of a two-inch-long piece of thirty-five-pound-test clear monofilament. Wrap the thread back up the bend, binding the end of the monofilament to the hook. Now tie the fly. Next, tie the other end of the monofilament behind the hook eye. The monofilament should loop slightly below the hook point to shield the point when the fly contacts objects in the water, yet it bends easily out of the way when a fish strikes.

A loop of monofilament prevents this squid imitation from catching weeds and other debris.

A small piece of monofilament makes this saltwater pattern weedless.

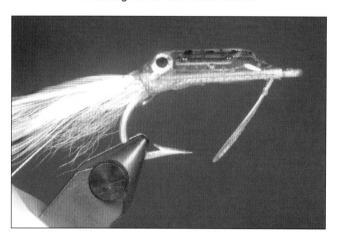